advanced JAVA networking

PRASHANT SRIDHARAN

To join a Prentice Hall internet mailing list, point to http://www.prenhall.com/mail_lists/

Prentice Hall PTR
Upper Saddle River, New Jersey 07458
http://www.prenhall.com

Library of Congress Cataloging-in-Publication Data

Sridharan, Prashant
Advanced Java networking / by Prashant Sridharan.
         p.   cm.
Includes index.
ISBN 0-13-749136-0
1. Java (Computer program language) 2. Internet programming   I. Title.
QA76.73.J38S75   1997
005.2'762—dc21   97-1264
                                                         CIP

Acquisitions editor: *Mark Taub*
Editorial assistant: *Tara Ruggiero*
Marketing manager: *Dan Rush*
Editorial/production supervision
        and composition: *Eileen Clark*
Manufacturing manager: *Alexis Heydt*
Cover design: *Anthony Gemmellaro*
Cover design director: *Jerry Votta*
CD Web page design: *Cynthia L. Mason*

Prentice Hall books are widely-used by corporations and government agencies for training, marketing, and resale.
The publisher offers discounts on this book when ordered in bulk quantities.
For more information, contact:

        Corporate Sales Department
        Phone: 800-382-3419, Fax: 201-236-7141
        E-mail: corpsales@prenhall.com
Or write: Prentice Hall PTR
        Corp. Sales Dept.
        One Lake Street
        Upper Saddle River, NJ 07458

Printed in the United States of America
10 9 8 7 6 5 4 3 2 1

ISBN 0-13-749136-0

Prentice-Hall International (UK) Limited, *London*
Prentice-Hall of Australia Pty. Limited, *Sydney*
Prentice-Hall Canada Inc., *Toronto*
Prentice-Hall Hispanoamericana, S.A., *Mexico*
Prentice-Hall of India Private Limited, *New Delhi*
Prentice-Hall of Japan, Inc., *Tokyo*
Simon & Schuster Asia Pte. Ltd., *Singapore*
Editora Prentice-Hall do Brasil, Ltda., *Rio de Janeiro*

For my mom, my sister, and my puppy.
Thanks for everything.
I love you very much.

Contents

Introduction,   xvii

Thanks a million!   xvii

How to read this book,   xviii
What this book is all about,   xix
Who should read this book,   xix
How to read this book,   xx
Where to begin,   xx
Conventions,   xxii

Fixes and Updates,   xxiii

Chapter 1

Advanced Java,   1

Basic Java,   3
Object-oriented design using Java,   4
Applying good object-oriented design skills,   10
OOP—strong, efficient, and effective,   12

Java I/O Routines,   13

  Streams,   13

  The Java core system,   15

  The Abstract Window Toolkit,   18

  I/O in short,   19

Introduction to Threading in Java,   19

  What are Threads?   20

  Threading in Java,   21

  Thread summary,   29

Object Serialization,   29

  Handling object relationships,   30

  The output streams,   31

  Handling object webs,   32

  Reading objects,   33

  Security and fingerprinting,   33

  Serialization overview,   34

Performance,   34

  Performance Issues,   34

  Summary of performance issues,   38

A First Look at Java Networking in Action,   39

  Pulling it all together,   40

  Summary,   44

Chapter 2

Java Sockets,   46

Sockets and Inter-Process Communication,   47

  Introduction to IPC,   47

  Summary of sockets,   57

Protocols,   58

  The OSI stack,   58

  TCP/IP,   59

  HTTP,   59

IIOP, 59
Protocols and sockets, 60
It all ends with protocols, 60

TCP/IP Client, 60
Developing clients for servers, 60

TCP server, 67
Server methodology, 67
Setting up the server, 68
Initializing the server socket, 68
Creating the thread, 69
Detecting information and starting the thread, 70
Gathering information, 72
Clients and servers in short, 75

UDP client, 75
Datagrams, 76
Creating a UDP sender, 77

Featured application, 87
Messaging format, 88
Client, 88
Server, 92

Summary, 93

Chapter 3

Java IDL: Interface Definition Language, 95

CORBA, 96
CORBA-style communication, 96
The CORBA vision, 97
Communication with CORBA, 98
The Interface Definition Language, 99
Different vendors, different ORBs, 100
Advantages of CORBA, 101
Common Object Services, 102

Object administration, 103
Clients, servers, oh my! 104
What CORBA means for you, 105

The Interface Definition Language, 105
Interfaces, 106
Modules, 106
Interface inheritance, 107
Variables and structures, 108
Methods, 109
Constructed data types, 109
Exceptions, 110
Overview of the IDL, 111

Language Mappings, 111
What exactly are language mappings? 111
The Sun Microsystems Java Language Mapping, 112
Interfaces, modules, and methods, 113
Interface inheritance, 114
Variables and structures, 115
Constructed data types, 116
Exceptions, 117
Java and CORBA together, 117

CORBA Clients, 117
Designing a User Interface, 118
Defining the problem, 118
The cooler interface definition, 119
The cooler user interface, 119
Initializing the client ORB, 122
Client overview, 128

CORBA Servers, 128
Defining an interface and generating code, 128
Server overview, 136
Java callbacks, 137

Creating a callback,   137
Registering a callback,   139
Receiving and handling a callback,   142

A Java IDL Version of the Featured App,   144
Server interface,   144
Network module,   145
Calendar server,   148

Summary,   153

Chapter 4

Java RMI: Remote Method Invocation,   155

Distributed Objects,   155
What is RMI?   156
How does RMI work?   157
Local vs. remote objects,   160
Applet vs. application,   162
Dynamic method invocations,   163
Overview of RMI,   163

Client,   163
RMI client methodology,   163
Catching exceptions,   167
Handling security constraints,   168
Client overview,   170

Server,   170
RMI server *classes,   170*
RMI Registry *classes,   173*
RMI server security constraints,   174
Generating stubs and skeletons,   176
Server overview,   177

RMI Dynamic Server Creation,   178
The factory solution,   178
Dynamic server overview,   184

Callbacks,   184
  Why callbacks?   184
  Creating the callback,   184
  Implementing the callback client,   185
  Filling in the callback method,   186
  Registering callbacks,   187
  Invoking callbacks,   190
  Callbacks in short,   192

A Java RMI Version of the Featured App,   193
  RMI interface,   193
  RMI client,   194
  RMI server,   199

Summary,   203

Chapter 5

Java Database Connectivity,   205

Inside JDBC,   205
  Database drivers,   206
  JDBC in general,   208

Databases and SQL,   209
  Creating an Access database,   209
  Simple SQL,   210
  Summary,   213

Retrieving information,   213
  Creating the user interface,   213
  Database security,   215
  Using the JDBC driver,   215
  Creating queries,   217
  Database and SQL overview,   219

Storing information,   219
  Creating the connection,   219
  Forming a statement,   221

A JDBC version of the featured app,   223
  Creating the database,   223
  Mapping the network module to database queries,   225
  Developing the client,   226
  Establishing the connection,   227
  Making an SQL Invocation,   228
  Invoking SQL to make a change,   229
  Shutting down the connection,   230
Summary,   231

Chapter 6

The Java Web Server,   235

Inside an HTTP Server,   235
  Web server architecture,   236
  Using a Web server,   236
  Advanced Web server features,   237
  HTTP Server overview,   238
Servlets,   238
  What is a servlet?   238
  Servlets overview,   242
Dynamic Documents,   242
  Creating the servlet,   242
  Dynamic documents overview,   251
Multi-Purpose Servers,   251
  Client invocations,   252
  Server architecture,   253
Summary,   254

Chapter 7

Java Beans,   257

Component Models,   257
  The competition,   258

Overview of Beans Component Model,   259
  Interface publishing,   259
  Event handling,   260
  Persistence,   260
  Layout,   260
  Builder support,   261
  Distributed Beans,   261
  Why use Beans?   261
Java Beans,   262
  Component interaction,   263
  Network communication,   264
  User interface issues,   265
  Persistence,   266
  Events,   266
  Properties,   266
  Beans in a nutshell,   266
Using Java Beans,   267
  Creating a Java Beans application,   267
  A simple example,   268
  Instantiating components,   270
  Connecting Beans events,   274
  Bean introspection,   275
  Summary,   276
ActiveX,   276
  What is ActiveX?   276
  The Microsoft "vision",   279
  ActiveX controls,   279
  ActiveX and Java,   280
  Summary,   280
OpenDoc and CyberDog,   281
  OpenDoc components,   281
  Cyberdog,   282
Summary,   282

Chapter 8

The Networked Java World, 285

Marimba, 285

How does it work? 286
Castanet vs. Java IDL and Java RMI, 288
Why Castanet? 289

Active Software, 290

How ActiveWeb works, 290
ActiveWeb and Java, 292
ActiveWeb vs. IDL and RMI, 292

Netscape, 292

What is Netscape ONE? 293
Netscape ONE and Java, 293

ICE-T, 294

How does it work? 294
ICE-T and Java, 295

Summary, 295

Chapter 9

JMAPI: Java Management API, 299

What is Network Management? 299

Network management at a glance, 300
Simple network management protocol, 301
The unique management problems of Java, 302
Network Administration Overview, 302

Modifying Clients for JMAPI, 302

AVM base classes, 302
AVM help classes, 303
Managed object interfaces, 303
Setting up notifications, 306
Modifying servers for JMAPI, 308

Summary, 315

Chapter 10

Java Hardware,   317

JavaOS,   317

Why JavaOS?   318
High-level JavaOS system architecture,   318
JavaOS Virtual Machine,   320
Drivers and networking,   320
Uniqueness of JavaOS,   321

JavaStation,   321

Introduction to the JavaStation,   321
Writing Networked Applications for JavaStation,   324
The Java Revolution makes it to your desktop,   324

Java Chips,   324

The Java Chip family,   325
The picoJava architecture,   326
Why Java Chips?   327

Summary,   327

Chapter 11

Java and Security,   329

Safety in Java,   329

Java Class Security,   330

Encryption,   333

Authentication,   336

Governments and Security,   338

The "Clipper" controversy,   338

Summary,   339

Chapter 12

Making an Architectural Decision,   341

Java sockets,   341
   Flexibility,   342
   Simplicity,   342

Java IDL,   343
   Advantages of JavaIDL,   343
   Disadvantages of JavaIDL,   343
   JavaIDL implementations,   344
   JavaIDL is robust,   344
   JavaIDL is difficult,   345
   Java IDL is powerful,   345

Java RMI decisions,   346
   RMI Advantages,   346
   RMI Disadvantages,   346
   Three-tier applications in RMI,   347

JDBC,   348
   Why JDBC is not enough,   348
   JDBC and JavaIDL or JavaRMI,   350
   JDBC Alone,   351

Other Java technologies,   351
   When to use Beans,   351
   When to use Servlets,   352

Summary,   353

Appendix A

Glossary,   355

Appendix B

CD-ROM Installation,   361

Contents,   361

Software Installation,   361
>   *JDK 1.02 to JDK 1.1,   362*
>   *A note about Java IDL,   362*
>   *Installation of Examples,   362*

Index, 363

Introduction

Thanks a million!

Writing a book is a time-consuming and arduous process with incredible rewards from both a career and personal perspective. While this entire book is written in the plural first person as a nod to my contributing author, Bill Rieken, I want to take a moment and thank each and every single person who helped me in this endeavor. It has always been my lifelong dream to write a book, and now that I've actually done it I realize it could never have been possible without the great many folks who stood by me.

The first thing moonlighting authors begin to realize is that the free time they once had to hang out with friends, watch "ER," and take a weekend flight to the Redskins game is lost. I actually met my girlfriend three weeks before I began writing. Amazingly, she's still with me after several nights of "sorry sweetie, I gotta write." I love you Jenn! My mom and my sister may be the women behind this man, but Jenn is most definitely the woman beside him. Thanks to all three of the most incredible women on the face of the planet!

Extra special thanks go to Bill Rieken, who helped me by getting those darn sockets straight! He was an extraordinary help in outlining some of the security problems that the Internet brings to the network programming table. Bill is a mad scientist, a jolly old man, and a two-year old all rolled into one. Working with him has been and always will be a blast.

My friends were terrific throughout the entire process. Dave Krause dutifully called me after every Redskins loss to cheer me up, (Ensign) Daniel Orchard-Hays tried to get me to golf, Jon Hogue was around (somewhere), and somehow I managed to make it to Doug Jelen's wedding where I didn't even stumble with my best man's speech ("I've known Doug forever, and I would be the first to say that his garbage collection algorithm was implemented exceptionally well.")

Sydney Springer and Maurice Balick gave me my start in Silicon Valley, and they are two of the most wonderful people in the world. Hellene Garcia whined constantly about 49er superiority, Karin Stok-Harrison was a sweetheart, James McIlree made fun of my BMW, Janet Koenig made me laugh, and Laraine Peterson was a scout leader. I love all the engine ears and marketeers at SunSoft Object Products, especially Ken Oestreich and Manish Punjabi, my marketing conscience. Also, special appreciation goes out to Terena Fujii and Cynthia Mason for helping out with the CD. My manager, Jeff Zank, was incredibly understanding and belied my experience with managers when I told him I needed "time to edit." This business is about people, and Jeff understands that.

Over at Prentice Hall, Ralph Moore made sure my manuscript was nice and neat. And, Mark Taub got me signed up to write a book to begin with. He showed remarkable trust in letting a kid write a book! Sean Donahue masterfully corrected my engineering-tainted English, and Eileen Clark made sure the production schedule didn't go through the roof.

Finally, Larry Pass, Fred Kuhl, Bill Rieken, Laraine Peterson, and Bob Goldberg helped me make sure everything I wrote was correct and useful. Ultimately, however, the onus is on me to make sure everything is right, and I accept the blame for anything that may have gone wrong. It amazes me that a Computer Science-dropout-turned-English-major could end up in Silly Valley, in the hottest field imaginable, writing a book, and evangelizing Java for the best company in the Valley. Thanks to all the men and women of Silly Valley without whose passion, drive, and energy I would have been a lost soul long, long ago.

Prashant Sridharan

How to read this book

By now you've seen all the hype, read all the books, and discovered all the wonders of Java. But, most of us still use C++ or C to create our hard-core applications, saving Java for our Web pages or leaving it to HTML jocks to fiddle with. Doing so denies us the opportunity to use a programming language that makes interfacing with a computer infinitely easier, with less frustration and faster results.

Java is much more than "Dancing Dukes" or a programming language for Web pages. It is a strong alternative to the masochistic programming of the past—Programming in which countless months were spent debugging, in comparison to the mere days it took to code the initial concept. Java allows us to spend more time in the conceptual phase of software design, thinking up new and creative ways to bring the vast knowledge of the Internet and its many users to our desktop.

Gone are the days of reliance solely on the machines sitting in our offices, resting in the living room, or gathering dust in the kitchen. Today, our information, and the steady flow thereof, is garnered from the millions of our fellow computer users around the world, not only from a shiny disc we slip into the little slot on the front of our machine.

Up until now, you've no doubt designed programs to interface with that knowledge using C or C++. Java, however, will change all of that. Residing alongside its ability to create adorable and functional user interfaces quickly and easily is the capability to easily connect to the Internet. Java, after all, is The Internet Language.

What this book is all about

Advanced Java Networking is designed to present you with a myriad of alternatives to connect your applications to the Internet. It is neither a programming reference nor a marketing brochure. We'll leave that to the geeks and marketeers to battle out. Instead, we wanted to explore each alternative without marketing bias or engineering snobbery.

One part of the engineering community will tell you that plain vanilla sockets are the only true way to communicate information over a network. Another will purport that Java-only applications relying on Remote Method Invocation (RMI) will solve all your communication problems. Then, of course, there is the Common Object Request Broker Architecture (CORBA) camp. We will present you with an honest account of each alternative, as well as guidelines for choosing what's best for your business or programming needs. In addition to the hundreds of lines of sample code we will supply to help you start from scratch with Java communication, we will place an additional emphasis on migration of your existing desktop-centric applications to an Internet-ready world.

Who should read this book

We assume that you have a strong object-oriented programming background, preferably in Java. You should have a strong grasp of Java fundamentals such as how to create a class, how to compile and execute programs on your native system, and how to deploy Java applications. Furthermore, you should understand a good deal of the terminology of the object-oriented world. In this book, we do not attempt to cover these details as this is not an introductory Java text.

How to read this book

We've divided this book into parts, and each part into chapters. Each part addresses one aspect of Internet programming, be it **Java Fundamentals**, **Core Networking** like RMI, CORBA, or Java Database Connectivity (JDBC), **Advanced Networking** like Beans and Java Web Servers, or some general **Java Networking Information** in which we've included a special chapter on Internet security that will address simple Applet Security restrictions, as well as more complex subjects such as good ol' Kerberos.

Finally, we want to show you that Java programming is much more than an animation floating by a Web page, or interactive Internet content. Java is a language that the authors of this book truly, honestly believe in. We make no effort to contain our enthusiasm for it, and certainly don't apologize for our delight in working with it. We hope that you will come to love this language as much as we have.

Where to begin

It's hard to believe, but Java is a little more than a year old! In the span of one year, a hundred or so books have been written on Java! Following is our honest appraisal of what we believe are the top three Java programming books on the market today. We feel these books, along with this one, will give you one heck of a Java library.

You will find that our code samples, as robust and well-documented as they are, sometimes will contain Java routines that seem esoteric. While we consider them essential, Java programmers who are unfamiliar with the language's powerful communication tools will find them strange and daunting. We do our best to explain them as well as we can, but we make no attempt to be exhaustive in our summary. These books will give you the proper foundation to build your networked applications.

In addition, there are several Java workshops and classes from which to choose. We have seen or have attended a few of them, and we chose one that we feel promotes the language properly, and teaches the material in a pleasing and fun manner. After all, Java should be fun. No more pointers!

Core Java, Gary Cornell and Cay S. Horstmann, SunSoft Press (Prentice Hall), 1996, 607 pages

Core Java is an essential component of your Java library. While most of the SunSoft press Java titles are geared towards highly differing audiences, *Core Java* explains just about every feature of the Java language in a manner amenable to the hard-core programmer. If you are reading this book, more than likely you subscribe to the "Java as Internet Language" theory, so you will find the Socket section particularly enlightening. The new second edition covers the Java Developer's Kit version 1.1 in depth and introduces JDBC.

Java in a Nutshell, **David Flanagan, O'Reilly and Associates, 1996, 438 pages**

O'Reilly and Associates have another gem on their hands with *Java in a Nutshell*. This book is a programming reference in the purest of terms. Most of the analysis is somewhat unhelpful, but the explanation of Java's core classes is unsurpassed. The diagrams are wonderful, and you will appreciate having the headers for every class in front of you.

Exploring Java, **Patrick Niemeyer and Joshua Peck, O'Reilly and Associates, 1996, 407 pages**

Think of this book as the perfect companion to *Java in a Nutshell*. Niemeyer and Peck are a bit wordy and are sparse on coding examples, but they make up for it with a decent explanation of the concepts behind the language.

"Advanced Java Networking," Visigenic Professional Services (Palo Alto, CA)

Salil Deshpande has developed a course that we believe highlights Java's communication aspects in a frank, informative, and fun manner. Salil steps through the various communication alternatives using a fast-paced, hands-on approach that ought to be the envy of any Java course available. A course syllabus is included in the following sidebar for your reference. Please contact Visigenic Professional Services directly through their Web site: `http://www.customware.com/`.

"Advanced Java Networking" Course Syllabus

This five day course is essential for architects, software engineers, and technical managers who want to learn how to build distributed applications using various Java networking facilities provided with Java and available as extensions.

Students will learn how to build non-trivial distributed applications with Java, Java's Socket APIs, Remote Method Invocation (RMI) and Object Serialization, and Visigenic Inc.'s CORBA implementations, VisiBroker for Java and VisiBroker for C++.

Format
50% lecture, 50% lab exercises

Prerequisites
This course assumes some experience programming in a Unix or Windows environment, good knowledge of OO concepts, and at least one object-oriented programming language, preferably Java!

We assume that students have been exposed to all the hype about Java, are familiar with Java syntax, have a good idea of the facilities offered by Java, and perhaps even written some simple applets. (This is not an introductory Java course).

Objectives

Upon completion of this course, you will be able to architect, design and build non-trivial applications with Java's Socket classes and other built-in networking facilities, Java Remote Method Invocation (RMI) and Object Serialization facilities, and VisiBroker for Java, Visigenic Inc.'s CORBA-based distributed object system.

In particular you will be able to:

- Make intelligent tradeoffs while choosing between various networking APIs for your application
- Write Java applications that communicate with other Java, C, or C++ applications using Sockets
- Use Java's stream classes to make application development easier
- Build client/server applications with Java
- Describe interfaces to remote Java services using RMI
- Implement an RMI server in Java
- Use the RMI stub compiler to generate client stubs for remote services
- Implement RMI clients in Java
- Use the RMI Registry
- Pass complex data structures easily between Java clients and servers
- Implement RMI clients that receive callbacks from RMI servers
- Understand the relationship between RMI and HTTP servers
- Describe interfaces to remote services in CORBA IDL
- Write Java clients that make invocations on remote CORBA objects, implemented in C, C++, Java, or any other language.
- Pass complex data structures between Java clients and Java or C++ servers
- Implement Java clients that receive callbacks from CORBA servers
- Perform distributed applet-to-applet communication
- Use exceptions as a design tool, and throw and catch exceptions between clients and servers, across networks.
- Understand the abstractions and facilities provided by the CORBA Common Object Services, and be able to design applications that make use of them.

Conventions

We use the standard `Courier` font to denote source code and type out our code listings. If you see a `Courier` word within a sentence (for example "Java `Vectors` are cool"), it is the name of a class or object. We are also firm believers in the step-by-step approach we take to code samples. Therefore, we have generally shown the entire code listing and the additions from the previous instance of it. The changes are in **Courier Bold**. For example, the first time we show a code snippet, it looks like this:

```
public class Jennifer

{

}
```

And, when we make an addition it is bolded:

```
public class Jennifer

{

    String loves = "Prashant";

}
```

Also, when we show a command prompt, the part you type is also bolded:

```
%prompt% dir c:\games
```

There are several icons throughout this book that highlight certain parts of the text, as follows.

The "Tip" icon informs you of a special or unique way to accomplish something in Java networking.

The "Alert" icon tells you of any bugs or "gotchas" that you should be aware of while programming your applications.

The "Note" icon simply points out any information that might be useful to you in your network programming endeavors.

Fixes and Updates

We would also like to take a moment to apologize in advance for any errors that we may have committed. This book has been a total blast to write, and we might have gotten caught up in our own excitement here and there. In any event, we hope you have fun reading and exploring the Java networked world!

The CD-ROM that accompanies this book (see Appendix B, "CD-ROM Installation," for complete details regarding the CD-ROM) contains several of the applications that we have developed in this book. Additionally, a special Web page has been created as a front-end to navigating the CD-ROM and for linking to related Web sites. To access that Web page, please load the file named `index.html`, found in the root directory of the CD-ROM, into your browser.

To err is human, and the authors of this book are as human as can be. Despite our testing every example thoroughly, both from an installation and compilation perspective, problems sometimes do arise. If we find a problem with any of the programming examples in this book, we will post a fix as soon as possible on our Web site, located at:

`http://www.prenhall.com/~java_sun`

This online Web supplement can also be linked to from the Web page included on the CD-ROM included with this book.

Java Language Fundamentals

Java Language Fundamentals covers the basics of object-oriented programming, serialization, threads, and streams that are required before any further investigation into networked applications may begin. It contains a quick summary of the design and analysis of object-oriented applications, with an emphasis on Java. Included is a simple primer on threads and threaded applications, and how to implement them in Java. This part forms the basis for the remainder of the book and should be, at the least, skimmed for terminology and an understanding of the foundation on which Advanced Java Networking takes place.

Introduction
Chapter 1: Advanced Java

CHAPTER
1

A Quick OOP Primer

Input and Output Routines

Threading in Networked Programming

Object Serialization

Our First Java Networking Project

Advanced Java

Our tour of Java networking begins with a simple and quick tutorial on several of the advanced features of the Java programming language. From there, we dive straight into the APIs associated with connecting Java objects across disparate machines and networks. Each of these APIs has both strengths and weaknesses, and we certainly highlight the strengths while exposing the weaknesses. Finally, we describe the tools necessary to provide a safe environment for your Java applications, while not having to sacrifice the power of the language itself. Our discussion begins here, with the fastest object-oriented tutorial this side of the Mississippi....

Basic Java

When beginners first take to C++, their primal screams can be heard for miles. Often, emergency crews are dispatched immediately to prevent the serious injuries that are typically endured when beginners are first confronted with the dreaded `*pointer->`. Enough to make a grown man cry, C++ is a powerful yet incredibly difficult language.

Enter Java. Java is object-oriented, modular, elegant, and—in the hands of a master--quite poetic! Java code can be beautiful and powerful, fun and exciting, and, most importantly, incredibly useful!

This chapter focuses on some of the advanced concepts you need to grasp in order to support your further endeavors using Java. Throughout the discussion, you will see sample code that highlights some of Java's inherently object-oriented features: encapsulation and information hiding, modularity, inheritance, and elegance. We intend this chapter to provide you with a base of terminology, not a comprehensive Java language tutorial. Beginners should be forewarned: This book assumes you know the language.

Much of what is discussed in this chapter are the fundamental design aspects of an object-oriented language. For seasoned programmers, the urge to skip this chapter will be strong. However, many of the advanced features of Java, as well as the architectural decisions that must be made for a Java networked application, are based on the fundamental concepts we describe in this chapter and are of great importance to both veteran and rookie networking programmers alike.

Object-oriented design using Java

In Java, you declare classes as a collection of operations performed on a set of data. Because data cannot be passed by reference (Java is a pointer-free language—let the cheering begin!), Java classes are needed to contain data so that it can be modified within other classes.

Classes vs. interfaces

The prevailing assumption about Java is that you are unable to separate implementations from interfaces. However, this assumption is false. Java provides an interface component that is similar to its class counterpart except that it is not permitted to have member functions. Indeed, this interface must be reused by other objects that will implement its method and variable definitions, as illustrated in the following snippet.

```
public interface MyAdvancedJavaInterface
{
        public abstract void methodOne();
        void methodTwo();
}


public class MyAdvancedJavaClass implements MyAdvancedJavaInterface
{
        MyAdvancedJavaClass()
        {
        }

        public void methodOne()
        {
```

```
        ...
    }

    public void methodTwo()
    {
        ...
    }
}
```

All member functions declared within interfaces are, by default, `public` and
`abstract`. This means they are available for public consumption and must be
implemented in a class before they can be used. Furthermore, interfaces do not
have constructors and must be extended before they can be used.

Data members

Good object-oriented style dictates that all data members of a class should be
declared private, hidden from any operations other than those included in the
class itself. But, any experienced OO programmer will tell you in no uncertain
terms that this is often stupid and inane for small classes. Because structs are not
available in Java, you can group data into one container by using a class. Whether
you subscribe to the artificially enforced private-data-member scheme of C++ or
the language-enforced scheme of Smalltalk is entirely up to you. Java, however,
assumes data members are public unless otherwise instructed, as the following
snippet suggests.

```
public class MyAdvancedJavaClass
{
        public int numItems;
        private int itemArray[];
};
```

Methods

Another important component of the Java class is the operation, or method. Methods allow outside classes to perform operations on the data contained in your
class. By forcing other classes to utilize your data through the classes, you enforce
implementation hiding. It doesn't matter to other classes that your collection of
data is an array, for as far as those classes are concerned, it could be a `Vector`.
Somewhere down the line, you could change the implementation to a `Hash-`
`Table` if efficiency becomes a concern. The bottom line is that the classes that use
your methods don't care, and don't need to know, so long as the *method signature*
(the method name and its accompanying parameters) remains the same. The following code shows how a method can be introduced within a class.

```java
public class MyAdvancedJavaClass
{
        public int numItems;
        private int itemArray[];

        public void addItem(
            int item
        )
        {
            itemArray[numItems] = item;

            numItems++;
        };
};
```

Constructors

But, there is one small problem with this example. The data is never initialized! This is where the notion of constructors comes in. Constructors set up a class for use. Classes don't need to specify a constructor, indeed a constructor is, by default, simply a function call to nothing. In this case, however, our class must call a constructor because our data needs to be initialized before it can be used.

In Java, everything is inherited from the superclass `Object`. All `Object`s must be initialized, or allocated, before they are used. For example, the declaration

```java
public int numItems;
```

specifies an integer value. The int is a primitive type, but just like an `Object`, and therefore int needs to be initialized. We can do so either in the declaration itself

```java
public int numItems = 0;
```

or we can use the constructor and initialize the array as well

```java
public class MyAdvancedJavaClass
{
        public int numItems;
        private int itemArray[];

        MyAdvancedJavaClass()
        {
            numItems = 0;
            itemArray = new int[10];
        }

        public void addItem(
```

```
        int item
    )
    {
        itemArray[numItems] = item;

        numItems++;
    };
};
```

Keep in mind that initializing a variable at its declaration affords little flexibility for any classes or methods that subsequently will use your object. A constructor can be modified easily to accept incoming data as well, enabling you to modify your object depending on the context of its use:

```
public class MyAdvancedJavaClass
{
    public int numItems;
    private int itemArray[];

    MyAdvancedJavaClass(
        int initialValue,
        int arrayLength
    )
    {
        numItems = initialValue;
        itemArray = new int[arrayLength];
    }

    public void addItem(
        int item
    )
    {
        itemArray[numItems] = item;

        numItems++;
    };
};
```

An object is allowed to have several constructors, so long as no two constructors have the same method signature (parameter list):

```
public class MyAdvancedJavaClass
{
        public int numItems;
        private int itemArray[];

        MyAdvancedJavaClass()
        {
            numItems = 0;
            itemArray = new int[10];
        }

        MyAdvancedJavaClass(
            int initialValue,
            int arrayLength
        )
        {

            numItems = initialValue;
            itemArray = new int[arrayLength];
        }

        public void addItem(
            int item
        )
        {
            itemArray[numItems] = item;

            numItems++;
        };
};
```

Sometimes, confusion may arise when there are several constructors that all do the same thing, but with different sets of data. In Java, constructors are allowed to call themselves, eliminate duplicate code, and enable you to consolidate all of your constructor code in one place:

```
        MyAdvancedJavaClass()
        {
        /*  Instead of...
            numItems = 0;
            itemArray = new int[10];
        */
```

```
        // call the more specific constructor
        this(0, 10);
}


    MyAdvancedJavaClass(
        int initialValue,
        int arrayLength
    )
    {
        numItems = initialValue;
        itemArray = new int[arrayLength];
    }
```

Constructors are powerful tools. They enable you to create classes and use them dynamically without any significant hard-coding. As we will see, good constructor design is essential to an object-oriented architecture that works.

Creating and initializing an object

We mentioned earlier that all Java classes inherit from the Object superclass. The constructor for an Object is invoked using the **new** operation. This initialization operation is used at object creation, and is not used again during the object's life-cycle. One example of an object being initialized is the array initialization in our sample class. The **new** operation first allocates memory for the object and then invokes the object's constructor.

Because we created two kinds of constructors, our sample class can be invoked in one of two ways:

```
myAdvancedJavaInstance1 = new MyAdvancedJavaClass();
myAdvancedJavaInstance2 = new MyAdvancedJavaClass(10, 100);
```

The first instance of our class is initialized to the default values 0 and 10. When we invoked the new operation on this instance, the new operation set the values appropriately, and created a new instance of Array within the class instance. The second instance of our class set numItems to 10 and created a 100 item Array.

As you can see, this kind of dynamic class creation is very flexible. We could just as easily create another instance of our class with entirely different (or the same) initial values. This is one of the basic principles of object-oriented design espoused by languages such as Java.

Each instance of the object maintains a similar-looking, but *entirely different* set of variables. Changing the values in one instance does not result in a change in the values of the variables of the other instances. Remember, an instance of a class is like your BMW 328i Convertible. As the analogy in Figure 1-1 illustrates, it looks as cool as every other BMW 328i, but just because you modify yours to remove the annoying electronic inhibition of speed, doesn't mean every other Beemer also will be changed!

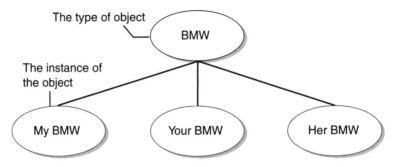

Figure 1–1 Just as customizing your BMW makes it different from other BMWs, modifying variables in one instance doesn't change them in all instances.

Applying good object-oriented design skills

Maybe you're tired of driving your minivan because your husband (or wife) makes you! What you really want is a BMW Z3 Roadster. So, you drive your behemoth Toyota van down to the nearest BMW dealer and trade it in for the Z3. Now, because you have a different car, does that mean you have to learn how to drive all over again? Obviously not (unless you just traded in a Volvo, in which case you have to learn to drive to begin with). That's because the world, yes the same world that brought you Elvis, and Bob Dole, is inherently object-oriented.

Inheritance

Your Z3, and every other car on the road, is a car, pure and simple. All cars have accelerators, brakes, steering wheels, and, even though you don't use them in a Beemer, turn signals. If we take this analogy further, we can say that every car inherits from the same "base class," as illustrated in Figure 1-2.

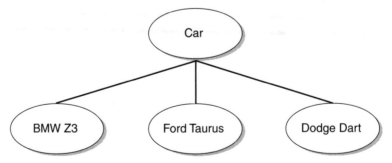

Figure 1–2 In any object-oriented environment, classes inherit the characteristics of their base classes.

A base class is a special kind of object that forms the foundation for other classes. In Java, a base class is usually inherited later on. Think of derived classes as "kinds of" base classes. In other words, "a BMW Z3 is a kind of car." With that in mind, we create the following class structure:

```
public class Car
{
}


public class BMWZ3 extends Car
{
}
```

The `extends` keyword tells the BMWZ3 class to utilize the properties, values, and behavior of the `Car` base class. But there is one small problem. Can you ever drive a generic "car?" No, because there is no such thing. There are always kinds of cars, but never a specific thing that is known simply as a car. Java gives us the notion of an "abstract base class."

An abstract base class is, quite simply, a class that must be inherited from. It can never be used as a stand-alone class. In Java, the abstract keyword gives a class this unique property.

```
public abstract class Car
{
        int topSpeed;
}


public class BMWZ3 extends Car
{
}
```

In this situation, the `Car` class can never be instantiated or used as is. It must be inherited. When the BMWZ3 class inherits from `Car`, it also obtains all of the variables and methods within the `Car` class. So, our BMWZ3 class gets to use `topSpeed` as if it were its own member variable.

Somewhere in your code you might want to check what type of variable you are using. Java provides the `instanceof` keyword to enable you to inquire as to what the abstract base class of an object is. For example, the following two code snippets would return the value true:

```
BMWZ3 bmwVariable;
FordTaurus fordVariable;
```

```
if(bmwVariable instanceof Car) …

if (fordVariable instanceof Object) …
```

Whereas the following code snippet would return the value false.

```
if(bmwVariable instanceof PandaBear)
```

Notice that Java's inheritance model is quite simple. In C++, objects are allowed to inherit from one or more abstract base classes and can be made to inherit the *implementation* of those interfaces as well. Java, as a matter of simplicity, does not allow this, nor does it plan to at any time in the future. There are ways to get around multiple implementation inheritance, but they do not really involve inheritance at all. The bottom line is that if you need to use multiple implementation inheritance, you probably won't want to use Java.

Code reuse

Let's say you are putting together your son's bicycle on Christmas morning. The instructions call for you to use a Phillips-head screwdriver. You take the screwdriver out of the toolbox, use it, and put it back. A few minutes later, you need the screwdriver again. Surely you would use the same screwdriver, not go to the hardware store and buy a new one!

Likewise, code reuse is of vital importance to the programmer on a tight schedule. You will need to streamline your code so that you can distribute commonly used tasks to specific modules. For example, many of the online demonstrations we provide with this book include animation examples. Rather than recreate the animation routines, we reused the same set of animation tools we developed beforehand. Because we coded the animators with reuse in mind, we were able to take advantage of a strong interface design and an effective inheritance scheme.

OOP—strong, efficient, and effective

Whew! Whether this is your first foray using the Java language or your 101st, all of your design begins in this one place. There are three steps to creating an object that you can use time and again:

1. Strong interface design
2. Efficient class implementation
3. Effective Inheritance

With the fundamentals of object-oriented programming under your belt, you are ready to explore the simplicity with which you can create programs in Java that handle input and output. The Java I/O routines are not only easy, but extremely powerful. Bringing your C++ I/O to Java will result in as little functional loss as migrating object-oriented design techniques to Java from C++.

Java I/O Routines

Java provides several tools for the input and output of data, ranging from the Abstract Window Toolkit (AWT) to the core System functions of Java classes. The AWT is exactly what it says it is; a set of routines for designing windows and graphical user interfaces. The core System classes are built-in routines for gathering and disseminating information from Java objects.

This section highlights some of the input and output routines provided by both the core Java capabilities as well as by the Abstract Window Toolkit. As we delve further into the realm of networked programming, we will discover that much of what drives our decisions on a networked architecture will be that which is detailed in this section. As input and output are the most important actions a computer program performs, we must develop a strong understanding of the I/O capabilities and limitations of Java.

Streams

Imagine your grandfather fishing in a stream. He knows that as long as he stays there, he's going to get a bite. Somewhere, somehow, sometime a fish is going to come down that stream, and your grandfather is going to get it.

Just as your grandfather is the consumer of fish, your applications are either consumers or providers of data. In Java, all input and output routines are handled through *streams*. An input stream is simply a flow of data, just as your grandfather's stream is a flow of fish. You can write your application to fish for data out of your input stream, and eventually to produce data as well. When your application spits out information, it does so through a stream. This time, your application is the producer, and the consumer is another application or device down the line.

Java provides several different kinds of streams, each designed to handle a different kind of data. The standard input and output streams form the basis for all of the others. `InputStream` and `OutputStream` are both available for you to use as is, or you can derive more complicated stream schemes from them. In order to create the other kinds of Java streams, first you must create and define the basic streams.

Perhaps the most-used stream formats are the `DataInputStream` and the `DataOutputStream`. Both of these streams enable you to read or write primitive data types, giving you the flexibility within your application to control the results of your application's execution. Without this kind of functionality, you would have to write specific bytes rather than reading specific data.

File buffers are a method commonly used to increase performance in an input/output scheme. `BufferedInputStreams` and `BufferedOutput-Streams` read in chunks of data (the size of which you can define) at a time. When you read from or write to the buffered streams you are actually playing with the buffer, not the actual data in the stream. Occasionally, you must `flush` the buffers to make sure that all of the data in the buffer is completely read from or written to the file system.

Sometimes you will want to exchange information with another application using a stream. In this case, you can set up a pipe. A pipe is a two-way stream, sort of. The input end of a pipe in one application is directly connected to the output end of the same pipe on another application. If you write to the input of the pipe, you will read the same exact data at the pipe's output end. As you can see in Figure 1-3, this is a pretty nifty way to promote inter-application communication.

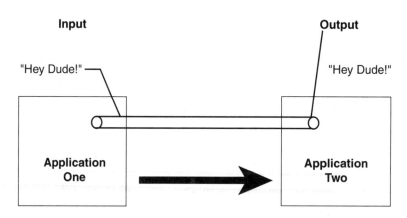

Figure 1–3 Pipes enable interaction between two or more applications.

Lastly, you will eventually want to fiddle with files on your local file system. The `FileInputStream` and `FileOutputStream` enable you to open, read, and write files as we will show you in a moment. Remember, Java has strict restrictions on applet security, so most file streams can be manipulated only by applications. For more information, consult Chapter 11, "Java and Security."

The Java core system

In Java, applications are allowed to write to the standard output devices on a machine. If you use a Web browser such as Netscape, the standard output to which Java writes is the "Java Console" mentioned in one of Navigator's windows. If you write a Java application (i.e., a stand-alone applet), the standard output device is the command line from which you execute the program.

The System class

One of the classes Java includes in every applet or application, whether you specify that it do so or not, is the System class. The System class contains several basic objects that provide a few, albeit limited, alternatives to input and output using the AWT. Keep in mind that Java was designed primarily as an object-oriented language, not necessarily as a language for Web pages or GUIs. Indeed, one of the beauties of Java is that it is a language in its own right, not simply an Internet publishing tool such as Shockwave or Microsoft's failed Blackbird.

In a way, promoting the System routines over the AWT is bucking the recent trend of Java applications, but as Java begins to mature as a language and encroach upon C++ as the object-oriented language of choice, the System routines will become more and more valuable as building blocks for more complex and thoughtful input and output mechanisms.

Input using the System class

Input in the System class is actually handled by the InputStream class contained in the Java I/O routines. System.in is an object of type InputStream that is created, maintained, and initialized by the System class. In other words, it's yours for the taking; you don't have to do a thing to use it.

The InputStream class assumes that you will be reading from the standard input stream. A stream is a sequence of characters retrieved from somewhere. The standard input stream is the location that your operating system uses to get data from you. Because streams are defined as characters from a source, it is entirely conceivable that a stream could be a file, a modem, or even a microphone. As a matter of fact, files and other peripherals are treated as streams by Java.

So, how do you get input from the user? Simply use the System class's input stream to get the information you require. The input stream is an object with several methods to facilitate data input. For example, there are primitive, yet useful, routines to get characters and strings, to read integers and other numbers, and even to get a stream of unfiltered and untranslated bytes. Deciding which routine to use is simply a matter of which kind of data you wish to read. In our example, we will read and write strings:

```
public class InputOutputTest()
{
        String str;

        public void getInput()
        {
            str = System.in.getln();
        }
}
```

Output using the System class

As with input, output is handled through streams. How can output be a stream if a stream is a sequence of characters from a source? Well, the source is your application, and the stream is routed to a device known as the standard output. The standard output is usually your monitor, but it could be other things as well. Most notably, the standard output is set to be the Java Console when an applet runs within Netscape Navigator. When you run the following example from within an applet, watch your Java Console for the output. If you run it from within an application, the output should show up on the command line.

```
public class InputOutputTest()
{
        String str;

        public void getInput()
        {
            str = System.in.getln();
        }

        public void drawOutput()
        {
            System.out.println(str);
        }
}
```

Files

The stream classes would be pretty useless if you couldn't manipulate files as well. There are several applet security mechanisms in place to prevent unguarded file access, many of which we will discuss in Chapter 11, "Java and Security." But for now, simply assume that as long as you are not writing an applet, you will be able to manipulate files. In the purest sense, standard input and output are files. As such, they are sometimes subject to the same applet security restrictions, so be forewarned.

The basics

When reading and writing to and from files, there are three steps that must be followed:

1. Open the file for reading or writing.
2. Read or write from the file.
3. Close the file.

It is important to do each step. Failing to open a file will, obviously, prevent you from reading. But perhaps not as intuitively, you must still close the file or you may wreck your file system. Every application is allowed a certain number of file descriptors, doohickeys that maintain the status of a file. If you run out of available file descriptors, you will no longer be able to open any other files.

When opening a file, you have three options. You can open the file for reading so you can extract data from it, but you will be prevented from writing to the file unless you close it and open it for writing. You can open it for writing, but you will be prevented from reading from it. Finally, you can append to a file, which is similar to writing except that it preserves any data already in the file.

Taking files one step further

So what do files have to do with networked computing? Well, the diagram in Figure 1-4 offers a graphical representation of input and output streams. Remember that streams are merely interfaces to collections of data. What if that data is located on a network connection rather than in a flat file or a keyboard?

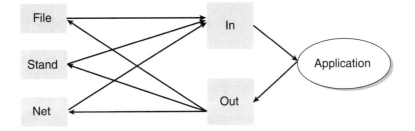
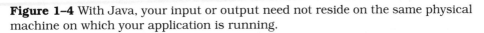

Figure 1–4 With Java, your input or output need not reside on the same physical machine on which your application is running.

The standard interface to a network in the computer world is a socket. A socket is a connection between processes across a network. The processes can be located on the same physical machine, the same Local Area Network, or even across the world on different LANs. The three basic steps still apply:

1. Open a connection to the remote process.
2. Read or write data.
3. Close the connection.

Again, as with file manipulation, you can use the `InputStream` and `Output-Stream` objects to interface to the socket. In fact, sockets are nothing but files in the purest sense. The advantage to this file-centric hierarchy is perhaps not as obvious as it should be. In the end, all three forms of input sources are completely interchangeable. You should not write your applications to be specific to a specific kind of file. In an object-oriented design, the objects you create should simply know that they will have to read or write data down the line.

The Abstract Window Toolkit

The AWT is a half-baked attempt to create a user interface toolbox for programmers. Because all of the various classes, containers, and widgets in the toolkit are capable of being used in both the applets embedded in Web pages as well as in the stand alone applications on your desktop, it is a powerfully extensible tool. At the heart of this kind of flexibility is the idea that the Toolkit is an abstraction—in other words, a layer on top of your current windowing system.

Your current windowing system may be anything from X11/Motif to Windows 95's own window system. In any event, the AWT ensures that native calls are made to these windowing systems in order to allow applications to run on top of the desktop. For applets within a Web page, the browser manufacturer essentially creates a windowing system that renders the AWT's widgets within itself.

The end result of all of this is that eventually a native call is made for each action taken by the AWT. Your applications need not be aware of this, for Java's platform independence assures that no matter the platform on which you execute byte-codes, the results will be identical.

Input alternatives

The AWT contains several widgets designed to elicit response from the user. From simple text areas to more complex dialog boxes, each one is designed to funnel information from the user's keyboard to your application. Most of them are very easy to use and program, so we'll leave it to the several Java books on the market to provide you with a reference, and a basic list and explanation of the elements that are included.

Remember, input in a windowing system is not limited to typing words on the screen. Every push button, checkbox, or scroll bar event is a form of input that you may or may not choose to deal with. Every AWT class has some way or another of checking the status of its input mechanism. For example, your scroll bar will be able to tell you if it has been moved. You may choose then to take some action, or let the AWT do it for you. There is no need to implement scrolling text for a scroll bar when the AWT is fully capable of doing it.

Output alternatives

Obviously, the easiest way to display output with the AWT is to display something graphically. The AWT supports simple graphics routines for drawing, as well as for the usual suite of labels, multimedia, and widget manipulation. Output is significantly easier using the AWT. Without the toolkit, you would have to manage not only what to do with the input you receive, but also how to display your response.

I/O in short

Input and output is at the heart of every program you create. No matter what the objective of your application, somehow you will need to get either a response from the user, display a response, or maybe even both. To take things one step further, your input or output need not reside on the same physical machine as that on which your application is running. Indeed, that is the very subject of this book. By stretching your applications to fit a networked model, you will be able to take full advantage of the input and output schemes offered to you by Java.

When your applications receive several inputs, they will often get inundated with processing. To alleviate this, Java provides a full suite of threading utilities, which we discuss in the next section. Threads allow your applications to execute steps in parallel. So, when your application receives two different inputs simultaneously, you can use threads to simultaneously resolve them and produce output.

Introduction to Threading in Java

Multithreaded programs are the current rage in computer science. Books upon books upon books have been written that describe the benefits of threading, the threading features inherent in various operating systems, and the various forms of threaded architectures.

So, what on earth are threads? How can you use them in your programs? Will threading continue to work in those applications that run native on operating systems that do not support threading? What does it mean to be MT-safe, and how do you design an MT-safe program?

The entire realm of multithreaded and multitasked programming transcends the scope of this book. We will confer that knowledge of the topic that is directly related to the ideas of networked programming, and in cases where more research may be warranted, direct you to the appropriate resources.

What are Threads?

Let's say you're sitting in your living room watching another Washington Redskins victory. You get bored watching the massacre of the Dallas Cowboys, and you decide that you would like to see the 49ers game in progress. In the good old days, you would have to actually switch channels and choose between one or the other. But, these days, televisions have Picture-in-Picture (PIP) capability. By pressing the PIP button on your trusty remote control, you can watch the Redskins demolish the Cowboys on a little box in the corner of the TV while watching the 49ers on the rest of the screen.

This is a prime example of multithreaded programming. The little screen and the big screen share resources (in this case, the area of the full television screen), but are not able to affect one another. In the areas in which the two games collide, one screen gives way to another.

Threads in your computer

In the computer world, multithreaded applications exist similarly to the television world. They share the same area, in our case the television screen, in reality the physical process in which the application resides and is permitted to execute. MT applications, as they are known, are simultaneously able to execute multiple series of executable steps. Each of these series of steps is known as a thread.

Threads are implemented differently by different operating systems. In Solaris, for example, threads are defined and maintained in the user environment. The operating system maintains responsibility over the process, regardless of what the process decides to do with itself. In a sense, the operating system treats the process as an object. The OS only cares about the interface to the process, or how it starts up, shuts down, begins execution, and similar operations. It has no feelings whatsoever over how the process executes information.

In fact, this is the fundamental concept of threads. Threads exist as a user-created and user-managed aspect of a program. The operating system could care less if there are multiple threads in the executable or if it is single threaded. Furthermore, the operating system will not help you resolve conflicts. All it cares about is the integrity of the process, not about what goes on inside of it.

Handling conflicts

Let's say you have a couple of threads prancing along merrily within your application. Suddenly, they both access the same piece of data at the same time. This results in what is known as *concurrent access*. Concurrent access errors occur as a result of poor thread management.

Access errors occur in everyday life, too. Let's say you've scheduled an appointment from eleven in the morning to one in the afternoon. Carelessly, you forgot your all-important staff meeting at twelve-thirty. Obviously, you can't be in two places at once! The end result is that you've placed yourself in two meetings. The threads within our applications similarly have accessed identical data at the same time.

When creating a thread, the first thing you must determine is what data that thread will touch. You then have to fence off that data so that only one possible thread can ever touch it at any given moment. In Solaris, this is done with a concept called *mutual exclusion*. A mutual exclusion lock that is placed around your data ensures that it will never be permitted to enter a concurrent access situation.

Imagine a relay team of four people competing at the Olympics in Sydney. The first runner on the relay team is given a baton that must be passed to a teammate before that teammate is allowed to run. If the teammate runs without the baton, she is disqualified. However, if the baton is passed properly, the runner can continue until she arrives at the finish line or must pass the baton to another teammate.

Likewise, different threads can obtain the lock around the data *so long as the lock is available*. If the lock is unavailable, the thread must wait, effectively suspending itself, until the lock is available. There are specific settings to allow threads to continue without waiting, but these settings are beyond the scope of this book. If one thread grabs a lock but never lets go, then it will have *deadlocked* the entire application. When your methods obtain a thread, make sure that they give it up somehow. Otherwise, the rest of your application will wait for a lock that will never come free.

For more information on threads, consult the excellent Sun Microsystems title, *Threads Primer* by Bill Lewis and Daniel J. Berg.

Threading in Java

Creating and debugging threads in Java is considerably simpler than doing so in C++. Deadlocks in Java are much easier to prevent, and a ton more intuitive. But MT applications in Java are not as robust or as powerful as their C++ counterparts. In short, there are trade-offs to threading in Java, for it is not an all-encompassing answer to the MT question.

Java treats threads as user-level entities as well. A Java applet or application runs within a process space defined in the Java Virtual Machine (Java VM). The VM allocates processes and the resources for each process, and allows the applet or application to define how that process space is used. Java programs that implement threads must do so using the `Thread` class or a derivative thereof.

The `Thread` class

Java's language hierarchy, which includes the likes of Strings, Integers, and so on, also contains a powerful, yet incredibly simple `Thread` object that you can implement within your programs. The Thread class provides all of the functionality necessary for you to create fully multithreaded and MT-safe applications using the Java language.

NOTE: Two approaches to spawning threads in Java are worth noting, as outlined in the following sections. Many of our networking examples later on will make heavy use of one or the other method. As always, there are trade-offs and benefits for each architectural decision you make.

Using the entire class as a thread

The first method we could employ involves spawning threads in which an entire class can reside. For example, we spawn a thread, then create a `runnable` class and attach it to the thread. Now the entire class exists within the thread and the stream of execution for that class is maintained by the thread. If the thread is killed, the stream of execution is likewise destroyed.

The biggest advantage to this method is that the class need not know anything about how it is to be implemented. Take a look at the following example:

```
public class Animator extends Panel implements Runnable
{
        Animator() { ... }

        public void run() { ... }
}


public class AnimatorManager
{
        Animator animations[];
        Thread animationThreads[];

        AnimatorManager() { ... }
```

```
    public void createAnimation(
        Animator anim
    )
    {

        // first spawn a thread for the class

        // now let the thread continue...
    }
}
```

The AnimatorManager class is responsible for creating a series of Animator objects, spawning a thread for the object to execute in, and shutting down, suspending, resuming, or inquiring about the status of the thread. Note how the Animator does not know or care whether it will be in a thread of execution or in an entire process. It is a runnable class, meaning that whatever is contained within the run function will be executed *if the parent process or thread allows*.

The object is created normally, and our AnimatorManager assumes that the object is already created. The Thread is created, but the object is passed to it as a parameter. The corresponding constructor in the Thread class knows that the runnable object will reside solely within its thread of control.

```
public class AnimatorManager
{

    Animator animations[];
    Thread animationThreads[];

    AnimatorManager() { ... }

    public void createAnimation(
        Animator anim
    )
    {

        // first spawn a thread for the class
        animationThreads[currentThreadCount] = new Thread(anim);

        // now let the thread continue...
        animationThreads[currentThreadCount].start();
    }
}
```

NOTE: Remember that Java is inherently object-oriented, so this kind of thread creation is quite within the reach of the language. There is no funny business going on here. A thread is created and an object is told to live within it. It is actually quite intuitive in an object-oriented sense. The next method hearkens back to the days of structured programming.

Inheriting from the Thread class

The second way to implement threads is to create a class that inherits from the Thread class. In the first method, we created an object that was a free-standing object in its own right. In this case, we will create an object that is a Thread object from the beginning. In essence, the Java VM treats both methods as similar and reasonable means to spawning threaded objects, and both are acceptable from a style perspective.

Inheriting from the Thread class is actually quite simple. Instead of extending from Panel or Applet, your class simply extends from Thread. In your init method or constructor, you must initialize the thread as well. Obviously, your class must be aware that it is running in a thread.

The thread code for a class that inherits from Thread is in the run method. As in a class that implements Runnable, inheriting from Thread automatically enables you to implement the run method. Any code you want to manage the thread should be placed there. If you need to make the thread sleep or suspend, that's where you should place it.

The difference, however, between extending Thread and implementing Runnable is that when you inherit from Thread, your entire class is a thread. The thread must be started and stopped from within the class, unlike the other method in which the thread controls are outside the class itself (see Figure 1-5).

Take a look at the following example, and notice how the constructor calls the start method or the thread:

```
public class Animator extends Thread
{
        Animator()
        {
            start();
        }

        public void run() { ... }
}
```

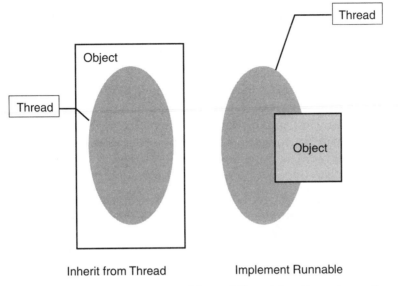

Inherit from Thread   Implement Runnable

Figure 1–5 Thread controls are accessed from different locations depending on the method chosen.

As you can see, the class is clearly a threaded class. What happens if you want to use the class' methodology without using threads? You'll have to create a new class that doesn't use threads, or you'll have to revert to the first method. Implementing `Runnable` and placing your thread controls outside the target class is the preferred way of using threads, but inheriting from threads can be particularly useful for highly modular code in which you want to package an entire object that does not rely on anything else.

Thread controls

A Thread has several control methods that affect its behavior. Simply starting and stopping a thread's execution are but two of the many tools available to you to manipulate how programs execute. For example, on several occasions, you will want to pause a thread's execution, and eventually resume it.

Let's say we had a stopwatch class. We want our counting to occur in a thread so that it doesn't impact any other classes or applets that will want to use it. In order to have complete control over the stopwatch, we must implement a few methods:

1. Start
2. Stop
3. Suspend
4. Resume
5. Sleep

In fact, Java implements all five of these options for us in the `Thread` class. The `start` method does exactly what it says. It tells the thread that it may begin execution of all the steps contained in the `run` method. The `run` method itself may call any of the above thread controls, but obviously you will want to restart the thread somewhere if the `run` method decides to suspend it!

The `stop` routine terminates the thread and prevents the `run` method from executing any further steps. It does not, however, shut down any sub-threads that it may have created. You must be careful and make sure that every thread you create eventually either terminates on its own or is terminated by its parent. Otherwise, you could very well have several threads executing and consuming resources long after the applet or application has terminated.

The `suspend` and `resume` routines are pretty self-explanatory. When `suspend` is called, the thread ceases execution of its run method until `resume` is called somewhere down the line. If your parent thread needs to inquire about the current running status of a thread it may call the `isAlive` method and find out if the thread is stopped. Obviously, if the thread isn't stopped, and it isn't running, it must be suspended.

Lastly, the `sleep` method tells the thread to pause for a given number of milliseconds. It is particularly useful for the clock because we want it to "tick" every second.

The state diagram in Figure 1-6 should make clear the thread timing you need to be aware of. Remember, before anything can be done to a thread, you must call start on it. Once you are finished with the thread of execution, you must call stop.

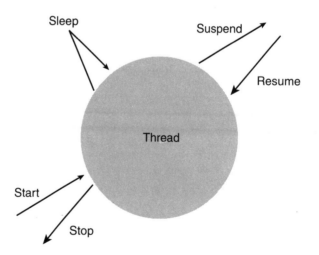

Figure 1–6 The five control methods that affect a thread's behavior are start, stop, suspend, resume, and sleep.

synchronized methods

Conflict handling within Java is implemented using method synchronization. If you have data that could potentially deadlock between two threads, then you must declare the functions in which the data is modified as *synchronized*. Java prevents multiple threads from entering the synchronized methods and thereby eliminates the possibility of deadlock.

Creating a synchronized method is actually quite easy. It is simply a matter of declaring that the function will be synchronized in the method signature, as can be seen in the following snippet.

```
public class ThreadClass
{
        int data;
        . . .

        public void synchronized addToData(
            int addend
        )
        {
            data += addend;
        }
        . . .

}
```

There are a couple of important caveats to synchronized functions. Because multiple threads may require entry to a synchronized function, it is better to keep any function that is declared as synchronized short and sweet. When one thread enters a synchronized function, keeping its time spent in the function to a minimum will keep your programs running smoothly. After all, the idea behind threading is to get your programs to execute steps in parallel, not to spawn threads that end up waiting forever for each other to finish with the data.

yield(), wait(), and notify()

In an application with multiple threads, often you will have many threads competing with one another for resources. One way to allocate those resources effectively is to set the relative priorities of each thread. We will discuss that in a moment, but right now let's discuss some of the specific steps you can take within the thread itself. Remember that when threads execute, they all share the same process space in which the application resides. Like a bunch of kids forced to share a toy, the threads compete and vie for control of the process. Like any good parent, however, you have several tools at your disposal to make sure the threads cooperate.

Sometimes you will want to control entry into a function and label the function as synchronized. Even though the function is long, you want to yield control of the function pretty early on. You can call the notify method to tell the parent thread that you are finished with the synchronized lock.

In order to make a thread stand by for a notify message, you must add the wait method to the thread's execution routines. The notify method is called somewhere in an executing thread. Once notify is called, any thread awaiting execution on a wait call automatically proceeds.

Another way to give up the process space in which a thread runs is to call the yield routine specifically. When yield is called within a thread, the thread gives up any scheduling priority, process space, or claim to its current turn in the sharing cycle.

Thread priorities

TIP: A more elegant, yet more confusing, way to control threads is by setting their priority. Obviously, when you set a thread to have a high priority, it gets first crack at any processing time and resources. You should be careful and judicious in setting thread priorities. Even with the best of intentions, you could very well defeat the purpose of using threads to begin with should you set every thread at a high priority.

In Java, threads may have one of three priorities: minimum, normal, and maximum. You may set the priority using the setPriority method of the Thread class and retrieve the priority of any thread by using the getPriority method, like so:

```
Thread threadOne;
Thread threadTwo;
Thread threadThree;

threadOne.setPriority(Thread.MIN_PRIORITY);
threadTwo.setPriority(Thread.NORM_PRIORITY);
threadThree.setPriority(Thread.MAX_PRIORITY);
```

As threads are a powerful and underused aspect of most Java programs, thread scheduling and prioritizing is a flexible and equally powerful way to control how your applications behave and execute.

Daemon threads

There are two kinds of threads. So far we have discussed application threads, which are tied to the process and directly contribute to the running of the application. Daemon threads, on the other hand, are used for background tasks that happen every so often within a thread's execution. Normally, an application will run until all the threads have finished their execution. However, if the only remaining threads are daemon threads, the application will exit anyway.

Java itself has several daemon threads running in the background of every application. Java's garbage collection is controlled by daemon threads known in computer science parlance as reaper threads, or threads that run through an application looking for dead weight. In the garbage collection thread's case, the dead weight happens to be unused but allocated memory.

If your application needs to set up a daemon thread, simply call the `setDaemon` method of the thread, as shown in the following snippet. The application in which the thread resides will know to ignore that thread if it needs to execute, and program execution will continue normally.

```
Thread t = new Thread(myClass);
t.setDaemon(true);
```

Thread summary

Threads are one way in which you can affect the behavior of an object. Serialization is another. Serialization allows you to store your objects as strings. When we use threads we do so to change how it behaves when it is running. Serialization does not allow us to preserve that run-time behavior, only the class' static behavior and characteristics. Whenever you reconstruct a serialized class, only your class will be reconstituted correctly, not any of the threads. Therefore, it is important that your threads be as object oriented as possible so that they can store their state when necessary.

Object Serialization

Serialization is a concept that enables you to store and retrieve objects, as well as to send full-fledged objects "over the wire" to other applications. The reason serialization is of such vital importance to Java should be clear: without it, distributed applications would not be able to send objects to each other. That means that only simple types such as `int` and char would be allowed in parameter signatures, and complex objects would be limited in what they could do. It's sort of like saying you would have to talk like a three-year-old whenever you spoke with your boss. You want to have a complex conversation, but you are limited in what you can say.

What is serialization?

Without some form of object storage, Java objects can only be transient. There would be no way to maintain a persistent state in an object from one invocation to another. However, serialization can be used for more purposes than maintaining persistence. The RMI system uses object serialization to convert objects to a form that can be sent over a communication mechanism. Java IDL also makes extensive use of serialization for its own parameter passing.

When an object is serialized it is converted to a stream of characters. Those characters can be sent over the wire to another location. Parameters passed in remote objects are automatically translated into serialized representation. Once an object is serialized, it can be safely sent via a communication method to a remote location.

The serialization routines have been incorporated into the standard Java Object class with several routines to facilitate the writing and reading of a secured representation. There are several security concerns that you must be aware of, and we will discuss those in a moment. Without object serialization, Java could never truly be an effective Internet language.

Handling object relationships

An important consideration of the object serialization facilities is that the entire process is executed in a manner transparent to any APIs or user intervention. In other words, you need not write any code to utilize serialization routines. When writing an object, the serialization routines must be sure to do so in a manner that allows full reconstruction of the object at a later time. Not only must the class structure be saved, but the values of each member of the structure must be saved as well. If you had a class with the following representation:

```
public class CuteBrownBear
{
        Color eyeColor;
        float heightInches;
        float weightPounds;
}
```

It must be saved so that the values of `eyeColor`, `heightInches`, and `weightPounds` are preserved and can be restored once the reading functions are invoked. Sometimes, however, things can become complicated when objects begin to refer to one another. For example, the following class contains `Cute-BrownBear` as well as several other toy objects that we must save as well:

```
public class ToyBox
{
        CuteBrownBear bearArray[5];
        ActionFigure actionFigureArray[5];
}
```

The serialization routines must not only serialize the ToyBox object, but the CuteBrownBear objects and ActionFigure objects as well. To handle this kind of situation, the serialization routines traverse the objects it is asked to write or read. As it traverses an object representation, it serializes any new objects automatically. If, down the line, it finds another object of a type already serialized, it merely modifies the earlier serialized representation to refer to the new instance. In this manner, serialized objects are compact and efficient without much duplicated code.

For example, when we need to serialize the ToyBox object, the serialization routines first serialize CuteBrownBear in array position one. Array positions two through five are not serialized on their own; rather the original serialized representation is modified to point to their locations and values. So, the final serialized object has one reference to the CuteBrownBear object, plus five sets of data values.

The output streams

Serialization output is handled through the ObjectOutputStream. Serialization calls refer to the writeObject method contained within the stream, passing it the instance of the object to be serialized. The stream first checks to see whether another instance of the same object type has been previously serialized. If it has, the routines handle it as we discussed in the previous section, merely placing the new values alongside the representation. If, however, the object has yet to be serialized, the routines create a new serialized representation and place the values next to it.

Most serialization is handled transparently. But, an object may at any time begin to handle its own serialization by reimplementing the writeObject method. The writeObject method is part of every Object class, and can be overridden on command. If you need a finer-grained serialized representation, or would like to include some kind of encryption or other technique between serialization endpoints, this is where and how you do it.

As an example, let us instantiate a CuteBrownBear object and serialize it:

```java
// create the streams here…
FileOutputStream fileOut = new FileOutputStream("filename");
ObjectOutputStream objectOut = new ObjectOutputStream(fileOut);

// instantiate the new bear object
CuteBrownBear bear = new CuteBrownBear();

// serialize the bear
objectOut.writeObject(bear);
```

Handling object webs

An object web is a complex relationship between two or more objects in which objects refer to other objects that may eventually refer back to it. If you were to serialize such an object representation, you could potentially be caught in an infinite loop. Let's say we had a system of roads between three cities, Seattle, Washington, and San Francisco. We want to take an end-of-summer road trip and visit each city. The only instruction the auto association gave us was "if you hit one of these three roads, follow it until it ends."

Following that logic, we would start at San Francisco, go to Seattle, visit the Redskins, come back to the Golden Gate, and go to Seattle, and so on (see Figure 1-7)..

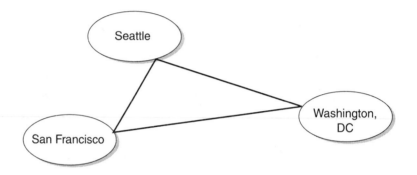

Figure 1–7 An example of serialization in which you need to store objects that are linked by a circuitous route

Likewise, if we were to serialize San Francisco, then Seattle, followed by Washington, and keep following the path back to San Francisco, we would end up following the same loop an infinite number of times. This lattice arrangement ensures that a simple tree-based algorithm will not suffice. Java's object serialization routine accounts for this kind of structure in the same manner that it handles multiple objects of the same type in the same stream.

Because of these object webs, any serialization must take into account those objects that have already been serialized. So, in addition to the serialization methods, Java's object serialization routines also keep track of the object's serialized state. Moreover, Java also keeps track of whether object *types* have been serialized as well. In so doing, it can keep track of the data contained in the object, not the entire object itself.

Reading objects

Reading objects is a matter of taking the serialized representation and reversing the process that created them in the first place. Remember to handle your deserialization in the same order as your serialization, traversing any trees in a similar fashion. The objective is to reconstruct the original object.

The deserialization routines are handled with a corresponding `ObjectInput-Stream` and the `readObject` method contained therein.

Once again, to obtain control over serialization routines for your object, you need to override and reimplement the `writeObject` and `readObject` routines.

Security and fingerprinting

Sometimes objects can be serialized surreptitiously by other objects linked in by your application. If your object does things that you would prefer to keep private and unknown to the world, then you need to disable your objects. Serialization can be disabled for an object by adding the `private transient` tag to the class definition:

```
private transient class CuteBrownBear
{

        ...

}
```

Or, the object itself can override the serialization routines and return a `NoAccess Exception`. The `NoAccessException` tells any object that attempts to serialize your implementation that it may not do so. Furthermore, it gives a sufficient debugging warning to any applications that may reuse your object.

```
public class CuteBrownBear
{
        ... the rest of the CuteBrownBear class goes here ...

        public void writeObject(...) throws NoAccessException
        {
        }

        public void readObject(...) throws NoAccessException
        {
        }

}
```

Serialization overview

Java automatically handles its own object serialization for you. However, if you are so inclined, you may reimplement the serialization routines within your own objects. We have presented you with several serialization concerns in this chapter. If you are going to handle the serialization for a given object, make sure you conform to the various restrictions we have given you. If your objects do not handle their serialization properly, your entire object system may not be serializable.

Yet another issue of importance to Java programmers is performance. While serialization ensures that our objects can be saved and restored, performance issues strike at the very limitations of the language. The greatest programmers in the world can build the applications seen only in science fiction, but they are prevented from doing so by limitations in their hardware and the speed with which their software can be run.

Performance

Performance issues are the primary reason why most major corporations have not yet begun wholesale revisions of their existing computer systems to use the Java language. While many of these issues are real and Java has yet to become the perfect language in all respects, it is not necessarily true that performance is a major show-stopper. Often, the perception is not reality.

Performance Issues

When we speak of performance in Java, we are actually speaking of two very different problems. The first is the download performance of an applet. Today, your hard-core applets will often contain upwards of 20 to 30 classes. Incorporate a mechanism such as Java IDL or Java RMI, and the communication infrastructure may add up to 100 different classes of its own. In order for the applet to run, each of those classes must be downloaded in order to be used.

The second major issue behind performance is runtime performance. For both applets and applications, the speed with which Java computes is pretty slow. Compared to comparable statistics for similar applications written in C++, Java does not measure up. There are several initiatives and technologies becoming available that may render that issue moot.

Download Performance

For applet writers, download performance is the single most important hurdle to overcome. While most programmers can create truly artistic programs that can accomplish a wide variety of things, they often meet a brick wall when their customer tries to download them within a browser. In order to study the download performance of an applet, we must first discuss how an applet is downloaded to begin with.

Java incorporates an object called the class loader. The class loader locates the class to be downloaded, goes about fetching it, and recognizes any other dependent objects and downloads those as well. The browser does the actual downloading and the class loader merely tells it what to do. When the browser downloads an object, it first establishes the connection to be used (see Figure 1-8). Once the connection is made, the object is checked to make sure it has not been downloaded previously. If it has been downloaded before, it is not downloaded, and the connection is closed. If the class has not been downloaded before, it is downloaded, and then the connection is closed.

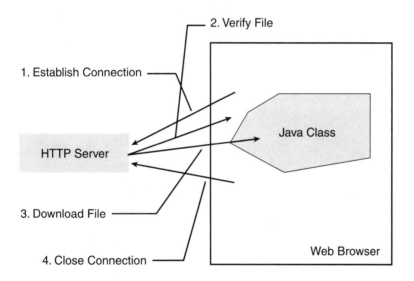

Figure 1–8 Download performance is measured by the time it takes to perform the steps involved.

So, the time in which it takes to download an object is determined by four factors as illustrated in Figure 1-8:

1. Time to open a connection
2. Time to verify a file
3. Time to download the file
4. Time to close the connection

And most importantly, the same four steps are applied to every single class in your entire object system. No matter what you do, you will have to spend the time to download the files. There's no getting around that part because you need those files to run your applet. However, the time spent establishing and closing connections is a waste because you are essentially doing the same thing to the same location each time.

The brilliant engineers behind Java recognized this problem and created the Java Archive. A Java Archive enables you to gather all of your files, stick them in one large archive file, and let everything get downloaded in one fell swoop. This means that there need only be one open connection, one download, and one closure for the entire system of object files.

Using Java Archives is a rather simple process. You must first use the jar utility, which UNIX users will find quite similar to their tar program, to archive your files. This is not unlike "zipping" a bunch of files into one. Once completed, you simply specify the archive in the applet tag in your HTML code:

```
<applet archive="archivename.jar"
           codebase="../classes/"
           code="PrashantIsCool.class">


        ...HTML text here...


</applet>
```

Java Archives greatly improve the download performance of your applets. Without something like them, applets would be restricted to small, compact programs that accomplish little more than animating a dancing duke. The trick is that the browser has to support archives. Currently, Netscape Navigator and Internet Explorer support ZIP files, and both plan to support the JAR standard once it is completed.

Runtime Performance

Runtime performance is a different beast altogether. Where download performance was a relatively simple issue to resolve, runtime performance requires a significant investment in compiler technology. Thankfully, the Java engineers are ahead of the curve on this as well. They have put together a specification for a Just In Time (JIT) compiler.

Remember, Java is an interpreted language. This means that the code you develop is only halfway compiled into bytecodes. The bytecodes are then translated by your local virtual machine into native code. Finally, that native code is run on your machine. When an application executes, the bytecodes are washed through the virtual machine, and the result is then executed on your platform. This ensures platform independence because the bytecodes are translated by the virtual machine into native code as indicated by the flow diagram in Figure 1-9.

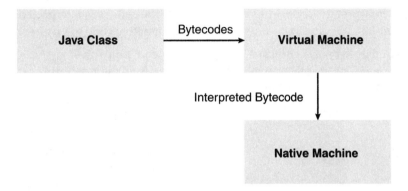

Figure 1–9 Performance of Java using a virtual machine.

Today, non-Java applications are always compiled for the native machine, meaning that you are locked into the platform for which you bought the software but can bypass the Virtual Machine altogether (see Figure 1-10).

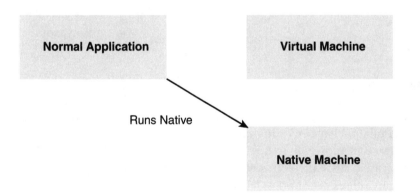

Figure 1–10 Performance of native, non-Java code.

When Java came out with its promise of platform independence, people rejoiced because they no longer had to develop for every computer under the sun. However, the enthusiasm was tempered by the fact that Java was an interpreted language, meaning that the extra steps involved in translating Java code into native code made applications significantly slower. Furthermore, the bytecodes generated by the Java compiler were created with platform independence in mind. This meant that in order to preserve an adequate middle ground, Java bytecodes were arranged so that no platform necessarily got an advantage when it came time to translate into native code. The end result was that not only did it take a bit more time to interpret the code, but also the fact that the code was interpreted from a platform-independent state caused the resulting native code to execute slower.

The JIT compiler solves most of these issues by enabling you to generate native code from your interpreted bytecode. The native code then performs exactly as it would had the program been originally programmed in a native language.

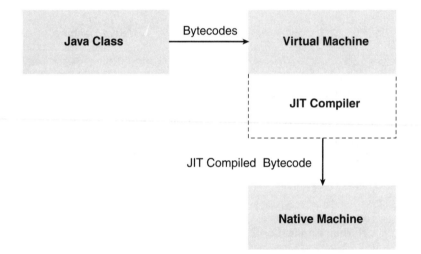

Figure 1–11 Performance of Java using a JIT compiler.

As you can see from Figure 1-11, the JIT exists as part of the virtual machine, and JIT compilation happens automatically if the compiler is installed. Some virtual machines will allow you to turn off JIT compilation, but that should be necessary in only rare cases. Currently, several vendors including Sun, Microsoft, Symantec, and many others are offering JIT compilers that can either be purchased as add-ons to a native virtual machine or are bundled as part of their own virtual machine.

Summary of performance issues

Performance is an issue of vital importance to Java programmers. Because of Java's promise as a platform independent language, several architectural decisions were made to create the language. However, some of these decisions have contributed to Java's faults. Many of these issues have been addressed, namely download and runtime performance. Further deficiencies in the Java language will be corrected as time goes on if Java is to achieve its potential. Ultimately, the growth in applications using the language will uncover these faults as well as the corrections to them.

With several of the major benefits of the Java language under our belt, we can turn to finally developing a networked application. Our networked applications will use many of the techniques we have discussed thus far, as well as several more we will introduce along the way. Congratulations! Your first foray into Java networking is about to begin....

A First Look at Java Networking in Action

So far you have learned the three basic things you need to know in order to write Networked applications in Java:

- Object-oriented design
- Input and output fundamentals
- Threading

 A good object-oriented design will allow you great flexibility in creating clients and servers. You can extend the functionality of a well-designed class very easily: You can simply alter the nuances of the class's architecture in order to facilitate the kind of communication you desire, and you can publish your class to the "world" so that it can be used as it was intended to be.

Solid input and output fundamentals enable your classes to process data quickly and efficiently. With a strong I/O functionality, your classes can accept, manipulate, and return data without much hassle. And once again, you can publish your class to the "world," specifying exactly which data you will accept, streamlining the processing power of your objects.

Effective threading principles will enable your class to produce fast turn-around times on object requests (those methods invoked upon your object), make good use of system resources, and begin to create an entire collection of objects that work together without affecting system performance. Figure 1-12 illustrates how a server can effectively handle information by spawning threads to process that information.

Good networked applications have three things in common:

- Useful interface definitions
- Pragmatic data definitions
- Efficient processing of data

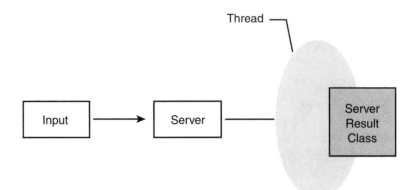

Figure 1–12 Threading can prevent servers from being bogged down.

Hopefully, the treatment of these three topics in this chapter so far provide you with a means to satisfy the criteria set forth above and publish networked Java objects that take full advantage of the language.

Pulling it all together

Throughout this book, we will reimplement the following featured application. Our Internet Calendar Manager is a simple tool designed to enable you to schedule appointments over a network. Because of Java's platform independence, you will be able to run this application on both your Windows 95 laptop as well as your SPARC station. Because the data is held in a central repository with the Internet used as the communication mechanism between the two, it will not matter where you run the application because—no matter what—you will be manipulating the exact same data.

Road map for Success

Your first task is to outline a clear object-oriented strategy to complete your project. For example, the Internet Calendar Manager was designed with modularity as its most crucial element. We wanted to be able to remove and replace certain parts of the program as often as we needed to without affecting the rest of the application. With that in mind, we created the class structure as shown in Figure 1-13.

As you can see, changing a component in the `Scheduler` does not at all affect the `Calendar` portion of the application. Each module is entirely separate from the other. This is an example of code reuse and modularity. Furthermore, the Network module keeps our network interaction limited to one module. All initialization, data exchange, and remote invocations take place only from within the module itself.

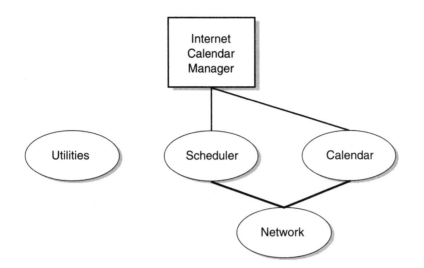

Figure 1–13 The class structure of our Internet Calendar Manager was created with modularity in mind.

Furthermore, we recognized a series of objects that we would require throughout the application. Most of these are not specific to the implementation of any module, rather they are helper objects that deal with wide ranging things from multimedia (sounds and pictures) to animation. These objects were placed in the Utilities module, intended to be used as they are needed.

Project planning

Once the project is divided as we did in the previous section, we must define the interfaces with which each object would talk to one another. In particular, the modularity of the Network component enabled us to redo it for each section without in any way affecting the rest of the application. In fact, the entire Network module wasn't even completed until two weeks before press time. The rest of the application was finished and working, talking to the Network module, but was never communicating with any remote objects.

User interface

The Internet Calendar Manager we created is a stand-alone Java application. We made it so for ease of use. An applet version of the same application will reside on the Web site for this book. In any event, the UI components are the same. A series of buttons along the top of the application control which of the two tasks you can do: add an appointment or delete an appointment.

Pressing the "Scheduler" button takes you to the add an appointment section. There, you can specify the reason for the appointment and the time for which you would like to schedule it. Pressing the Schedule button sends the appointment to the network module which, in turn, talks to the server and places the appointment in the data repository.

The other button takes you to the Calendar application. The Calendar application allows you to view a list of all the appointments scheduled, and the reasons and times for them. You may also delete appointments from within this application.

The buttons switch between the cards created within the card layout, as shown in Figure 1-14.

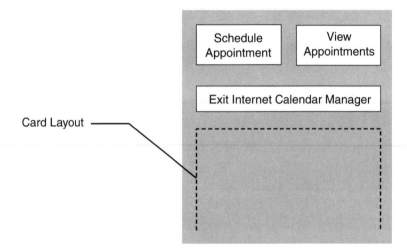

Figure 1–14 An example GUI for our featured application.

Finally, the exit button gracefully terminates the connection, telling the Network module that it wants to exit.

Network modules

The Network module will be changed from chapter to chapter to reflect the new form of network communication. However, the APIs will remain the same. The Network module provides an abstracted layer above the network communication mechanism of choice. In so doing, we can provide a series of four methods that are of importance to the user, while keeping the network hidden from the rest of the application:

```
public class NetworkModule
{
        public void scheduleAppointment(
            String reason,
            int time);
```

```
        public Vector getAppointments();

        public void initNetwork();

        public void shutdownNetwork();
}
```

As far as the rest of this application is concerned, the Network module will accept information and do something with it over the network. Precisely what that something is is of no concern to the application itself.

Servers

The Network module would be useless without a server for it to talk to. Every server implements the same exact routines, regardless of whether it is a JDBC server, an RMI server, or an IDL server. In fact, the server itself is interchangeable, enabling us to choose on the fly to which one we want to talk. Simply run the proper application to take advantage of the communication mechanism of your choice.

```
public interface InternetCalendarServer
{
        void scheduleAppointment();

        void getAppointments();
}
```

The interface definition in this snippet does not take into account any kind of data structure in which to store an appointment. The server code implements both of the methods above, as well as establishes and defines the following data structure:

```
public interface InternetCalendar Server
{
    Appointment Type
    {
       String reason;
       int time;
    }

    void scheduleAppointment(
       AppointmentType appointment
    );

    AppointmentType[] getAppointments();
}
```

Keep in mind that the interface definitions shown are pseudo-code only. As we will see later, server definition varies widely between each communication alternative. In Java IDL we will see how an entire language is available with which to define servers. In Java RMI we can create servers using Java itself.

NOTE: In an effort to show you how easy and fun network programming can be with Java, we have devised a simple application that we will redo every chapter. In one chapter we will use sockets, in another CORBA. Eventually, you will have four different applications that do the same thing. With the four applications, you can compare ease-of-use and performance, as well as figure out what all the hubbub is about network programming. The next four chapters will explore the basic alternatives available to network programmers intent on using the Java language.

Summary

Wow! Not only have we learned the nuances of the Java programming language, but we've delved into the wide world of Threads, explored some of the important performance issues we need to deal with, and seen how easy it is to save and restore our creations. These are great tools to have as we begin our journey through the realm of inter-process communication, networked programming, and distributed design.

Core Java Networking

Core Java Networking covers the four major technologies for building client/server applications in Java. First, Java Sockets examines the Java Developer's Kit's built-in socket functionality. Sockets are the backbone of all networked communication, and this chapter covers them in detail. Java IDL, the Interface Definition Language, covers the Java binding to the CORBA standard. Using Java IDL, Java applications can use legacy systems and CORBA objects directly. Java RMI, Remote Method Invocation, takes a look at Java-to-Java client-to-server systems. RMI enables Java client applets and applications to seamlessly connect across networks to Java servers. JDBC, Java Database Connectivity, allows Java applications to connect to existing data stores without any unnecessary overhead.

Chapter 2: Java Sockets
Chapter 3: Java IDL: Interface Definition Language
Chapter 4: Java RMI: Remote Method Invocation
Chapter 5: JDBC: Java Database Connectivity

CHAPTER 2

Inter-process Communication and Protocols

Point-to-point Communication

Broadcast Communication

A Sockets Project

Java
Sockets

Sockets and Inter-Process Communication

At the heart of everything we discuss in this book is the notion of inter-process communication (IPC). In this chapter, we will show you some examples using Java mechanisms for inter-process communication. IPC is a fancy way of saying "two or more Java programs talking with each other." Usually the programs execute on different computers, but sometimes they may execute on the same host.

Introduction to IPC

When you call Charles Schwab to check on your stock portfolio, you dial a telephone number and, once connected, you press some telephone buttons to request various services and press other buttons to send parameters, such as the numeric codes for stock symbols in which you are interested. You may think of your account as an object with different methods you can invoke to purchase or to sell stocks, to get current quotes, to get your current position in a stock, or to request a wire transfer to a Swiss bank. You are a *client* and the other end is a *server*, providing the services (methods) you request.

Of course, the server also provides services to many other clients. You can be a client of other servers, such as when you order a pizza with a push-button telephone. Sometimes a server can be a client as well. A medical records query server may have to send a request to two or three hospitals to gather the information you request for a patient. Thus your server becomes a client of the hospital servers it queries on your behalf.

All of these situations are examples of inter-process communication. Each client and each server reside in different processes. Sometimes you, the individual, are the client; other times it is a computer. Sometimes the server is an application that listens in on what you type on your telephone pad and processes the information; other times it will be a program, perhaps written in Java as we will do later in this chapter. IPC is how our applications communicate, but it also refers to the mechanism we use. This chapter explores the fundamentals of IPC using something called a socket.

Sockets

The communication construct underneath all of this communication is more than likely a *socket*. Each program reads from and writes to a socket in much the same way that you open, read, write to, and close a file. Essentially, there are two types of sockets:

- **One is analogous to a telephone (a connection-oriented service, e.g., Transmission Control Protocol (TCP))**

- **One is analogous to a mailbox (a connectionless "datagram" service, e.g., (Unreliable Datagram Protocol (UDP))**

An important difference between TCP connection sockets and UDP datagram sockets is that the TCP protocol makes sure that everything you send gets to the other end, while the UDP protocol does not. Much like mailing a letter, it is up to you, the sender, to check that it was received by the recipient.

Sometimes when you use the postal service, your letter becomes "lost in the mail." When the letter absolutely, positively has to be there, you may need a more reliable form of postage. Similarly, your choice between using a datagram or a connection socket is easily determined by the nature of your application. If all your data fits in an 8K datagram and you do not need to know if it was received at the other end, then a UDP datagram is fine. Mailing party invitations is one example where UDP is more appropriate than TCP. If the length of service warrants the expense of establishing a connection (three handshake packets), or it is necessary that all the packets be received in the same order as they were sent, such as transferring a file that is more than 8K bytes long, then a TCP socket must be used. Likewise, if we were to mail our important package using something like Federal Express, we would be able to track the package and know when it arrives at its destination.

NOTE: A socket is sometimes called a "pipe" because there are two ends (or points as we occasionally refer to them) to the communication. Messages can be sent from either end. The difference, as we will soon see, between a client and a server socket is that client sockets must know beforehand that information is coming, whereas server sockets can simply wait for information to come to it. It's sort of like the difference between being recruited for a job and actively seeking one.

In this chapter, we will write an online ordering application, using TCP, and a broadcast communication application, using UDP. These applications will use the following classes from the java.net package, as illustrated in Table 2-1.

Table 2–1 Java socket types and their corresponding protocol

Mechanism	Description
Socket	TCP endpoint (a "telephone")
ServerSocket	TCP endpoint (a "receptionist")
DatagramSocket	UDP endpoint (a "mailbox")
DatagramPacket	UDP packet (a "letter")
URL	Uniform Resource Locator (an "address")
URLConnection	Connection to a web object (e.g., a CGI-bin script)

Writing to a port

When we speak about applications communicating, they are really speaking to ports on either end of a communication link. Ports are sort of like a telephone line. When you talk to your mommy on a telephone, she is on one end of the line, you are on the other. The telephone link itself could be viewed as a port. On a computer, these ports are available on any TCP/IP-based network machine. One of the ""well-known ports" is:

```
echo     7/tcp
```

which means that TCP port 7 provides an "echo" service. It is straightforward to write an echo program in Java. First, we must create an EchoTest class that contains one variable, the stream to which we will connect our socket:

```
public class EchoTest
{
    DataInputStream in;
}
```

Then we must initialize the data stream within our constructor. We supply the system's standard input (the keyboard) as the variable specifying the source of the input stream:

```
public class EchoTest
{
    DataInputStream in;
```

```
    EchoTest()
    {
      in = new DataInputStream(System.in);
    }
}
```

Now we complete our Java-only echo program by creating an infinite loop in which we get a line then immediately write it out to the screen.

```
public class EchoTest
{
    DataInputStream in;

    EchoTest()
    {
      in = new DataInputStream(System.in);
    }

    public static void main(
      String args[]
    )
    {
      String line;

      while(true)
      {
       line="";

       try

         {
           line = in.readLine();
         }
         catch (IOException e)
         {
           System.err.println(e.getMessage());
         }

         System.out.println(line);
        }
      }
}
```

You can execute the program that we created by doing the following, and get similar results:

```
%prompt% java MyEcho
abc                    input...
abc                        ...output
def                    input...
def                        ...output
xyz                    input...
xyz                        ...output
^C
%prompt%
```

Introducing sockets in Java

To take our first step toward proficiency using Java sockets, we modify our echo program to do the following:

1. Read a line from the keyboard
2. Write it to a socket connected to TCP port 7
3. Read the reply from the socket connection
4. Print the line from the socket to the screen

A socket object is created as follows:

```
Socket s = Socket("localhost", 7);
```

The two arguments to the `Socket` constructor are *hostname* and *port number*. We use "localhost" to keep it simple. The hostname is passed as a `String` variable, typically from the command line. Unlike operating system calls, note that the socket's protocol is not specified—*Java Sockets are always TCP sockets*.

Here is a simple TCP client written in Java. First, we must create the `EchoClient` class and import all of the Java libraries that we will use in our program.

```
import java.io.*;
import java.net.*;

public class EchoClient
{
}
```

Now, we must create a function in which we will place a loop similar to the one we created with our Java-only client. This loop must have two objects on which to act, the `DataInputStream` from the socket from which it will get data, and the

`DataOutputStream` from the socket to which it will write data. We assumed this was standard input and standard output for our Java-only client, but we will not make that assumption here:

```java
import java.io.*;
import java.net.*;

public class EchoClient
{
    public static void echoclient(
      DataInputStream  sin,
      DataOutputStream sout
    ) throws IOException
    {
    }
}
```

Now, we must get an input stream for the keyboard, and an output stream based on the socket. We will also add the loop here. The loop will first get input from the keyboard using the stream we just created. Then it will write that data directly to the socket.

```java
import java.io.*;
import java.net.*;

public class EchoClient
{
    public static void echoclient(
       DataInputStream  sin,
       DataOutputStream sout
    ) throws IOException
    {
       DataInputStream in = new DataInputStream(System.in);
       PrintStream out = new PrintStream(sout);

       String line;

       while(true)
       {
          line="";
```

```
        // read keyboard and write to TCP socket
        try
        {
            line = in.readLine();
            out.println( line );
        }
        catch (IOException e)
        {
            System.err.println(e.getMessage());
        }
    }
}
}
```

Just for the heck of it, now we will read the activity on the socket and stick it on the screen.

```
import java.io.*;
import java.net.*;

public class EchoClient
{
    public static void echoclient(
        DataInputStream   sin,
        DataOutputStream  sout
    ) throws IOException
    {
        DataInputStream in = new DataInputStream(System.in);
        PrintStream out = new PrintStream(sout);

        String line;

        while(true)
        {
            line="";

            // read keyboard and write to TCP socket
            try
            {
                line = in.readLine();
                out.println( line );
            }
        }
```

```
            catch (IOException e)
            {
                System.err.println(e.getMessage());
            }

            // read TCP socket and write to terminal
            try
            {
              line = sin.readLine();
              System.out.println(line);
            }
            catch (IOException e)
               {
               System.err.println(e.getMessage());
            }
         }
      }
}
```

Finally, we can create our main application here. In our main application, we will create the socket first, then get a `DataInputStream` and a `DataOutputStream` based on it. This enables us to read and write to the socket easily, as well as pass it on to the function we created earlier. Once we are finished, we must close the connection to the socket.

ALERT: As we will discuss later, too many open connections are a system liability. If a connection is not in use, but is still open, other applications may not be able to connect to the port to which you are connected.

```
import java.io.*;
import java.net.*;

public class EchoClient
{
    public static void echoclient(
       DataInputStream  sin,
       DataOutputStream sout
    ) throws IOException
    {
       DataInputStream in = new DataInputStream(System.in);
       PrintStream out = new PrintStream(sout);
```

```
    String line;

    while(true)
    {
      line="";

      // read keyboard and write to TCP socket
      try
      {
        line = in.readLine();
        out.println(line);
      }
      catch(IOException e)
      {
        System.err.println(e.getMessage());
      }

      // read TCP socket and write to terminal
      try
      {
        line = sin.readLine();
        System.out.println(line);
      }
      catch(IOException e)
      {
        System.err.println(e.getMessage());
      }
    }
}

public static void main(
  String[] args
)
{
  Socket s = null;

  try
  {
    // Create a socket to communicate with "echo"
```

```java
            // on the specified host
            s = new Socket(args[0], 7);

            // Create streams for reading and writing
            // lines of text from and to this socket.
            DataInputStream sin =
              new DataInputStream(s.getInputStream());
            DataOutputStream sout =
              new DataOutputStream(s.getOutputStream());

            // Tell the user that we've connected
            System.out.println("Connected to " +
                s.getInetAddress() +
                ":" +
            s.getPort());

        echoclient(sin, sout);
}
catch (IOException e)
{
    System.err.println(e);
}

    // Always be sure to close the socket
    finally
    {
      try
      {
        if(s != null)
          {
           s.close();
          }
          catch (IOException exc)
          {
              ;
          }
      }
    }
}
```

When we execute our program, we send a message to the echo socket, and then read whatever information comes back on the socket and print it out. Because the echo socket merely takes whatever input it gets and bounces it right back to the port, what we get in return on the socket is exactly what we sent. The output is displayed below. If you need to connect to another host, substitute its name for localhost.

```
%prompt% java EchoClient localhost
Connected to localhost/127.0.0.1:7
abc           request...
abc                 ...reply
xyz           request...
xyz                 ...reply
^C
```

This service (and any other) can be tested by using the TELNET command that is available on all networked computers. In this case, the TELNET program acts in the same manner as our client, sending information to the port and reading whatever it gets back.

```
%prompt% telnet localhost 7
Trying 127.0.0.1...
Connected to localhost.
Escape character is '^]'.
abc           request...
abc                 ...reply
^C
xyz           request...
xyz                 ...reply
^]     control-right-bracket
telnet> quit
Connection closed.
```

Summary of sockets

We have shown you what, in the most basic sense, sockets are and how they are implemented in Java. The subsequent sections in this chapter build on this material and show you how to create an entire client/server system using only sockets. The rest of this book showcases several other Java communication technologies that use sockets as their underlying mechanism to transfer data across networks. Sockets in turn depend on protocols to transfer information. Protocols are the "language" that sockets speak with one another.

Protocols

When a foreign dignitary arrives at the White House, certain protocols are observed. These describe who is introduced and when and with what fanfare. The President is always introduced last, and makes his or her entrance to the tune of "Hail to the Chief." In the geek world, a protocol ensures that certain formalities are observed when information is exchanged across networks. This includes the format of the message, the content of the message, and the type of connection used to send the message. There are several kinds of protocols, ranging from the time-tested TCP/IP or UDP to the newer Internet Inter-ORB Protocol.

The OSI stack

There are seven layers in the International Standards Organization (ISO) Open Systems Interconnection (OSI) reference model, referred to as the OSI stack, shown in Table 2-2.

Table 2-2 The OSI reference model for communication technology

Application	TELNET, FTP, SMTP, HTTP
Presentation	byte-order, ASCII-UNICODE, COM-CORBA
Session	Login session, RPC call, ORB/RMI invocation
Transport	End-to-end communication (with possible ack)
Network	Host-to-host communication (one hop in a path)
Link	Network adapter card device driver
Physical	Ethernet, ISDN, PPP, T3, CATV

Even though they are not specifically part of the OSI stack, if they were, TCP and UDP would be at the transport level (layer 4), while IP would be at the network layer (layer 3). A while ago, OSI, TCP, and UDP competed for network standards. Today, TCP and UDP stand alone. The Internet Protocol (IP) code maintains routing tables to make sure each IP packet gets to the next hop in a route toward its destination. Note that one UDP datagram or one TCP segment may be broken into many IP packets. Each IP packet may take a different route from the source to the destination, and the packets may arrive in a different order than they were sent. UDP sends the received packets upward toward the application code as soon as they arrive. TCP collects the IP packets and assembles a TCP segment before sending it upward, so the application receives data in the same order it was sent.

The TCP protocol also keeps track of IP packets, sending an acknowledgment when a whole segment is received, or requesting a retransmission if all IP packets

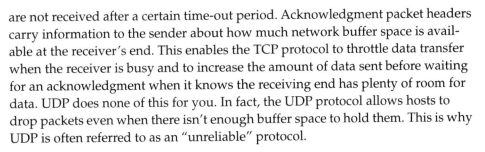

are not received after a certain time-out period. Acknowledgment packet headers carry information to the sender about how much network buffer space is available at the receiver's end. This enables the TCP protocol to throttle data transfer when the receiver is busy and to increase the amount of data sent before waiting for an acknowledgment when it knows the receiving end has plenty of room for data. UDP does none of this for you. In fact, the UDP protocol allows hosts to drop packets even when there isn't enough buffer space to hold them. This is why UDP is often referred to as an "unreliable" protocol.

TCP/IP

TCP/IP is a non-proprietary, ubiquitous network protocol. It gained wide acceptance, not because of a Department of Defense (DOD) design requirement that it survive a nuclear war, but because it came with many useful services such as remote terminal connections (TELNET—terminal emulation), file transfer (FTP—file transfer protocol), and electronic mail (SMTP—simple mail transfer protocol).

It was not just another propeller-head technical marvel; it provided some very useful services to end-users. Its design was based on an informal, grass-roots review, via e-mail, of Requests for Comments (RFCs) for protocol specifications, network addresses, and network services. Its acceptance has grown far beyond anyone's wildest dreams.

HTTP

The HyperText Transfer Protocol (HTTP)-based Mosaic Web browser was the "killer app" that made the Internet easy to use for non-technical users. HTTP enabled the development of the World Wide Web. Java is the next step to advance distributed computing in an object-oriented direction. HTTP is discussed in Chapter 6, "The Java Web Server," but it is important to realize that HTTP is a protocol on top of sockets. Furthermore, under the covers HTTP, uses TCP/IP.

IIOP

The Internet Inter-ORB Protocol (IIOP) is an open Internet protocol for communication between objects residing on a network. IIOP enables Java objects to invoke one another using an industry standard messaging system. Without IIOP, objects on the client end would not be able to talk to objects on the server end without first synchronizing their languages. IIOP standardizes the means clients and servers use to exchange information. As we will see later in this chapter, the format of the messages sent between clients and servers is of the utmost importance. Even we in our daily lives require a standard message format. If I were to start transposing my nouns and verbs (such as "were If I transposing to start my nouns and verbs"), then no one would understand me. Similarly, IIOP enables objects to understand one another.

Protocols and sockets

A socket is an endpoint for a network connection. Both ends have a socket, just as telephones and mailboxes are at both ends. Each socket has a "name" (port number) associated with it. For example, TELNET opens a file named "/etc/passwd" and a socket named "23." "Well-known" ports are listed in /etc/services on UNIX systems and in c:\solarnet\etc\services on Windows systems that use PCNFSPRO2.0 network software.

For example, port 25 is used by sendmail (facilitating the Simple Mail Transfer Protocol), port 23 is used by TELNET, port 21 is used by FTP, and port 80 is used by HTTP. Port numbers less than 1024 are reserved for use only by the privileged root (superuser) account on UNIX systems; port numbers between 1024 and 5000 are assigned by the TCP/IP code inside the kernel; and port numbers above 5000 are available for use by ordinary (non-root) users.

It all ends with protocols

The clients and servers that we develop in this chapter and in this book will use different protocols. This chapter explores the differences between TCP and UDP protocols, and does so by creating its own message formats and attaching to different ports. Subsequent chapters on Java IDL and Java RMI use different protocols. In the end, however, all communication alternatives eventually settle on either TCP or UDP as their base protocol. TCP and UDP are sort of like building blocks. Without a building block like them, communication between applications would be impossible.

TCP/IP Client

Clients are the senders of information. Servers are the recipients of that information. Think of a client approaching your restaurant with a wad of dough, and you, as the server, gladly accepting that money for your own, shall we say, charity. In this section we begin our discussion of client/server programming by developing an application that transmits information across a network connection to another program.

Developing clients for servers

Suppose you're home with your cronies watching the Super Bowl and the Mighty Washington Redskins on television. As invariably happens, you've run out of nachos and dip before half-time, so you decide to replenish the nutrition supply by ordering a pizza. Today, when you want to order that pizza, you pick up the phone and call your favorite pizzeria to request a delivery.

A few years ago, a small start-up company in the Silicon Valley called the Santa Cruz Operation (SCO) developed an Internet pizza ordering application. By today's standards, it was quite low-tech, based solely on HTML forms and requiring someone to read the information manually on the other end via e-mail. The nifty thing about this Internet Pizza Hut was the idea that you could simply use your computer and communicate with a faraway place and get a pizza. In this sense, SCO was pretty well ahead of the game—they were one of the first to genuinely use the Internet, not the corporate intranet, to conduct business with remote users.

In this section, we will develop our own Pizza client/server system as an ultra-hip high-tech alternative to the telephone and publish it to the world. This time, however, we will use Java and implement our `PizzaServer` using sockets. You'd begin by creating the client class. For our example, the `PizzaTool` we are about to create is a stand-alone Java application and will have a fancy GUI interface that you can design yourself. Our GUI code's framework looks something like this:

```java
import java.awt.*;
import java.net.*;
import java.io.*;

public class PizzaTool extends Frame
{
    // AWT Components
    … skip these for now …

    PizzaTool()
    {
       // initialize the application frame

    // create the GUIs
    }

    public boolean action(
      Event evt,
      Object obj
    )
    {
      if(evt.target == sendButton)
      {
    }
```

```
    return true;
  }

  public static void main(
    String args[]
  )
  {
    PizzaTool pizza = new PizzaTool();
    pizza.show();
  }
}
```

NOTE: As will be our practice throughout this book, we show you the completed GUI rather than showing the code development process for it. There are several GUI builders on the market, and we hope you will choose one to assist you.

Name

Address

Phone Number

○ Small   ○ Veggies

○ Medium   ○ Meat

○ Large   ○ California

Submit

Figure 2–1 A sample GUI for the PizzaTool.

When displayed, our pizza tool GUI will look like the one shown in Figure 2-1.

We need to modify this working client to send its information over the network to the other end. To do so, we must create a socket in our application's constructor and initialize it as we did earlier. We will use port number 8205 in this application.

```java
import java.awt.*;
import java.net.*;
import java.io.*;

public class PizzaTool extends Frame
{
    // AWT Components
    … skip these for now …

    // network components
    Socket socket;
    DataInputStream inStream;
    PrintStream outStream;

PizzaTool()
{
    // initialize the application frame

    // initialize the network
    try
    {
        socket = new Socket("localhost", 8205);
        inStream = new
          DataInputStream(socket.getInputStream());
        outStream = new PrintStream(socket.getOutputStream());
    }
    catch(Exception exc)
    {
        System.out.println("Error! - " + exc.toString());
    }

    // create the GUIs
}

public boolean action(
    Event evt,
    Object obj
    )
    {
    if(evt.target == sendButton)
```

```
        {
    }

    return true;
    }

    public static void main(
        String args[]
    )
    {
        PizzaTool pizza = new PizzaTool();
        pizza.show();
    }
}
```

Inside our `action` method, we need to send the information we gather from our GUI back to the server. The server then makes a calculation and sends us the total for the order. First, we must send information across the socket using the `outStream` variable we derived from the socket. Then, just as we did earlier, we must turn around and read information from the same socket using the `inStream` variable.

```
import java.awt.*;
import java.net.*;
import java.io.*;

public class PizzaTool extends Frame
{
    // AWT Components
    … skip these for now …

    // network components
    Socket socket;
    DataInputStream inStream;
    PrintStream outStream;

    PizzaTool()
    {
        // initialize the application frame

        // initialize the network
        try
```

```java
    {
     socket = new Socket("localhost", 8205);
     inStream = new
       DataInputStream(socket.getInputStream());
     outStream = new PrintStream(socket.getOutputStream());
}
catch(Exception exc)
{
    System.out.println("Error! - " + exc.toString());
}

// create the GUIs
}

public boolean action(
    Event evt,
    Object obj
)
{
  if(evt.target == sendButton)
  {
      // send the order to the server
      instructionField.setText("Sending Order...");
      try
      {
        outStream.println(
            nameField.getText() + "|" +
            addressField.getText() + "|" +
            phoneField.getText() + "|" +
            size + "|" +
            toppings);
      }
      catch(Exception exc)
      {
        System.out.println("Error! - " + exc.toString());
      }

      // get the price back
      instructionField.setText(
      "Receiving Order Total...");
```

```
      String totalString = new String();
      try
      {
        totalString = inStream.readLine();
      }
      catch(Exception exc)
      {
        System.out.println("Error! - " + exc.toString());
      }
    }
  }
}

public static void main(
    String args[]
)
{
    PizzaTool pizza = new PizzaTool();
    pizza.show();
}
}
```

Notice how we send information to the server. We have created our own protocol and message format to use to send the three important customer fields, as well as the kind of pizza ordered, directly to the pizza server. The format is delimited by the bar sign (" | ") and, as we will see in a moment, is interpreted on the server end.

```
outStream.println(
    nameField.getText() + "|" +
    addressField.getText() + "|" +
    phoneField.getText() + "|" +
    size + "|" +
    toppings);
```

Once complete, our application then is able to publish the information it received from the server.

NOTE: In order to conserve paper (save some trees), we have not shown you the entire code listing for both the GUI and the network portion of our application. As always, a full, working version of this application can be found on the CD-ROM that accompanies this book.

Socket programming is at the heart of everything we discuss in this book. Every communication technology involved with computers uses sockets in some fashion. Often, having control over the format and length of messages between clients and servers is of great importance. We could just as easily have created our pizza application using a mechanism found in other parts of this book. However, by using sockets we had full control over how the communication is implemented. In the next section, we need to create the server that resides on the other end of port 8205.

TCP server

A connection-oriented service is best for applications that require characters to be received in the same order in which they were sent, such as keystrokes typed from a terminal or bytes in an ASCII file transfer. Usually, the connection is kept open for a long time relative to the length of time to set up the connection (a "handshake" of three IP packets).

Connection-oriented protocols, such as TCP, send an acknowledgment when the data is received, and they retransmit data automatically if an acknowledgment is not received before the time-out period has expired. Each acknowledgment packet tells the receiving side how much buffer space is available at the other end. This enables both endpoints to transmit a "window" of data, perhaps several 8K packets, before stopping to wait for an acknowledgment from the other end. When the acknowledgment is received, the window size is updated from the packet header. This enables TCP to throttle data transfer when one side is running low on buffer space and to increase data transfer when the other side has plenty of room to receive data.

NOTE: Everything mentioned in the previous paragraph is done by the TCP protocol. A programmer need not worry about data acknowledgment, retransmissions, or the dynamic negotiation of data transfer rate. This is why TCP is referred to as a "reliable protocol."

Server methodology

A typical TCP application opens a "well-known" port to receive connection requests, and then it spawns a child process or a separate thread of execution to perform the requested service. This ensures that the server is always ready for more invocations. A single-threaded server must poll the sockets constantly, and when it detects activity it must spawn a new process to handle the incoming request. Our multi-threaded server can simply wait for information on a socket and spawn a thread to handle incoming requests.

The `PizzaServer` that we will implement will hang on port 8205 and wait for information. When the client sends its bar-delimited request, the server will spawn a thread to handle the request. The thread reads the information, processes it, and sends a reply.

Setting up the server

We must create the `PizzaServer` object itself. The `PizzaServer` is a stand-alone Java application with its own application main. We must also create a `PizzaThread` that inherits from the Java `Thread` class. This threaded object will be created every time we detect activity on the port. As we discussed in our Chapter 1 section on threads, it is one of two ways we could have implemented the server object. We leave the other threaded version as an exercise to the reader.

```
import java.net.*;
import java.io.*;
import java.lang.*;
import java.util.*;

public class PizzaServer
{
    public static void main(
        String args[]
    )
    {
    }
}

// threaded pizza!
class PizzaThread extends Thread
{
}
```

Initializing the server socket

Inside the main program, we must create a `ServerSocket`. The `ServerSocket` is a Java type whose sole purpose is to enable you to wait on a socket for activity. It is initialized by specifying the port on which you want to wait.

```
import java.net.*;
import java.io.*;
import java.lang.*;
import java.util.*;

public class PizzaServer
{
```

```
    public static void main(
        String args[]
    )
    {
        // initialize the network connection
        try
        {
          ServerSocket serverSocket = new ServerSocket(8205);
        }
        catch(Exception exc)
        {
          System.out.println("Error! - " + exc.toString());
        }
    }
}


// threaded pizza!
class PizzaThread extends Thread
{
}
```

Creating the thread

The `PizzaThread` object will accept one variable, the `incoming` socket from which it gathers information. We need to specify this here because the main server program has already grabbed hold of the socket and we don't want to do so twice. We merely pass the socket obtained by the main program on to the thread. We will also implement the `run` method for the thread.

```
import java.net.*;
import java.io.*;
import java.lang.*;
import java.util.*;

public class PizzaServer
{
    public static void main(
        String args[]
    )
    {
        // initialize the network connection
        try
          {
```

```
                ServerSocket serverSocket = new ServerSocket(8205);
            }
            catch(Exception exc)
            {
                System.out.println("Error! - " + exc.toString());
            }
        }
}


// threaded pizza!
class PizzaThread extends Thread
{
        // the socket we are writing to
        Socket incoming;

        PizzaThread(
          Socket incoming
        )
        {
            this.incoming = incoming;
        }

        // run method implemented by Thread class
        public void run()
        {
        }
}
```

Detecting information and starting the thread

Now, we must wait on the thread until activity occurs. Once we detect some sem-blance of information coming across the socket, we must pop a thread automati-cally and let the thread get and process the information. Our main program merely delegates activity to others.

```
import java.net.*;
import java.io.*;
import java.lang.*;
import java.util.*;

public class PizzaServer
{
    public static void main(
```

```java
            String args[]
        )
        {
            // initialize the network connection
            try
            {
                ServerSocket serverSocket = new ServerSocket(8205);

                // now sit in an infinite loop until we get something
                while(true)
                {
                    // accept the message
                    Socket incoming = serverSocket.accept();

                    // spawn a thread to handle the request
                    PizzaThread pt = new PizzaThread(incoming);
                    pt.start();
                }
            }
            catch(Exception exc)
            {
                System.out.println("Error! - " + exc.toString());
            }
        }
    }


// threaded pizza!
class PizzaThread extends Thread
{
    // the socket we are writing to
    Socket incoming;

    PizzaThread(
        Socket incoming
    )
    {
        this.incoming = incoming;
    }

    // run method implemented by Thread class
```

```
    public void run()
    {
    }
}
```

Notice also how we must call the `start` method explicitly on the thread. As we discussed in the Threads section of Chapter 1, if a class inherits from the Java `Thread` class, the thread must be started from outside the class.

Gathering information

Once the thread is running, it needs to go to the socket and get information from it. To do so, we must obtain in and out streams from the socket. Remember, the socket is merely a construct. In order to get information from it, it must be abstracted into an input/output mechanism. We will then be able to read and write to the socket. As we discussed in our client section, the data we are going to receive is in a bar-delimited format. We must use a `StringTokenizer` object to extract the information from the message.

```java
import java.net.*;
import java.io.*;
import java.lang.*;
import java.util.*;

public class PizzaServer
{
    public static void main(
      String args[]
    )
    {
      // initialize the network connection
      try
      {
          ServerSocket serverSocket = new ServerSocket(8205);

        // now sit in an infinite loop until
        // we get something
          while(true)
          {
              // accept the message
              Socket incoming = serverSocket.accept();

              // spawn a thread to handle the request
```

```
                PizzaThread pt = new PizzaThread(incoming);
                pt.start();
            }
        }
        catch(Exception exc)
        {
            System.out.println("Error! - " + exc.toString());
        }
    }
}


// threaded pizza!
class PizzaThread extends Thread
{
// the socket we are writing to
Socket incoming;

PizzaThread(
    Socket incoming
)
{
    this.incoming = incoming;
}

// run method implemented by Thread class
public void run()
{
    try
    {
        // get input from socket
        DataInputStream in =
            new DataInputStream(incoming.getInputStream());

        // get output to socket
        PrintStream out =
            new PrintStream(incoming.getOutputStream());

        // now get input from the server until it closes the
        // connection
        boolean finished = false;
```

```java
while(!finished)
{
    String newOrder = in.readLine();

    // convert to a readable format
    try
    {
    StringTokenizer stk =
            new StringTokenizer(newOrder, "|");
        String name = stk.nextToken();
    String address = stk.nextToken();
    String phone = stk.nextToken();
    int size =
      Integer.valueOf(stk.nextToken()).intValue();
    int toppings =
      Integer.valueOf(stk.nextToken()).intValue();

    // no exception was thrown so calculate total
    int total = (size * 5) + (toppings * 1);

    // send the result back to the client
    out.println("$" + total + ".00");

    // put our result on the screen
    System.out.println(
        "pizza for " + name + " was " + totalString);
    }
    catch(NoSuchElementException exc)
    {
        finished = true;
    }
 }
}
catch(Exception exc)
{
    System.out.println("Error! - " + exc.toString());
    }

    // close the connection
    try
```

```
        {
          incoming.close();
        }
        catch(Exception exc)
        {
          System.out.println("Error! - " + exc.toString());
        }
    }
}
```

Note in particular the two lines we actually use for reading information from the socket and sending information back:

```
      String newOrder = in.readLine();
      ...
      // send the result back to the client
      out.println("$" + total + ".00");
```

These two lines have the same syntax as they would if they were reading and writing a file. In fact, as we have discussed in Chapter 1's input/output section, to the programmer a socket is nothing more than a file. We are able to use streams, read and write information, and save sockets just as we would files. This is an important concept to grasp because the same security restrictions apply to sockets as do to files. We will discuss security in greater detail in Chapter 11, "Java and Security."

Clients and servers in short

So far we have implemented an application for which we know what is on both ends. This form of point-to-point communication is one way to create a networked application. We created a message, located the destination for the message, and shipped it off. While reliable, point-to-point communication is important, we also want to be able to form a message and broadcast it. In so doing, anyone, anywhere can grab the message and act on it. This form of broadcast communication can also be accomplished using Java sockets and is discussed in the next section.

UDP client

We have spoken so far about TCP communication, which we have mentioned is a "point-to-point, reliable protocol." Well, what makes an unreliable protocol? An unreliable protocol is one in which you send a chunk of information, and if it gets lost along the way, nobody really minds. TCP provides an infrastructure that ensures a communication is sent and arrives safely. Another protocol, Unreliable

Datagram Protocol (UDP), is a "spit in the wind" protocol. One day, you wake up, spit into the wind, and hope it will land somewhere. Likewise, with datagrams you can easily form a message, send it, and hope it gets to the other end. There are no guarantees that it will ever arrive, so be careful to choose wisely.

Datagrams

At the beginning of this chapter, we referred to datagrams as letters that we send to a mailbox. In fact, a datagram is a chunk of memory, not unlike a letter—a chunk of paper into which we put information and send off to a mailbox. Just as with the U.S. Postal Service, there is absolutely no guarantee that the letter will ever arrive at its destination.

Here's a sample "receive buffer" datagram:

```
DatagramPacket packet = new DatagramPacket(buf, 256);
```

You must give the constructor the name of a byte or character array to receive the data and the length of the buffer in bytes or characters. You get data as follows:

```
socket.receive(packet);
```

where socket is created as follows:

```
socket = new DatagramSocket();
```

The `DatagramSocket` class is an endpoint (mailbox) for UDP communication. Like the `Socket` class (which uses TCP), there is no need for a programmer to specify the transport-level protocol to use.

After a datagram is received, you can find out where it came from as follows:

```
address = packet.getAddress();
port = packet.getPort();
```

and you can return a reply as follows:

```
packet = new DatagramPacket(buf, buf.length, address, port);
socket.send(packet);
```

This datagram will go out the same UDP port (akin to a "mailbox"), to the other process receiving datagrams on that UDP port number. A UDP server can specify its service port number in its constructor, in this case port number 31543.

```
socket = new DatagramSocket(31543);
```

NOTE: Datagrams are sort of like that old "I Love Lucy" episode in which Lucy and Ethel go to work in a candy factory. As they stand in front of a conveyor belt, little candies begin to flow out. Lucy and Ethel are able to wrap and package the candies as they come out. Soon, their boss speeds up the belt and the candies begin to flow out really fast and Lucy and Ethel are unable to keep up. Similarly, datagrams happen along the port and are picked up by receiver programs that happen to be listening. Unlike Lucy and Ethel, however, if you miss one, nothing bad will happen.

Creating a UDP sender

To pay homage to Lucy and Ethel in our own bizarre, twisted way, let's create a cookie factory! In our factory, we will be able to build chocolate chip cookies and specify the number of chips we want in each one. Then we will send them along the conveyor belt to be packaged and shipped off to some Java engineer turned writer who is in desperate need of a Scooby Snack.

Real-world implementations of broadcast communication include stock tickers that constantly publish stock quotes for NASDAQ or the New York Stock Exchange. By simply plugging your receiver into the port, you can grab that information and do something with it (presumably selling your Microsoft stock and buying up all the SUNW shares on the exchange). Modifying our sample program to similarly broadcast and grab information is quite simple.

To begin our sender program, we must create a Java application for our `Cookie-Bakery`. The application will have a simple GUI in which you can specify the number of chips in the cookie using a slider and then simply press a button to send the cookie to the conveyor belt.

The GUI framework looks like this:

```java
import java.awt.*;
import java.net.*;

public class CookieBakery extends Frame
{
    // AWT components

    CookieBakery()
    {
        // initialize the application frame
    }
```

```
public boolean action(
  Event evt,
  Object obj
)
{
  if(evt.target == sendButton)
  {
      // determine the number of chips
      int numChips = chipsScrollbar.getValue();
      String messageChips = numChips + " chips";
  }
  else if(evt.target == exitButton)
  {
      System.exit(0);
  }

  return true;
}

public static void main(
  String args[]
)
{
  CookieBakery cookies = new CookieBakery();
  cookies.show();
    }
}
```

The GUI itself will resemble that shown in Figure 2-2 with a slider to select the number of chips, and a button to press so that you can "bake" it.

Number of chips

Bake Cookie

Figure 2–2 Sample GUI for the CookieBakery.

Formatting a UDP packet

In order to send a packet to the server, we must create and format one. Packets are created using buffers and contain an array of bytes. Therefore, any string message that you wish to send must be converted to an array of bytes as we do in a moment. Also, we need to define and obtain the Internet address of the machine on which this application runs. UDP requires it as part of its protocol.

```java
import java.awt.*;
import java.net.*;

public class CookieBakery extends Frame
{
    // AWT components

    // network components
    InetAddress internetAddress;

    CookieBakery()
    {
      // initialize the application frame

      // initialize the network
      try
      {
          internetAddress =
      InetAddress.getByName("localhost");
      }
      catch(Exception exc)
      {
          System.out.println("Error! - " + exc.toString());
      }
    }

    public boolean action(
      Event evt,
      Object obj
    )
    {
      if(evt.target == sendButton)
      {
```

```java
        // determine the number of chips
        int numChips = chipsScrollbar.getValue();
        String messageChips = numChips + " chips";

        // convert the chip message to byte form
        int msgLength = messageChips.length();
        byte[] message = new byte[msgLength];
        messageChips.getBytes(0, msgLength, message, 0);

        // send a message
        try
        {
            // format the cookie into a UDP packet
            instructionField.setText("Sending Cookie...");
            DatagramPacket packet = new DatagramPacket(
            message, msgLength, internetAddress, 8505);
        }
        catch(Exception exc)
        {
            System.out.println("Error! - " +
                exc.toString());
        }

        // display final result
        instructionField.setText("Sent Cookie!");
    }
    else if(evt.target == exitButton)
    {
        System.exit(0);
    }

    return true;
}

public static void main(
    String args[]
)
{
    CookieBakery cookies = new CookieBakery();
    cookies.show();
}
}
```

Sending the packet to the server

In order to send the cookie to the conveyor belt, we must create a Datagram-Socket. Then we can send the packet we just created using the send routine.

```java
import java.awt.*;
import java.net.*;

public class CookieBakery extends Frame
{
        // AWT components

        // network components
        InetAddress internetAddress;

        CookieBakery()
        {
            // initialize the application frame

        // initialize the network
        try
        {
            internetAddress =
        InetAddress.getByName("localhost");
        }
        catch(Exception exc)
        {
            System.out.println("Error! - " + exc.toString());
        }
}

public boolean action(
        Event evt,
        Object obj
)
{
        if(evt.target == sendButton)
        {
            // determine the number of chips
            int numChips = chipsScrollbar.getValue();
            String messageChips = numChips + " chips";
```

```
        // convert the chip message to byte form
        int msgLength = messageChips.length();
        byte[] message = new byte[msgLength];
        messageChips.getBytes(0, msgLength, message, 0);

        // send a message
        try
        {
            // format the cookie into a UDP packet
            instructionField.setText("Sending Cookie...");
            DatagramPacket packet = new DatagramPacket(
             message, msgLength, internetAddress, 8505);

            // send the packet to the server
            DatagramSocket socket = new DatagramSocket();
            socket.send(packet);
        }
        catch(Exception exc)
        {
            System.out.println("Error! - " +
                exc.toString());
        }

        // display final result
        instructionField.setText("Sent Cookie!");
    }
    else if(evt.target == exitButton)
    {
        System.exit(0);
    }

    return true;
}

public static void main(
    String args[]
)
{
    CookieBakery cookies = new CookieBakery();
    cookies.show();
}
}
```

Now that we have created an application that sends a message containing "xx chips" to a port, we need something on the other end to receive and decode the message into something useful. After all, we don't want to waste our delicious chocolate chip cookies!

Creating a UDP receiver

The UDP Receiver we will create will listen in on a port and wait for cookies. When it gets one, our `CookieMonster` will let us know by printing a "Yummy, tastes good" message. As with our `CookieBakery`, the `CookieMonster` will listen in on port 8505, a totally random selection. To start our `CookieMonster`, first we must create the `CookieMonster` object with its own application main containing the packet that we will read and the socket from which we will get it. Note that we are importing the `java.net.*` package once again.

NOTE: We find throughout this book that servers, in this case a receiver, must be applications, while clients very easily can be applets as well. The reason is that Java's security mechanism will not allow a downloaded applet to have unlimited access to a port on the machine to which it is downloaded. Because of the highly protective Java security model, you are prevented from developing downloadable servers. This may change with the introduction of browsers that are able to change those security restrictions.

```java
import java.awt.*;
import java.net.*;

public class CookieMonster
{
    public static void main(
      String args[]
    )
    {
      // our socket
      DatagramSocket socket = null;

      // our packet
      DatagramPacket packet = null;
    }
}
```

Now we must create and initialize the packet that we will receive. Note that we have to specify a buffer into which the packet will read the message. A packet by itself is composed of four elements. The first is shown in the following code.

```java
import java.awt.*;
import java.net.*;

public class CookieMonster
{
    public static void main(
        String args[]
    )
    {
        // our socket
        DatagramSocket socket = null;

        // our packet
        DatagramPacket packet = null;

        // create a receive buffer
        byte[] buffer = new byte[1024];

        // create a packet to receive the buffer
        packet = new DatagramPacket(buffer, buffer.length);
    }
}
```

Once our packet is put together, we need to sit on a socket and wait for someone to fill it with information. We use the DatagramSocket's receive routine to hang on a UDP port and get information. We must pass the method the packet we created so that it knows where to put the information it gets.

```java
import java.awt.*;
import java.net.*;

public class CookieMonster
{
    public static void main(
        String args[]
    )
    {
        // our socket
        DatagramSocket socket = null;
```

```java
// our packet
DatagramPacket packet = null;

  // create a receive buffer
  byte[] buffer = new byte[1024];

  // create a packet to receive the buffer
  packet = new DatagramPacket(buffer, buffer.length);

  // now create a socket to listen in
  try
  {
      socket = new DatagramSocket(8505);
  }
  catch(Exception exc)
  {
      System.out.println("Error! - " + exc.toString());
  }

  // now sit in an infinite loop and eat cookies!
  while(true)
  {
      // sit around and wait for a new packet
      try
      {
          socket.receive(packet);
      }
      catch(Exception exc)
      {
        System.out.println("Error! - " + exc.toString());

      }

  }

}

}
```

So now we have a cookie in our hands, and we have to somehow eat it. To do so, we must first extract the cookie from the packet by retrieving the packet's buffer.

ALERT: Because we specified the buffer size when we created the packet, the CookieMonster waits until the buffer is filled before it returns the packet. This means that if the packets on the sending end are smaller than the packets we are reading here, we will end up with a packet, plus a little bit of the packet that comes down the pike afterwards, causing havoc in our messaging system. If our buffer is too large on the sending end, we will receive only a little bit of the message. It is important that you synchronize both the receiver and the sender so that they receive and send the same size buffer.

```java
import java.awt.*;
import java.net.*;

public class CookieMonster
{
    public static void main(
      String args[]
    )
    {
      // our socket
      DatagramSocket socket = null;

      // our packet
      DatagramPacket packet = null;

      // create a receive buffer
      byte[] buffer = new byte[1024];

      // create a packet to receive the buffer
      packet = new DatagramPacket(buffer, buffer.length);

      // now create a socket to listen in
      try
      {
          socket = new DatagramSocket(8505);
      }
      catch(Exception exc)
      {
          System.out.println("Error! - " + exc.toString());
      }
```

```
    // now sit in an infinite loop and eat cookies!
    while(true)
    {
        // sit around and wait for a new packet
        try
        {
            socket.receive(packet);
        }
        catch(Exception exc)
        {
          System.out.println("Error! - " + exc.toString());
        }

        // extract the cookie
        String cookieString = new String(buffer, 0, 0,
            packet.getLength());

        // now show what we got!
        System.out.println("Yummy!  Got a cookie with " +
            cookieString);
    }
  }
}
```

Now that we have learned how to create point-to-point and broadcast communication mechanisms, let's apply our knowledge to implement our featured application. In this real-world scenario, we must create a mechanism that enables a client to change its state and to send that information to a server to be stored and retrieved at a later date. To develop such an application, we need a point-to-point protocol because reliability is of the utmost premium. After all, we don't want to schedule an appointment and not know if it actually got on our calendar.

Featured application

As we discussed in Chapter 1, "Advanced Java," we will be reimplementing the same "featured application" in this chapter and in each of the next three chapters. We hope this gives you an insight into the advantages and disadvantages of each of the four major communication alternatives that we present in this book. Our sockets implementation needs to be preceded by a discussion on how we plan to implement messaging between the client and the server. Once that is complete, we can implement the client and the server to exchange information in that format.

Messaging format

Our messaging format must incorporate the two major elements contained in our notion of an appointment: the time of the appointment and the reason for the appointment. Therefore, we will create a message format akin to the pizza tool's message. In the pizza tool we implemented a few sections ago, we delimited our message with the bar symbol (" | "). Once again, we will use the bar symbol to separate the time and reason in our message from the client to the server.

From the server to the client, we need a slightly similar but more robust format. When the server sends information to the client, we will need to string a whole bunch of bar-delimited appointments together. The client can then use the `StringTokenizer` object to extract the information it needs.

But, the client cannot accept messages without asking for them first. Therefore, we need a header to the message. When we schedule an appointment (i.e., send a message from the client to the server), we precede the message by the word "store." When we merely prompt the server to send the client a message (i.e., the client sends a message to the server telling it to go ahead and reply), we precede the message with the word "retrieve."

Therefore, our message will be in one of the following two formats:

```
store|Take Fleagle to dentist|1
retrieve
```

The retrieve message prompts the server to send a message back with appointments strung together but delimited by the bar symbol.

Client

Because implementing the client for the featured application is quite similar to the pizza tool's client, the code we are about to produce will look remarkably similar to the code for the pizza tool. In order to plug our featured application socket implementation directly into the Calendar Manager, we must implement the `NetworkModule` that we declared in Chapter 1.

```
public class NetworkModule
{
    public void scheduleAppointment(
      String reason,
      int time);

    public Vector getAppointments();
```

```
   public void initNetwork();

   public void shutdownNetwork();
}
```

Specifically, we need to implement the `scheduleAppointments` and `getAp-pointments` methods. We will also have to create and implement a constructor to open and establish the socket connection. We will first implement the constructor. The code is basically cut and pasted directly from the pizza tool:

```java
import java.awt.*;
import java.util.*;
import java.net.*;
import java.io.*;

public class NetworkModule
{
        // network components
        Socket socket;
        DataInputStream inStream;
        PrintStream outStream;

        NetworkModule()
        {
          try
           {
             socket = new Socket("localhost", 8205);
             inStream = new
               DataInputStream(socket.getInputStream());
             outStream = new
               PrintStream(socket.getOutputStream());
           }
           catch(Exception exc)
           {
           System.out.println("Error! - " + exc.toString());
           }
        }
        public void scheduleAppointment(
          String appointmentReason,
          int appointmentTime
        )
        {
        }
```

```
public Vector getAppointments()
{
}

public void initNetwork()
{
}

public void shutdownNetwork()
{
}
}
```

Now we must implement the `scheduleAppointment` method that goes to the server with a formatted message containing the new appointment. Notice how we put together the message so that it conforms to the messaging format we just agreed upon.

```
public void scheduleAppointment(
    String appointmentReason,
    int appointmentTime
)
{
    try
     {
      outStream.println(
       "store|" +
       appointmentReason + "|" +
       appointmentTime + "|");
      }
     catch(Exception exc)
     {
      System.out.println("Error! - " + exc.toString());
     }
}
```

Once again, the mighty `StringTokenizer` comes to our rescue as we begin to decode the server's message to us in the `getAppointments` method. In order for the server to send us a message, we must prompt it to do so. That way, a socket connection is established, and a reply can be sent along the same route. It isn't entirely necessary to do things this way, but it is the preferred and time-honored method. Once we get our string from the server, we must tokenize it, step through each field, and convert it into a `Vector`.

```java
public Vector getAppointments()
{
   // the variable to store all of our appointments in
   Vector appointmentVector = new Vector();

   // the string to put our appointments in
   String appointmentString = new String();

   // now get the appointments
   try
   {
      // tell the server we want the appointments it has
      outStream.println("retrieve|");

      // now listen for all the information we get back
      appointmentString = inStream.readLine();
}
catch(Exception exc)
{
        System.out.println("Error! - " + exc.toString());

}

      // tokenize the string
      StringTokenizer stk =
         new StringTokenizer(appointmentString, "|");

      // translate into a Vector
      while(stk.hasMoreTokens())
      {
         // create a variable to stick the appointment in
         AppointmentType appointment = new AppointmentType();

         // now get the next appointment from the string
         appointment.reason = stk.nextToken();
         appointment.time =
            Integer.valueOf(stk.nextToken()).intValue();

         // put the appointment into the vector
         appointmentVector.addElement(appointment);
      }

      // return the Vector
      return appointmentVector;
}
```

Server

To implement the server, we will blatantly plagiarize code from the pizza application earlier in this chapter. Basically, we take all of the server code from there, including the thread portion, and modify it for our needs. First, we need to implement the store method. We will store our appointments in a `Vector` for simplicity's sake. The code snippet that follows is from the `run` method of the `CalendarThread`.

NOTE: You could just as easily use some kind of serialization or even a file to keep your appointments persistent. When the server shuts down, we will lose all of the appointments in our current implementation. Our server keeps data in a *transient* state, meaning that it is not maintained between executions.

```java
// convert to a readable format
try
{
    StringTokenizer stk =
        new StringTokenizer(newOrder, "|");
    String operation = stk.nextToken();
    if(operation.equals("store"))
      {
        String reason = stk.nextToken();
        int time =
          Integer.valueOf(stk.nextToken()).intValue();

      // no exception was thrown so store the appointment
      AppointmentType appt = new AppointmentType();
      appt.reason = reason;
      appt.time = time;
      appointmentVector.addElement(appt);

      // put our result on the screen
      System.out.println("stored" + reason + "|" + time);
   }
}
catch(NoSuchElementException exc)
    ...
```

Now we must implement the retrieve function. The retrieve function creates a new string, delimited by the bar symbol, of course, that contains every appointment in our `Vector`. It then sends that information back to the client using the same socket on which it received the original message.

```
    else
    {
        String returnValue = new String();

        // put together a string of appointments
        for(int x = 0; x < appointmentVector.size(); x++)
        {
            AppointmentType appt   =
            (AppointmentType)appointmentVector.elementAt(x);

            returnValue += appt.reason + "|" + appt.time + "|";
        }

        // now write the appointments back to the socket
        out.println(returnValue);

}
```

Summary

Sockets are the backbone of any communication mechanism. Everything we talk about in this book from here on will use them in some way or another. For example, in the past some CORBA implementations used UDP for their socket infrastructure, eliminating complex webs of point-to-point connections. This sped up their implementation because they spent less time routing messages, and more time sending them. When new objects were added to the system, UDP enabled them to be plugged in with little effort and little impact on the rest of the system. Lately, however, the onset of TCP-based IIOP has pushed almost all CORBA vendors to the more reliable protocol.

TCP is a reliable protocol system that has been used by generations of computer geeks. We all somehow, somewhere get our start in network programming by first using TCP/IP and writing to pipes and sockets. In the next chapter, we explore another reliable communication mechanism built on top of sockets. Java IDL, regardless of whether it is implemented in TCP or UDP, brings communication to a level above sockets. Where we were concerned with packet size or message format when we created the three client/server systems above, IDL keeps us from worrying about those details.

CHAPTER 3

What is CORBA?

The Basics of the Interface Definition Language

Translating an IDL File with Language Mappings

CORBA Clients and Servers

Understanding and Creating CORBA Callback

Modifying the Featured Application

Java IDL: Interface Definition Language

The Common Object Request Broker Architecture is an industry standard that has been around for sometime. Before Java, creating CORBA-based objects was a difficult and time-consuming process. With Java, much of the bellyaches associated with it have been limited or removed altogether. Along with Java's simplicity and elegance, CORBA frameworks give your applications the underlying machinery necessary to produce large-scale mission-critical applications that are distributed across platforms, machines, or networks.

By the end of this chapter you will have a strong understanding of what CORBA is, how to create your own CORBA clients and servers, and why CORBA is still around after spending so many years in the ivory tower of computer science. As high-browed intellectuals have contended for the past few years, CORBA may well be the cog that finally makes Java the true Internet Programming Language.

Once again, we will reimplement the Internet Calendar Manager from the previous chapter, this time to use Java IDL. Our application will use CORBA for its communication protocol rather than sockets. In so doing, we can compare the performance, reliability, and ease of development of the two.

CORBA

The Common Object Request Broker Architecture (CORBA) is a standard developed by the Object Management Group, the world's largest computer consortium. It is not a product; it is not a vision; it is not vapor ware. Many companies have chosen to implement CORBA, most notably Iona Technologies and SunSoft. The CORBA community is by far the more academic of the various communities behind the other communication alternatives we cover in this book. Indeed, their academic nature is both a benefit and a detriment to the average programmer.

Like all academic projects, CORBA has become a kitchen sink standard. Everything you could possibly want is covered in the specification, if not actually implemented by the various CORBA vendors. Much of what CORBA has to offer is intended to be hidden from the programmer. The programmer APIs are not defined; rather each vendor is charged with creating its own API. SunSoft NEO, for example, implements its own Object Development Framework to facilitate interaction between programmers and the ORB.

In this chapter, we refer to the ORB as an entity, not as a concrete product. Much of our code is from SunSoft's NEO product, chiefly because it is the project the authors actually work on. However, we have created objects for which we will always specify the object's definition, with the idea that any ORB can be used.

CORBA-style communication

Let's say your Aunt Fran calls you from South Dakota. When she dials your number, the phone eventually rings on your side. You pick up the phone, have a conversation, hang up the phone, and terminate the connection. Your Aunt Fran is the requester, or client, and you are the called party, or server. Aunt Fran doesn't care where your phone is in your house. She doesn't care if it's a cordless phone. She doesn't care if it's a conventional phone or a cell phone. All she knows is that she dials a number, you answer, you talk, and you hang up. In other words, Aunt Fran does not care how the call is implemented; she only cares that the call goes through.

If Aunt Fran were to dial using the socket paradigm, she would have to dial the number, specify which phone to ring, specify who should answer the phone, and it would be a shot in the dark. If the call doesn't go through, she won't be told why. She'll probably wait and wait and wait for a phone to ring even though it never will.

Remember also that CORBA does not specify how something will be implemented. Aunt Fran should be just as happy using a satellite phone as she would be using a regular phone. Java is the only language you can use to create a networked object with most of the alternatives in this book. While Java may be the greatest thing since the fork-split English muffin, many large-scale distributed systems are still written in C++, C, or, heaven forbid, COBOL. CORBA enables you to use those legacy systems without having to rewrite everything in Java.

The CORBA vision

As an example, let's say your beanbag has a beautiful interface. You can employ a few operations on it: you can fluff it and you can sit on it. Do you care what goes on underneath? If someone were to come by one day and replace your cloth bean-bag with a vinyl beanbag would you still know how to use it? Yes, because the interface didn't change, only the implementation did.

The beauty of CORBA is that you can create a whole bunch of interfaces that are implemented in a variety of different ways. If you want to talk to an object, you have the interface: in essence a contract that states what you will give the object and what you will get from the object in return. Because of that, objects are inter-changeable so long as they share the same interfaces.

For the Internet, this means that we can deploy an object and tell people what they must do in order to use it. Later on, if we discover an enhancement to the object, we can merely swap the old inferior object with my new enhanced one, and no one will ever know or care. One of the ways we do this at Sun is with our support feedback tool. Our customers can submit problem reports for our products using a Java interface that communicates over the Internet with an object. From time to time we upgrade or fix the object, but our customers never know. To them, the interface remains the same. Figure 3-1 shows a graphical representation of how object implementations are different from their interfaces.

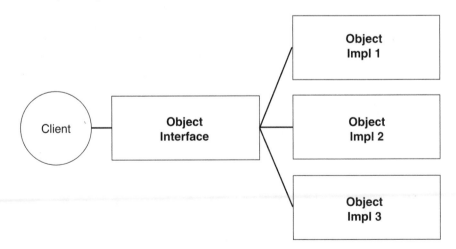

Figure 3-1 Clients only care about interfaces, not implementations.

In geek terms, this is referred to as "three-tier client-server computing." The first tier is your client, whether it is a Java applet or a Windows 95 OLE client, and it communicates with the second tier. The second tier is the object you implement in CORBA using the IDL. Finally, the third tier is your data source, perhaps a database or other implement. Information is passed through the three tiers with the idea that changes may be made to any tier, and no effect will be seen on any of the other tiers. Figure 3-2 shows how the data is kept from the client by using object servers as the middleman.

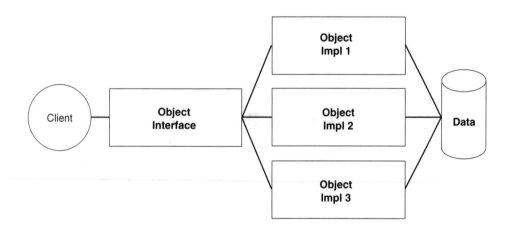

Figure 3-2 The three tier client server architecture consists of a client, an object, and a data source.

Communication with CORBA

Similarly, when you request information from a CORBA object, you don't care how it is implemented, you only care that your request goes through and that the object responds. CORBA, the ORB specifically, ensures that your request gets there, and if it doesn't, you will find out. Moreover, the ORB will start up a server if one isn't already running.

Unlike TCP/IP and sockets, CORBA ensures reliability of communication. If a request does not go through, you will know about it. If a server isn't there, it will be started up, and you will be told if there is a problem. Every possible communication contingency is covered in the specification.

But this kind of reliability does not come without a price. CORBA lends a ton of functionality to devise object schemes that work. However, it also places a heavy burden on the programmer with all of the overhead required in a call. In short, CORBA programming is far from easy, but as a trade-off you receive significant gifts for your effort.

The Interface Definition Language

Just as Java objects are defined as collections of operations on some state, CORBA objects are defined similarly. Unlike Java, CORBA enables you to define your interface definition separately from your implementation. As you can see in Figure 3-3, splitting the interface from the implementation enables you to create multiple objects from the same interface, each handling the method signatures differently. In the end, however, the greatest advantage to the split is that your interfaces are likely to remain static, while your implementations will change dramatically over time.

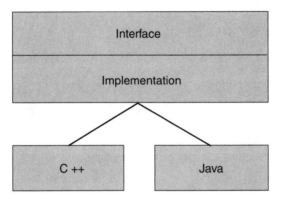
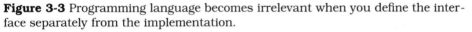

Figure 3-3 Programming language becomes irrelevant when you define the interface separately from the implementation.

Software architects will spend considerable time and energy creating objects and their interfaces, leaving the implementation up to their staff. The interface implementers will code their objects in the ORB of their choice. Once the objects are finished and registered with the system, they are ready to be invoked. One of the few advantages to C++ over Java is this kind of separation between implementation and interface, and CORBA allows you to have the same kind of functionality.

A client that invokes on an object knows only the interface definition. The implementation of the object is of no concern to the requester, who cares only that the object request gets to the server and that a response is sent back. Theoretically, client programmers and server programmers don't need to know any of the details of each other's implementations. The interfaces are defined using the Interface Definition Language. The IDL enables us to know what methods can be invoked on an object. A typical CORBA object lifecycle requires the most time in developing the interfaces. Once you are satisfied with the interface, you move on to the implementation.

In the business world today, a great push towards Java is taking place. Because of its tremendous advantages over C++, many organizations are planning an eventual move to Java programming with the idea that several of the language's drawbacks will be addressed appropriately in subsequent revisions. If these organizations had taken a CORBA-like approach to their original software design, then the migration would hardly be an issue. Because each CORBA object has an interface that is published and well known, changing its implementation does not involve changing the implementations of any other object that talks to it. As you can see in Figure 3-4, objects in CORBA talk to interfaces, while objects not written using CORBA talk directly to one another.

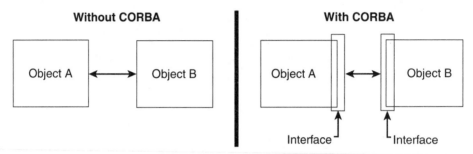

Figure 3-4 Objects talk to interfaces, not to implementations.

CORBA objects can be written in any language for which a *language mapping* is specified. Therefore, the implementation can vary between objects, but the client should not care. The language mapping is defined by the OMG, and the various vendors then choose to implement the mapping. NEO, for example, does not implement the Smalltalk mapping, but has created its own Java mapping. Language mappings are discussed in detail in the next section..

Different vendors, different ORBs

What if you create a client that accesses your chosen ORB and another object comes along, written in another ORB, and you would like to talk to it? In the early days of CORBA, you would have to rewrite your client : no small task considering that clients are where the pretty stuff is at. You'd have to redo all of your pretty graphics and recompile your client for the new ORB. For that reason, ORB consumers often stayed a one-ORB shop. If their servers were created in Orbix, their clients generally were as well.

In the new CORBA world, all objects and clients speak to one another using the Internet Inter-ORB Protocol, or IIOP. IIOP (usually pronounced "eye-op") ensures that your client will be able to talk to a server written for an entirely different

ORB. Note how this takes advantage of the client abstraction we spoke of earlier. Now, your clients need not know what ORB the server was written in and can simply talk to it.

Furthermore, the ORB is the only fully native portion of the entire CORBA system. The ORB is specific to the platform on which it runs. Orbix, Iona Technologies' entry into the CORBA market, runs on just about every platform imaginable because they have made the effort to port Orbix to every platform imaginable. SunSoft's NEO, on the other hand, runs exclusively on Solaris, but does so better than any other CORBA option.

NOTE: Because Orbix's ORB was written with quick portability in mind, they tend to offer less power than NEO does and also have significant problems with scalability. Again, this is a trade-off issue, and one that must be evaluated on a case-by-case basis. With the universal acceptance of IIOP, there is no reason why your CORBA objects need to be written in one ORB only.

Advantages of CORBA

CORBA is an example of Distributed Object programming. If you were to create two objects, say a Character object and a String object, you would be splitting up functionality across different objects. Your String object would instantiate several Character objects, and all would be happy in your plain vanilla object-oriented world (see Figure 3-5).

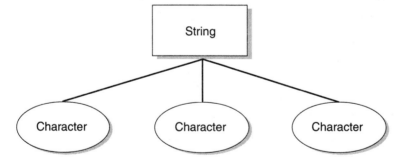

Figure 3-5 Objects are composed of other objects.

If, however, you were to take things one step further and have your String object instantiate its Character objects on a different machine, you would be entering the distributed object world and all the insanity that revolves around it (see Figure 3-6). When instantiating objects across multiple machines, certain precautions and measures must be taken to ensure the proper routing of messages. If you were to use CORBA as your basis for creating these objects, all of those situations would be addressed already.

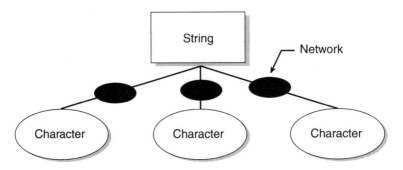

Figure 3-6 Distributed Objects allow objects to be composed of other objects residing on other networks.

CORBA gives you the tools you need to distribute your objects across multiple machines running on perhaps several different networks. You need only to instantiate your object before using it just as you normally would use a local object.

As mentioned already, CORBA makes a big distinction between interface and implementation. The interface is the list of methods with which you will communicate; the implementation is how those methods are created. Let's say I were to talk to a marketeer. We would both be speaking English (the interface), but I would have to talk slowly, explaining everything in a clear and concise manner (the implementation).

Common Object Services

When you programmed in C++, chances are you used a class library of some sort. The famous Rogue-Wave class libraries give you a great number of classes and objects that you can reuse in your code, ranging from the sublime `String` classes to the vastly more complex `HashTables`.

Likewise, part of the CORBA specification deals with a set of distributed class libraries known as the Common Object Services. The Common Object Services refer to specific types of objects that are beneficial to programmers in a distributed environment, including transaction objects, event service objects, relationships objects, and even lifecycle objects.

Perhaps the most useful of all the Common Object Services is the Naming Service. The Naming Service provides you with a directory-like system for storing and organizing your objects so that other programmers can access and invoke them.

In Figure 3-7, we map the string "Object One" to the physical object "1," but are able to map "Object Two" to the physical object "3." The Naming Service allows us to also change that on-the-fly. In fact, the Naming Service, and all Common Object Services for that matter, are nothing more than CORBA objects. Therefore, if you can get the interface to the Naming Service, you can create a client that modifies it yourself.

TIP: Some CORBA customers even use the Naming Service as a sort of versioning system, creating a new directory in the Naming Service for each new version of their object system. If you can do it with a directory, you can do it with the Naming Service.

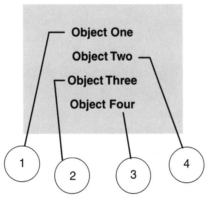

Figure 3-7 With the Object Naming Service, every string is mapped to an object.

Object administration

One of the biggest obstacles to distributed computing is the management of objects across multiple platforms and multiple networks. Though the CORBA specification does not specify an administration scheme, several vendors have created administration tools you can use to manage your entire system.

Tasks that run the gamut from server startup and shutdown all the way to machine-specific parameters are addressed in these tools. Often the tools are written in the same CORBA implementation that they manage, and many even have Java interfaces. Most of the tools address the issue of object registration and invocation. When an object is registered, it is stored in a location called the *Interface Repository*. Accessing objects from the Interface Repository is often quite difficult, has great overhead, and requires a significant knowledge of the OS. The Naming Service addresses some of these concerns by creating a user-friendly front end to objects that are stored in the Interface Repository. But in order to manipulate objects directly within the Interface Repository, you need object administration tools.

NOTE: Because the object administration tools vary widely among CORBA vendors, we will not address them in detail. The OMG, as a matter of fact, does not even specify the kinds of administration tools that are required to support an object system; that determination is left to the vendors. NEO includes a full suite of Java-based tools to manipulate your objects, and Orbix has similar tools available from the command line.

Clients, servers, oh my!

Client programming in CORBA is significantly easier than creating a server. Because, in the simplest sense, all you are doing is instantiating a class that just happens to be on a remote machine, it is quite intuitive as well. When you instantiate a class in CORBA, you specify not only the name of the class but the location as well. The location can be a specific machine or a specific server, but is usually determined by referencing the Naming Service.

The Naming Service contains a `find` method that enables you to retrieve an object by using a string name that you specify:

```
. . .
myFirstObject = NamingService.find("MyFirstObject");
myFirstObject.myFirstMethod();
. . .
```

Once an object is retrieved, invoking it is exactly the same as invoking a locally instantiated class. In fact, underneath the covers a local class is instantiated. Let's say you get an object called `MyFirstCORBA` from the Naming Service and invoke `myFirstMethod` on it. In reality, the local copy of `MyFirstCORBA` maps that call to a method that invokes across the ORB to the remote object, as illustrated in Figure 3-8.

Writing a server is much more complicated and many vendors do not yet support full Java server capability. In later parts of this chapter, we will discuss full Java server capability and what it means for the future of C++ objects in CORBA. Needless to say, the ease-of-use aspects of Java help to minimize overhead and the learning curve of CORBA in general. Yet, Java is thus far not as capable of the performance numbers generated by identical C++ applications.

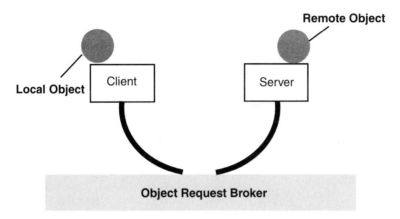

Figure 3-8 Objects invoke on remote objects via the Object Request Broker.

What CORBA means for you

CORBA is perhaps the single most developed of all the various communication alternatives we discuss in this book. Without much effort, you will be able to create clients that you can publish on the World Wide Web and make available to anyone who wishes to take advantage of your objects. With a significantly greater investment of time and energy, servers can be generated that take full advantage of client/server computing over the Internet. While the learning curve is greater compared to other alternatives, the payoff is also potentially greater. Even though CORBA may be difficult for you to grasp, once you learn it you will agree that it is the best of any alternative presented in this book, or potentially available in the Java industry.

The Interface Definition Language

As we discussed in Chapter 1, "Advanced Java," one of the most important concepts of object-oriented programming is implementation hiding. In CORBA, the implementation can be any number of things, ranging from different programming approaches to different programming languages altogether. In light of this, the OMG created the Interface Definition Language to help make clear the separation between interface and implementation.

The IDL does exactly what it says: define interfaces. The IDL, as the name implies, is a language in and of itself, but there are no assumptions made as to how (or if) an object will be created. Rather, the IDL specifies what the object will look like *from both a client and a server perspective.* In this section, we will examine closely the basics of the IDL. Subsequent sections will explain how you can implement the interfaces you create here in Java. Keep in mind, however, that we choose to implement our objects in Java because this is a Java book, but you could just as easily implement your objects in any language for which a language mapping exists.

Interfaces

Interfaces are the backbone of the IDL. In an object-oriented language, you can create interfaces as well as implementations, but here we are allowed to specify only the method signatures and the variables associated with them. For example, if we were to create an interface to our television, it would look something like this:

```
interface TelevisionSet
    {
        long currentChannel;

        void changeChannel(long newChannel);
        void increaseVolume();
        void decreaseVolume();
}
```

As you can see, we do not imply either that this is the 50-foot giant screen TV in our break room or the 13-inch TV in our kitchen. Rather, we mention only the common interfaces to both. It will be up to the implementer to define how his interface will behave. Note also that we have not included any kind of method for powering the set on or off. In fact, the underlying CORBA mechanisms take care of that for us. Remember that merely invoking an object instantiates its implementation and readies it for further use. Not using the object for a while has the reverse effect. After a specified time-out period, the object will shut itself down, not unlike the new Energy Saver computer monitors!

Modules

Let's say we now want to model all of the appliances in our home using the IDL. The first step is to create an interface for each appliance (we've done a few in this section), then to implement each as we see fit. After that we need to group the appliances together in a *module*. A module is essentially a name space for a group of interfaces. It enables each interface to have a common name when referred to in code, as evidenced in the following snippet.

```
module Appliances
    {
        interface TelevisionSet
        {
            ...
        }
```

```
    interface Radio
    {
        string currentBand;   // can be "am" or "fm"
        long currentStation;

        void changeBands();
        void stationUp();
        void stationDown();
    }


    … many more as well …
}
```

As you can see, modules are highly logical extensions to object-oriented interface design. In fact, the module itself could be enclosed in yet another module, allowing groups of modules to be grouped together. In order to call the `Radio` object's `stationUp` method, you would probably make a call like:

```
    Appliances.Radio.stationUp();
```

Keep in mind, of course, that the syntax of this call is entirely language dependent, and that the IDL makes no assumptions whatsoever about language use. Notice that `Appliances` is set as the parent object for `Radio`, as it would be for `TelevisionSet` as well.

Interface inheritance

There are several situations in which we would like our interfaces to inherit from one another. Just as we did with Java objects, we can define language specific inheritance that is translated through the language mapping down to the implementation.

```
interface TelevisionSet
{
    …
}


interface EnhancedTelevision : TelevisionSet
{
        void activatePIP();
        void deactivatePIP();
}
```

In this example, EnhancedTelevision inherits from TelevisionSet, getting all of the features from our initial TelevisionSet object, as well as adding a few of its own. When you instantiate EnhancedTelevision, you get not only the features you added, but the TelevisionSet properties as well, integrated by the language mapping with the EnhancedTelevision object as if they were part of the EnhancedTelevision to begin with. Any client that uses EnhancedTelevision has no idea that it is an inherited object.

Because the IDL is an interface language, inheritance does not imply implementation inheritance. When you inherit methods from another object, you do not get the implementations that go along with that method. Remember, the IDL does not care what kinds of implementations you create for an interface. In keeping with that neither does IDL link implementations together for inherited objects. In order to enact your own implementation inheritance, you need to create client code within your server that contacts the object implementation you want to use.

Variables and structures

When you include variables within an interface, you have to be careful. Are those variables matters of implementation (you do not want to start creating counter variables, for example) or are they a matter of interface definition (the current channel is vital for the operation of the TelevisionSet object)? In the previous examples in this section, we showed you several examples of variables including type enumerations, simple variable types, and parameter values. There are a few simple types available for use within the IDL, as you can see in Table 3-1.

Table 3-1 Available types within IDL

Type	Explanation
long	Integer type ranging from -2^{31} to 2^{31}
short	Integer type ranging from -2^{15} to 2^{15}
float	IEEE single-precision floating point numbers
double	IEEE double-precision floating point numbers
char	Regular 8-bit quantities
boolean	TRUE or FALSE
octet	8-bit quantity guaranteed to not be changed in any way
string	A sequence of characters
any	Special type consisting of *any* of the above

But, the IDL also gives you a means to create complex data types in containers known as *structures*. A structure is, essentially, a class with no methods. The IDL makes the distinction because some languages make the distinction. C++, for example, gives you the benefit of structures as a legacy from its C ancestry. Java, however, does not provide structures, and forces you to make the more logically object-oriented choice of classes. A complex data type is, by definition, a group of simple data types. In the following example, AnsweringMachineMessage is a complex data type composed of a bunch of strings:

```
struct AnsweringMachineMessage
{
        string dateStamp;
        string timeStamp;

        string message;
}
```

Methods

In order to manipulate your IDL-defined servers, you need to declare methods. In the previous TelevisionSet example, we defined several methods such as changeChannel and increaseVolume. Each method may have a series of parameters, as in the case of changeChannel. These parameters may be simple types or complex types, or a special IDL-defined type called Any.

The Any type is a special type that is most often used within method declarations (although it is permissible to use them as variables as well). In C or C++, Any is mapped to a void pointer (void *), while in Java it is mapped to an Object (remember how everything in Java inherits one way or another from type Object). As in the implementation languages, you would use Any to represent an unknown (at interface design time) quantity.

Parameters may be passed in one of three ways. If you pass in a parameter as an in parameter, the parameter will not be sent back from the method in a modified state. Parameters passed as out parameters cannot be accessed from within the method, but can be set inside the method. Finally, inout parameters can be sent back both modified and accessed from within the method itself.

Constructed data types

Besides structures, there are a few more kinds of constructed types. A union is a form of a structure, but the members of a union, unlike a structure, can vary from instance to instance. Let's say you had two cars, a BMW Z3 convertible and a Volvo station wagon. For trips to the grocery store, you would use the Volvo because the Z3 has no trunk space. But, for fun trips to the Santa Cruz beaches, you would definitely take your Z3. The kind of car you drive depends on your situation.

The last structured type supported by the IDL is the enumeration. An enumeration is similar to an array except that its contents are determined beforehand and cannot be changed. In our radio example earlier, we had a variable called currentBand. The currentBand was set using a string, but in reality it can have only two values, AM or FM. The IDL enables us to define the enumeration as follows:

```
module Appliances
{
        interface TelevisionSet
        {
            ...
        }

        interface Radio
        {
            typedef enum _RadioBand { AM_BAND, FM_BAND } RadioBand;

            RadioBand currentBand;
            long currentStation;

            void changeBands();
            void stationUp();
            void stationDown();
        }

        ... many more as well ...
}
```

Exceptions

As in Java, exceptions are a great way to propagate errors back through your objects. You define exceptions using the exception keyword in the IDL. The Java Language Mapping translates those exceptions into Java exceptions that you can then use in your applications. In the following example, the exception Rotten is thrown whenever someone tries to eat an apple that happens to be rotten.

```
interface Apple
    {
        exception Rotten { };

        void eatApple() throws Rotten;
}
```

Overview of the IDL

The Interface Definition Language is a powerful tool both for CORBA programming and for software architecture. While it is primarily the foundation on which you can create CORBA objects, it can just as easily be used to define entire object systems. For this purpose alone, the IDL warrants further study. If you are a masochist and enjoy scintillating beach reading, check out the CORBA specification from the Object Management Group. If you prefer a less technical tome, Thomas Mowbray's *Essential CORBA* is, well, essential.

Now that we have learned the IDL, we can define interfaces using it. Eventually, those interfaces need to be translated into code. This is done by mapping every construct in the IDL to constructs in the language of choice. While we will only discuss C++ here, CORBA objects defined in IDL can be developed in any language so long as a language mapping exists. This is the greatest benefit to CORBA. Your language independence allows you to spend time intelligently creating interfaces, and worrying about implementations later. Today Java is the hot potato; tomorrow it could be a new language altogether. By defining good interfaces, you can protect yourself from being torn in the winds of change.

Language Mappings

Because CORBA is independent of the programming language used to construct clients or servers, several language mappings are defined to enable programmers to interface with the CORBA functionality from the language of their choice. The OMG's member organizations are free to propose mappings that must then be approved by the rest of the consortium. Needless to say, getting the likes of DEC, Hewlett Packard, and Sun to agree on something small is difficult enough without having to introduce an argument like a language mapping.

Language mappings are vast, complex things that underscore the different ways of doing the same thing from within a language. The beauty of a programming language, and what keeps programmers employed is that there are often several ways to accomplish the same thing. Indeed, one approach to a problem affects portability, while another impacts performance. No two approaches are the same, therefore no one approach is ever "better" than another. It may be better in a particular context, but often that overused term "trade-off" is bandied about to reflect why one OMG member prefers its mapping over another.

What exactly are language mappings?

A language mapping in CORBA refers to the means necessary to translate an IDL file into the programming language of choice. Currently, the OMG specifies mappings for C, C++, and Smalltalk. Because of its wide acceptance and object-oriented nature, C++ is the language most often used by CORBA programmers. Since the introduction of Java, however, the CORBA community is excited over the use of Sun's language to eliminate many of the pitfalls of the C++ mapping.

C++'s greatest problem so far is not its difficulty, for that is enough of a barrier as it is, but, its painful memory management requirements. In a distributed para-digm in particular, memory management becomes a significant issue. Let's say you instantiate a local String class, passing it an array of characters. In C++, you can easily define which object, the parent object or the child String object, will be responsible for deallocating that memory. If you expand the situation to instanti-ating a String object on a remote computer, then you begin to deal with memory on *two different machines!* You allocate an array on your local machine, pass that array to a String class on another machine, and you end up with a quandary. Which machine's object will deallocate the memory?

Once again, Java comes to the rescue. Because it is a garbage-collected language, memory deallocation is of no concern to you. Let's say you wrote the above situa-tion in Java code. Neither the remote object nor the local parent object needs to worry about memory because once the memory is no longer used, *Java automati-cally returns it to the system.* Because of this and countless other problems with the C++ mapping, and with the use of C++ in general, the OMG is beginning to con-sider Java language mappings from its member consortiums.

Because the authors of this book are Sun employees, we show a definite bias toward the Sun Microsystems Java IDL language mapping. We apologize for our behavior in advance, but we believe the Java IDL mapping designed in our own office building is much better than anyone else's. To be fair, we recognize that some of what we have to tell you may differ from other companies' efforts, and we will make every effort to point out such nuances as they occur.

The Sun Microsystems Java Language Mapping

 NOTE: The language mapping described in this section is in a state of flux. Because of the fast-moving Java and CORBA communities, Java IDL is always trying to stay in step with Javasoft and CORBA. Naturally, the language mapping may change slightly from month to month, but, in general, it remains the same overall.

Sun Microsystems bundles a program called `idltojava` that actually does the mapping and generates the necessary files. The Sun approach to CORBA files is to create several user-level files that are directly modified by the programmer, and several *stub files* that are not intended to be modified, but instead provide the mapping functionality.

Interfaces, modules, and methods

The mapping takes every IDL defined module and translates it into a Java package. For example, the IDL module `Appliances`, as follows:

```
module Appliances
{
...
}
```

becomes the following in the generated Java files:

```
package Appliances;

public class
{
    ...
}
```

Interfaces map directly to Java classes because IDL modules are, as discussed earlier, name-scoping mechanisms. The corresponding Java name-scoping mechanism is the package. For every interface in a module (if there is a module at all, for modules are not required), a Java class is generated in the code:

```
module Appliances
{
        interface TelevisionSet
        {
        }
}
```

Becomes...

```
package Appliances;

public class TelevisionSet
{
    ...
}
```

As for parameters, Java maps them, as we will discuss in upcoming sections on simple and complex types. However, Java does not support pass-by-reference variables because it is a pointer-free language. There is no way in the Java language to pass a parameter that can be modified in the method and sent back to the calling function. As a result, the IDL out and inout parameters cannot be supported in Java without some special workarounds.

The Sun mapping supports the notion of *holders* in order to circumvent the lack of a pass-by-reference model in Java. A holder contains not only the variable itself but methods to modify that method as well. So, when a variable is passed by reference, Java passes a class instead.

Interface inheritance

Inheritance is a difficult task to take on in the Java language mapping because IDL interfaces support direct multiple inheritance while Java classes do not. In order to make classes multiply inheritable, they must be first declared as interfaces and then implemented as classes. While it sometimes becomes counter-intuitive because inherited interfaces do not follow the norm for regular interfaces, it is the only way to complete the language mapping on the inheritance subject.

For example, the following multiply inherited class:

```
module Appliances
{
        interface Speaker
        {
        }

        interface Listener
        {
        }

        interface Phone : Speaker, Listener
        {
        }
}
```

Becomes the following collection of interfaces and classes in Java:

```
package Appliances;

public interface SpeakerRef
{
    ...
}
```

```
public interface ListenerRef
{
    ...
};

public interface PhoneRef extends Appliances.SpeakerRef,
Appliances.ListenerRef
{
    ...
}

public class Speaker
{
    ...
}
```

Variables and structures

Table 3-2 outlines each of the simple types supported by the IDL and their resulting Java representation.

Table 3-2 IDL types and their Java representations

Type	Java Mapping
long	Java `int`
short	Java `short`
float	Java `float`
double	Java `double`
char	Java `char`
boolean	Java `boolean`
octet	Java `byte`
string	Java's language module's `String` class (`java.lang.String`)
any	Special type consisting of *any* of the above

The Sun mapping does not support `unsigned` types, however, because Java has no corresponding manner in which to represent an `unsigned` type. The Sun mapping leaves the implementation of unsigned types up to the user. When you try to interface with an unsigned type in one of your programs, you need to provide the logic that converts the negative values into their corresponding positive representation. Eventually, when Java supports unsigned types inside its `java.lang.Long` and `java.lang.Integer` objects, the Sun Java mapping will follow suit with proper unsigned support.

Constructed data types

IDL structures are mapped directly to a Java class consisting of each member variable as well as two constructors. One constructor is for initializing each member variable to a statically defined value, while the other can accept data upon instantiation. So, the following IDL:

```
struct PhoneNumber
{
    // xxx-xxx-xxxx format
    string areaCode;
    string prefix;
    string suffix;
};
```

Becomes:

```
public class PhoneNumber
{
    public String areaCode;
    public String prefix;
    public String suffix;
}
```

IDL sequences and arrays are equally easy to map into their Java counterpart. Every sequence is mapped directly into a Java array. Every Java array consists not only of the array values, but of infrastructure to supply the length of the sequence as well. Furthermore, IDL arrays are directly related to Java arrays, and therefore fall in suit with sequences. The extra array subscripting features provided by IDL sequences also were not originally intended to be included in IDL arrays. Because no harm can come from including the extra details in the array mapping, the decisions make sense. The end result is that if both your client and server implementations are going to be written in Java, then there is no real difference between sequences and arrays.

```
sequence <Phone> allThePhonesInMyHouse;
```

Thus, the IDL declarations above map to pretty straightforward Java counterparts:

```
Phone allThePhonesInMyHouse[];
```

The Enumeration and Union constructed IDL types are much more complicated. Because Java supports neither enumerated types nor variable classes, several layers of additional Java infrastructure must be provided to implement the details of the IDL types properly.

Exceptions

Java supports an exception capability very similar to both IDL and C++. As a result, the mapping between the IDL and Java is extremely obvious. Furthermore, CORBA C++ programmers will find that the helper methods provided by Java exceptions are much more intuitive and easier to use than their C++ counterparts. In the end, the Java exception and the IDL exception are perfect partners in object-oriented error tracking.

Java and CORBA together

Because CORBA is designed as an all-encompassing standard designed to provide answers to most, if not all, object-oriented programming questions, it does not quite fit into the Java philosophy. Java was designed as the exact antithesis to C++. While both Java and C++ are object-oriented languages, Java does not attempt to, nor does it satisfy, C++ and CORBA's insatiable need to "solve world hunger."

But, for all their differences, Java and CORBA can be made to work well together. As we have seen in this section and we will see in the next few chapters, CORBA provides a ton of functionality. Most of it will never be required by the average programmer and thus can become quite a burden. Meanwhile, Java is accessible to all programmers, both beginner and highly experienced. Java actually makes CORBA manageable because CORBA provides the plumbing, while Java gives you, the programmer, a means to access the plumbing without knowing how it works. After all, you don't care how your car works, you just care that it does. Similarly, no one (outside of geeks who desperately need a little bit of sun) really cares how CORBA works.

Once you are comfortable with language mappings, it is time to move on to actually developing client/server applications using CORBA. We will use the IDL, and its corresponding Java language mapping, to develop a client and server.

CORBA Clients

Writing a CORBA client is pretty simple, if you can grasp the nuances of the language mapping. After you obtain the interface (usually by looking at the IDL) for the server you wish to contact, you have to generate Java stubs. Java stubs contain all of the underlying functionality needed to make a call across a network to a server in an unknown location. Remember, your server will not be in any definite location; in fact, the beauty of the Naming Service is that the corresponding string name can point you to any object at any time.

With that in mind, the last thing you want to concern yourself with is network code. Let the ORB deal with all of that, and you can concentrate on creating a client that works for you. Your client will be mostly a User Interface. The few instances in which it needs to make a network call are usually to relay information from the UI back to the server, and to refresh information on the UI with data stored on the server. In client/server parlance, this is called a "thin client," meaning that the functionality of the client related to the server is minimal.

Designing a User Interface

Since the beginning of the "Java revolution," an enormous number of GUI builders have been released, all with cute coffee-related names that were devised by a marketeer in a cold sweat. In this section, we assume that every client is a thin client, choosing to concentrate the hard work on the server side and leaving the fun, cool stuff on the client. Clients are sort of like your starving artist little sister, they're beautiful and fun, but they don't do much work.

With that in mind, we have chosen not to endorse any one GUI builder. We believe that there is no single tool out there that could possibly be all things to all people, though the lads up in Redmond always seem to put out a product that comes as close as possible to that ideal. Which GUI builder you choose is of no consequence to the rest of this chapter. Rather than step through the Java code for designing a GUI, we will let you just design the GUI as we describe in this section and we'll move on.

Defining the problem

One of the best things about working for Sun is our incredible break room. Every break room has a nifty little water cooler. Now, the first time you look at it you'll say to yourself, "Gee, big deal."

But, wait, there's more! That little water cooler also spits out warm and hot water! When you first gaze upon this marvel of technological prowess, you will be stymied and get the urge to write an applet to unveil your discovery to the world. This is precisely what we intend to do.

Typically, you will have some information that needs to be published to the outside world. In the realm of client/server computing, this is done by creating a server to publish that information. Clients are then able to access that information through the server. In our example, we want to publish information about our water cooler, and we will do so by creating a client to access that information followed by a server to provide it.

The cooler interface definition

We need to model the interface definition so that it is intuitive. For example, our IDL will need three operations, one for each of hot, warm, and cold water. We need three data accessors to get the level of each kind of water. With that in mind, the interface definition would look something like the following:

```
interface Cooler
{
        int getHotWaterLevel();
        int getWarmWaterLevel();
        int getColdWaterLevel();

        int getHotWater();
        int getWarmWater();
        int getColdWater();
};
```

We will also need to track errors in invocation, just in case there is no water to get:

```
interface Cooler
{
        int getHotWaterLevel();
        int getWarmWaterLevel();
        int getColdWaterLevel();

        exception NoMoreWaterException { };

        int getHotWater() throws NoMoreWaterException;
        int getWarmWater() throws NoMoreWaterException;
        int getColdWater() throws NoMoreWaterException;
};
```

The cooler user interface

Our User Interface will display three buttons, one each for hot, warm, and cold water. By clicking on the hot water button, you will diminish the level of hot water in the cooler; clicking the warm water button will diminish the level of warm water, and so forth. The server will store the current level of each one and make sure we don't take out water when there's none there. So, the UI for the Cooler client is pretty obvious (see Figure 3-9), and you can draw it in just about any of the GUI tools.

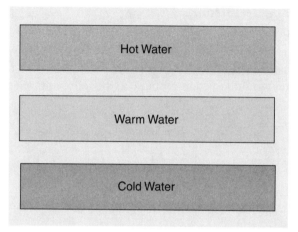

Figure 3-9 The user interface for our watercooler example is a basic three-button display.

We should also create another client that watches the server and shows the level of all three water sources at any given moment. This way, if we stick the applet on the Web, people all over the world can see how much water we Sun employees actually drink. The Monitor client also will have a button to reset the water source whenever we feel like it (see Figure 3-10).

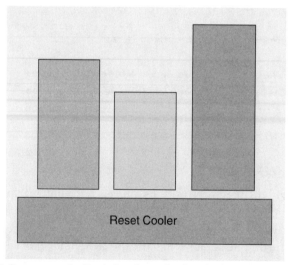

Figure 3-10 Our second client displays the level of water in our example cooler.

Once we are finished, we have two clients banging on the same server. One client will modify the server, the other will only do queries to the server to get information. For terminology's sake, we will call our Water Cooler applet the supplier and our Monitor applet the consumer (see Figure 3-11).

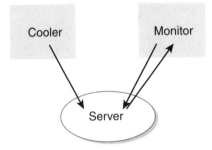

Figure 3-11 Our two clients operate with the same server to continually update our interface.

The full source code for the client is on the CD-ROM that accompanies this book, but there are two methods that we need to implement here for demonstration purposes. The `init` method will initialize both clients, just as you would any normal Java applet. We also need an `action` method to handle button events when they arrive.

ALERT: The source code we show you for Java IDL is practically pseudo-CORBA-code. Because we do not want to endorse any one ORB, we have decided to show you the methodology for developing CORBA applications. When you attempt to execute these examples on your own, you will need to consult the documentation for your ORB, be it NEO, VisiBroker, or Orbix, to be absolutely correct in your syntax. The source code included on the CD-ROM is NEO code, because, as a matter of practicality, it was the easiest for us, being NEO engineers, to get our hands on.

   If you think this is a problem, you are correct. The proliferation of ORBs, and the impact they could very well have over the course of the next few years, leads us to believe that someone, somewhere, needs to come up with a standard language mapping. This source code portability would ensure that everyone's CORBA implementation looked the same. After all, the IDL is the same among all of them, why can't the source code for that IDL be the same as well?

```
public void init()
{
        // do any of the UI stuff you need to do here...

}
```

```
public boolean action(
        Event evt,
        Object obj
)
{

        if(evt.target == hotWaterButton)
        {
        }
        else if(evt.target == warmWaterButton)
        {
        }
        else if(evt.target == coldWaterButton)
        {
        }


        return true;
}
```

Once your UI works to your satisfaction and you are able to generate events, run within a Web page, and do all of the other fun stuff that makes Java so wonderful, you are ready to move on to the next step . . .

Initializing the client ORB

At this point, you need to take your client and plug it into the ORB system. The actual steps involved in doing so are pretty simple and are outlined in the next few sections. The first, and most important, step is to actually import the ORB into your files:

```
import corba.*;
```

Once the ORB is included, you can have your applet class extend the ORB:

```
public class Cooler extends CORBAApplet
{
        ...
}
```

You then have to initialize the ORB so that your Applet is prepared to talk to the ORB itself. Because we extend the ORB to begin with, all we have to do is call the init method for the super class:

```
public void init()
{
        super.init();
}
```

Finally, your `init` method needs to obtain a reference to the remote object with which you would like to talk. Let's assume that we have stored the object in the Naming Service under the name "Cooler":

```
public void init()
{
        super.init();

        coolerObject = NamingService.find("Cooler");
}
```

Now that we have a reference to the object, we can communicate with the remote object just as if it were a local object. As we will see, the Java syntax looks exactly as it would were the remote object a local object.

Invoking a remote object

Now that we have the object and know that the server is ready to be started, we can go about the process of talking to the object itself. Up until now we have communicated only with the Naming Service in order to get the object; this will be our first invocation of the object. Note that even if the server has not been started, the ORB will allow us to talk to it. This is because the underlying CORBA mechanism makes sure the object has started and that it is ready to be invoked. Sometimes the latency between a client call and a server response is long, usually because the ORB is in the process of starting and initializing a server in order to handle the request.

```
public boolean action(
        Event evt,
        Object obj
)
{

        if(evt.target == hotWaterButton)
        {
            coolerObject.getHotWater();
        }
        else if(evt.target == warmWaterButton)
        {
            coolerObject.getWarmWater();
        }
        else if(evt.target == coldWaterButton)
        {
            coolerObject.getColdWater();
        }

        return true;

}
```

In this example, our invocations are pretty obviously triggered. For every button that is pressed, we will make a remote call to an object. The call will block the client until the server lets go of the invocation. If we wanted asynchronous communication rather than synchronous communication, we would need to take some steps in our IDL file to specify that a certain method should not block when invoked. For example, we could spawn a thread instead of making a direct invocation. For simplicity's sake, we have chosen not to do this. However, if your server side code is complicated and takes some time to execute, you may want to spawn threads to handle invocations for you.

Tracking errors

Java's exception handling mechanisms will enable us to track and report errors when they arrive. Furthermore, the exception handlers will prevent our program from crashing in the event a server encounters a problem somewhere down the line. If this were a mission-critical application, the client side would not experience any problems should the server flake out for some reason.

In order to make the most effective use of the exception handlers, you need to declare your own exceptions in the IDL file. After doing so, your servers must throw those exceptions when necessary. This enables us to obtain a specific exception for every error rather than a generic "an error has occurred" message.

```
public boolean action(
        Event evt,
        Object obj
)
{
        if(evt.target == hotWaterButton)
        {
            try
            {
                coolerObject.getHotWater();
            }
            catch (NoMoreWaterException exc)
            {
                // error handling here...
            }
        }
        else if(evt.target == warmWaterButton)
        {
            try
            {
```

```
                    coolerObject.getWarmWater();
            }
            catch (NoMoreWaterException exc)
            {
                // error handling here...
            }
        }
        else if(evt.target == coldWaterButton)
        {
            try
            {
                coolerObject.getColdWater();
            }
            catch (NoMoreWaterException exc)
            {
                // error handling here...
            }
        }
    }

        return true;
}
```

As you can see, exception handling enables us to protect our clients from server malfunctions. It also gives us the benefit of the doubt when making invocations that could be deemed risky (i.e., invocations across multiple networks, firewalls, and so forth). It is precisely those special conditions that gives CORBA the most fits when dealing with network traffic.

Implementing the monitor

The monitor is a client in the same sense as the cooler client we created previously. However, the monitor client is also required to routinely obtain the levels for each kind of water so that it can display each level graphically. In order to implement this pinging effect, we need to pop a thread within which the monitor will query the server every second:

```
public class Monitor extends Applet implements Runnable
{
        Thread monitorThread = null;

        public void start()
        {
            if(monitorThread == null)
```

```
    {
        monitorThread = new Thread(this);
        monitorThread.start();
    }
}

public void stop()
{
    if(monitorThread != null)
    {
        monitorThread.stop();
        monitorThread = null;
    }

}

public void init()
{
    super.init();

    coolerObject = NamingService.find("Cooler");
}
}
```

As you can see, we simply invoke and create a thread. Now we need to add the run method inside of which we will ping the server every second. While this is a very brutish approach to retrieving information at a steady rate from the server, it will have to suffice. In our section on callbacks, we will modify this client so that it obtains information from the server only when the information has changed.

```
public class Monitor extends Applet implements Runnable
{
    Thread monitorThread = null;

    public void start()
    {
        if(monitorThread == null)
        {
            monitorThread = new Thread(this);
            monitorThread.start();
        }
    }
```

```java
    public void stop()
    {
        if(monitorThread != null)
        {
            monitorThread.stop();
            monitorThread = null;
        }

    }

    public void init()
    {
        super.init();

        coolerObject = NamingService.find("Cooler");
    }

    public void run()
    {
        // prioritize the main thread
Thread.currentThread().setPriority (
            Thread.NORM_PRIORITY - 1);

while (kicker != null)
{
            // get the water level
            coolerObj.getHotWaterLevel();
            coolerObj.getWarmWaterLevel();
            coolerObj.getColdWaterLevel();

            // pause the thread
    try
    {
    Thread.sleep (pause);
    }
    catch (InterruptedException e)
    {
    break;
            }
        }
    }
}
```

Shutting down your connection

The final step to coding your client is to release the object reference. In Java, this is not as much a concern as it is in C++, for any memory management issues are of no concern. This does not mean, however, that object references are "free" in Java. On the contrary, the ORB keeps track of each object reference out there. If multiple clients possess object references, then the server will hunt down the necessary resources, allocating and deallocating memory as it sees fit, in order to keep the server functioning smoothly. By preventing multiple unused object references from being allocated, your server can function properly and to its utmost ability.

Client overview

In this section, we have constructed a simple client. More complex clients will follow the same model: Create the user interface first, then fill in the CORBA details. As your clients begin to get more and more complicated, your user interface and CORBA modules will begin to intersect. To make debugging and performance tuning much easier, it is highly recommended that you consider splitting your code as we did in the featured application that we described in Chapter 1 and that we will implement using IDL in a few sections.

Now that you're familiar with creating and implementing CORBA clients, let's turn the tables and see what's involved with setting up CORBA servers. In order for us to split our processing appropriately between the client and the server, the server should be the focus of all our attention. The client should do nothing more than funnel information back and forth between the user and server. You should limit the amount of processing you do in your client. Save all the hard work for your server.

CORBA Servers

One of the beauties of CORBA servers is that they are started up automatically by the Object Request Broker. When we used sockets we had to manually start our server, but here we simply create our server, register it with the ORB, and forget about it. Every time a client invokes the server, the server will start up (if it isn't running already), initialize itself, and ready itself for invocations. To the client, all of this happens seamlessly and with no additional work needed.

Defining an interface and generating code

In the previous section, we defined our interface as follows:

```
interface Cooler
{
        int getHotWaterLevel();
        int getWarmWaterLevel();
```

```
        int getColdWaterLevel();

        exception NoMoreWaterException { };

        int getHotWater() throws NoMoreWaterException;
        int getWarmWater() throws NoMoreWaterException;
        int getColdWater() throws NoMoreWaterException;
};
```

Now we need to implement the interface. The first thing we need to do is to generate all of our stub code. The stub code provides the underlying CORBA functionality to our server so that we can concentrate on developing the server logic itself. Because we generate code, we don't need to know the nuances of how CORBA works.

Java IDL includes an `idltojava` compiler that translates IDL code into Java code. The IDL file that we defined earlier gets six generated analogs that handle the CORBA plumbing for us. First, the Holder class is generated. As we discussed previously, a Holder allows us to pass a CORBA object as `inout` and `out` parameters to CORBA methods. We also get an Operations class that defines a simple Java `interface` from which the other files can inherit.

The meat of the generated server code lies in the Servant, Skeleton, and Stub code. A Skeleton is used by the client to obtain a basic framework for the object to which it desires to communicate. The Skeleton is sort of like a roadmap. Using it, you can get a good idea of where you are going, but you will get no information as to the scenery along the way. A Skeleton enables the client to know what is possible, but not how that is accomplished.

The Stub code is used by both the Skeleton and the Servant to handle the interaction of the Server code with the ORB itself (see Figure 3-12). While the Stub does all the work, the Skeleton and Servant are what we actually see.

As you can see from the diagram in Figure 3-12, the Stub is the foundation of the entire CORBA server. The other classes use the Stub to obtain information about how they will implement the IDL. We will see in a moment how Java RMI classes are generated after we create the server file. Java IDL works very differently. Whereas RMI works on generated classes, IDL generates code based on the IDL file. As we have noted before, interfaces defined using the IDL are inherently language independent. We could just as easily have created a C++ server rather than a Java server.

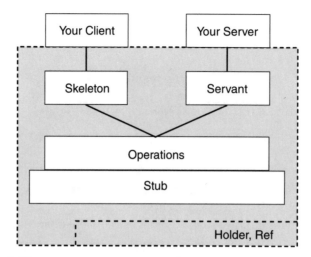

Figure 3-12 The generated components for a Java IDL server.

When we use the idltojava compiler on our Cooler.idl file, we get the following six classes:

1. CoolerRef
2. CoolerHolder
3. CoolerOperations
4. CoolerStub
5. CoolerServant
6. CoolerSkeleton

As we discussed previously, each of these classes plays an integral role in how our server behaves under the CORBA umbrella. It is highly recommended that you not modify these generated files.

Creating the server implementation

Once we generate code, we need to create a class that will contain the routines we want to provide when a method is invoked. Unlike RMI, we create our server after we generate the underlying code functionality for it. The skeletons, stubs, and servants are, as their names imply, placeholders. We must supply the logic for our methods, it just doesn't appear out of mid-air. By convention, our server class' name contains the name of the IDL object, followed by the "Impl" descriptor. Keep in mind that we don't have to name our class CoolerImpl, but we do because that is the general CORBA convention.

The first step in creating our server is to include all of the generated code:

```
import Cooler.*;
```

Once we have done that, we create a `CoolerImpl` class that implements the
`CoolerServant` we generated earlier. In so doing, our Cooler server obtains the
CORBA plumbing provided by the generated code.

```
import Cooler.*;


public class CoolerImpl implements CoolerServant
{
}
```

Now, we need to fill in the names of the functions we must implement in order to
fulfill our contract with the IDL definition and create a constructor:

```
import Cooler.*;

public class CoolerImpl implements CoolerServant
{
        CoolerImpl()
        {
            super();
        }

        public int getHotWaterLevel()
        {
        }

        public int getWarmWaterLevel()
        {
        }

        public int getColdWaterLevel()
        {
        }


        public int getHotWater() throws NoMoreWaterException
        {
        }
```

```
        public int getWarmWater() throws NoMoreWaterException
        {
        }


        public int getColdWater()throws NoMoreWaterException
        {
        }
}
```

Finally, we need to fill in each of the functions so that they do what they are intended to do.

```
import Cooler.*;

public class CoolerImpl implements CoolerServant
{
        private int hotWaterLevel;
        private int warmWaterLevel;
        private int coldWaterLevel;

        CoolerImpl()
        {
            super();

            hotWaterLevel = 0;
            warmWaterLevel = 0;
            coldWaterLevel = 0;
        }

        public int getHotWaterLevel()
        {
            return hotWaterLevel;
        }

        public int getWarmWaterLevel()
        {
            return warmWaterLevel;
        }

        public int getColdWaterLevel()
        {
```

```
            return coldWaterLevel;
    }


    public int getHotWater() throws NoMoreWaterException
    {
        if(hotWaterLevel >= 10)
            hotWaterLevel -= 10;
        else
            throw new NoMoreWaterException;
    }


    public int getWarmWater() throws NoMoreWaterException
    {
        if(warmWaterLevel >= 5)
            warmWaterLevel -= 5;
        else
            throw new NoMoreWaterException;
    }


    public int getColdWater()throws NoMoreWaterException
    {
        if(coldWaterLevel >= 3)
            coldWaterLevel -= 3;
        else
            throw new NoMoreWaterException;
    }
}
```

Die-hard CORBA veterans will attest to the charming simplicity with which this is done in Java. C++ servers contain the same steps, but can be drastically more complicated than they need to be. We have now completed the creation of our server implementation.

Creating the server executable

The code we created in the previous section is known as *servant code*. A *servant* is the physical process in which your server executes and the server implementation contained therein. A *server* is the set of interfaces and methods that is published in the IDL. The *interface definition* is the contract that the server fulfills and the servant executes.

That said, we must now create the server for our Cooler. The server must do three things:

1. Start itself up in a physical process;
2. Create a servant instance to reside in the process; and
3. Bind itself to a name in the Naming Service.

All of this is analogous to an ordinary table lamp. There are several table lamps in your home, all of which implement the same interface—namely "turn on" and "turn off." Just because they all implement the same interface doesn't mean that they all must be the same lamp. Indeed, you need many lamps, otherwise you would trip on your shoes as you went to bed. So, once we create several different lamps, we need to put them in their designated locations and plug them into the socket. Likewise, once we create a servant, we need to put it inside a server and plug it into the ORB.

To do so, first we must create the class so that the server can begin executing in its own process space. After we create a class, we need to supply it with a main routine and link up with the ORB. If we do not link up with the ORB here, subsequent invocations that create the stubs, skeletons, and servants will be unable to work properly.

```
import Cooler.*;

public class CoolerServer
{
        // private variables
        private CORBA corba;

        public static void main(
            String argv[]
        )
        {
            // link up with the ORB
            corba = new CORBA();
        }
}
```

Next, we need to create an instance of the `CoolerImpl` servant class that we created in the previous section. We also need to use the `CoolerRef` container class to support our servant instance. Remember, clients don't want servants to talk to, they want servers. With servers, they get a sketch of the contract provided for in the IDL. With servants, they get all of the legal mumbo jumbo in the contract itself. Clients don't need to know that stuff.

```
import Cooler.*;

public class CoolerServer
{
        // private variables
        private CORBA corba;
        private CoolerRef coolerRef;

        public static void main(
            String argv[]
        )
        {
            // link up with the ORB
            corba = new CORBA();

            // create the servant class
            CoolerImpl coolerImpl = new CoolerImpl();

            // create the container class
            coolerRef = CoolerSkeleton.createRef(
                corba.getORB(), coolerImpl);
        }
}
```

Finally, the server must take the `CoolerRef` instance and bind it to a unique name in the Naming Service.

```
import Cooler.*;

public class CoolerServer
{
        // private variables
        private CORBA corba;
        private CoolerRef coolerRef;

        public static void main(
```

```
        String argv[]
    )
    {

        // link up with the ORB
        corba = new CORBA();

        // create the servant class
        CoolerImpl coolerImpl = new CoolerImpl();

        // create the container class
        coolerRef = CoolerSkeleton.createRef(
            corba.getORB(), coolerImpl);

        // bind this server to the Naming Service
        corba.rebind("Cooler", coolerRef);
    }
}
```

Note how the name we have bound to is the same name that we referred to in the previous section on clients. After compiling all our code, we have a working server that the clients in the previous and next chapters can talk to.

Registering with the ORB

Finally, the CORBA server we have created must be placed inside the *Interface Repository,* the location of all objects known to the ORB. When the ORB receives an invocation from a client, it looks in the Interface Repository for the proper object, and, if it is found, starts the object up and readies it for invocation. Consult your CORBA vendor's documentation on how to register an ORB with the Interface Repository. For example, in NEO, registering an ORB is as simple as typing:

%prompt% **make register**

Server overview

As we did for our client, we created a simple CORBA server that accepts invocations and passes back results. This server is, in essence, no different from the most complex CORBA servers. The steps involved in creating servers remain the same:

1. Define your object using the IDL
2. Generate Stubs and Skeletons from the IDL
3. Fill in the code
4. Create the server container object
5. Register the object

In so doing, any object server you create will run efficiently, will be very reliable, and will have the flexibility to be changed often.

Sometimes, you do not want your Java IDL application to be a full-fledged server. For example, servers cannot be embedded within an applet and therefore cannot exist on a Web page. If you still require dynamic updates to your server, the only way to get them is to use a callback, which we'll discuss in the next section.

CORBA Callbacks

Let's say you've been pestering your Aunt Fran about the details for her latest wedding. You call her every day and she is getting sick of it. Finally, she tells you that she will call you "only when something happens."

In essence, the two of you are setting up callbacks between one another. When Aunt Fran gets an event that you should be aware of, you will get a call. Otherwise, her phone will be silent and she will not be bothered.

Java callbacks

Java IDL enables your client object to send itself to a server, setting up a *reference bridge* to the client object. Whenever the server must tell the client something, it will make calls on the client objects it stores. In this manner, a Java IDL server can keep track of all the clients that are speaking with it and funnel information back and forth between the objects.

For example, if Aunt Fran were being pestered by every member of the wedding party, not just you, she could tell them all that she will call when something happens. Aunt Fran will then be annoyed only when an event occurs. She would probably make a list of all the people she needs to call and go down the list when the time comes.

Likewise, a Java IDL server keeps track of all its clients and prevents an overload of the system. The alternative to callbacks is for each client to routinely *ping* the server every few seconds or so to get information. While this methodology may work for one or two clients, when several clients start harassing the same server, the server and the network begin to get unnecessarily burdened. With callbacks, the network traffic is high only when an event occurs, and never at any other time. In geek terms, this is referred to as *scalability*. Callbacks are *scalable* because they work just as efficiently for several thousand objects as they do for only a few.

Creating a callback

In order to use callbacks, you must create and define a callback object within your IDL file. The client that needs to setup a callback must first contact the server. In order for it to be allowed to call the server and setup a callback, the client must have access to a method defined for that purpose. Because the server is the one that will register client objects and call them back, the server must have that method as part of its suite of possible invocations.

```
interface CoolerCallback
{
        void waterLevelChanged (
           in long hotLevel,
           in long warmLevel,
           in long coldLevel);
}

interface Cooler
{
        int getHotWaterLevel();
        int getWarmWaterLevel();
        int getColdWaterLevel();

        int getHotWater();
        int getWarmWater();
        int getColdWater();

        // public method for the callback
        long registerCallback (in CoolerCallback coolerCB);
        void unregisterCallback (in long callbackID);
};
```

Notice how the `registerCallback` function contains a `CoolerCallback` object as a parameter. The `CoolerCallback` object will be implemented by your Java client. When the Java client sends itself as the parameter for the `registerCallback` invocation, it is essentially telling the server, "I'm the guy that you need to call when you get a change!" The register function also returns an integer specifying the ID of the object. If the object ever wants to unsubscribe to callbacks, it can give the server its ID number and the server will remove it from its callback list.

Furthermore, the client should implement callback methods just as we did in the server section. In essence, the callback will implement server methods without server infrastructure. The end result is that your client can be invoked by a server *as if it were a server*, but the client need not be burdened by the overhead of being a server (see Figure 3-13).

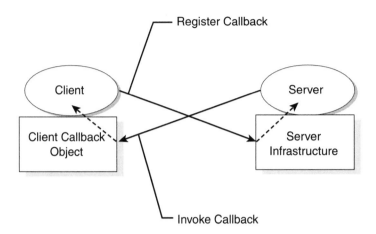

Figure 3-13 Clients must first register themselves with the server before the server will be able to call them back.

Registering a callback

In order for a callback to be invoked on a client by the server, the client must first register itself with the server as a callback object. This is done in the init function. We need to remove the code having to do with threads from our non-callback client, and instead place the following invocation in our init method. We may also remove the run method, because we need not bother with actually making invocations on the server. In addition, our client should implement the callback object:

```
public class Monitor extends CORBAApplet implements CoolerCallback
{
        public void init()
        {
            super.init();

            coolerObject = NamingService.find("Cooler");

            int callbackID = coolerObject.registerCallback(this);
        }
}
```

Notice how we pass the register method a copy of our own object, as we discussed earlier. The Monitor client is now ready to be invoked by the server. Later on we will implement the actual callback function that enables us to process the data we receive.

The Java IDL server should then keep track of the client object in some kind of storage mechanism. None of this is automatic, and all of it must be coded by the programmer. In the following example, we store the client object in a Vector because efficient searching is not required. We only need to call them all back sequentially. The two functions in the following code should be added to your server definition from the previous section:

```java
import Cooler.*;

public class CoolerImpl implements CoolerServant
    {
        private int hotWaterLevel;
        private int warmWaterLevel;
        private int coldWaterLevel;

        // our callbacks
        private Vector callbacks;

        CoolerImpl()
        {
            super();

            hotWaterLevel = 0;
            warmWaterLevel = 0;
            coldWaterLevel = 0;

            callbacks = new Vector();
        }

        public int getHotWaterLevel()
        {
            return hotWaterLevel;
        }

        public int getWarmWaterLevel()
        {
            return warmWaterLevel;
        }

        public int getColdWaterLevel()
```

```
    {
        return coldWaterLevel;
    }

    public int getHotWater() throws NoMoreWaterException
    {
        if(hotWaterLevel >= 10)
            hotWaterLevel -= 10;
        else
            throw new NoMoreWaterException;
    }

    public int getWarmWater() throws NoMoreWaterException
    {
        if(warmWaterLevel >= 5)
            warmWaterLevel -= 5;
        else
            throw new NoMoreWaterException;
    }

    public int getColdWater()throws NoMoreWaterException
    {
        if(coldWaterLevel >= 3)
            coldWaterLevel -= 3;
        else
            throw new NoMoreWaterException;
    }

    public int registerCallback(
        CoolerCallback coolerCallback
    )
    {

        callbacks.addItem(coolerCallback);
    }

    public void unregisterCallback(
        int callbackID
    )
    {

        callbacks.removeItemAt(callbackID);
    }
}
```

Once the callback is registered, the server can continue with its execution until an event is triggered to which it must respond. When Aunt Fran suddenly discovers that her husband turns out to be the Chia Pet she dated five months before, she can go down her list of wedding people and call each of them back. In the same manner, we will be able to look at our table of callback objects and respond.

Receiving and handling a callback

In order to receive a callback, you need to set up a *callback function*. This is analogous to giving Aunt Fran your phone number. When she needs to tell you something, she will have a specific place to call you. Likewise, your callback recipients need to let the server know where to call.

When the server gets an event, it invokes a remote procedure call on the callback function, passing any parameters as necessary. Your callback function accepts and processes the data given to it by the server. Figure 3-14 offers an illustration of this process.

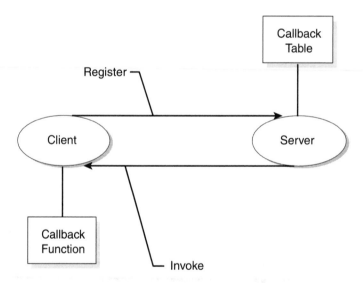

Figure 3-14 The callback registration and invocation process

 TIP: Remember, callbacks are an option to servers. Your callback recipient is acting like a server, but it is not quite a server. It cannot be instantiated on its own by a remote object. Each individual function must be setup with the callback server, and the flexibility you had with full-fledged servers is completely lost. On the other hand, your applet can receive events from a CORBA server without much overhead, it can be used within a browser, and it is easier to implement than a server.

Because our callbacks actually implement the `CallbackObject` interface, they automatically inherit the `waterLevelChanged` method. Our client should process all of its data in the `waterLevelChanged` function:

```
public class Monitor extends CORBAApplet implements CoolerCallback
{
        public void init()
        {
            super.init();

            coolerObject = NamingService.find("Cooler");

            int callbackID = coolerObject.registerCallback(this);
        }

        public synchronized void waterLevelChanged (
            int hotLevel,
            int warmLevel,
            int coldLevel
        )
        {

            System.out.println ("received a callback!");

            … handle the UI stuff you need to …
    }
}
```

Your callback function will merely receive the water levels for all three kinds of water. You can then effect the GUI however you please. Notice how we never actually invoke a method on the server after we register. Instead, we sit back, drink our Martinis (shaken, not stirred), and wait for the server to call us. As they say in Hollywood, "Hey babe, don't call me, I'll call you."

To that effect, the server will contain within it the code necessary to invoke the callback itself. Here, we have chosen to invoke on all the callbacks whenever the water level is changed in any way:

```
public int getHotWater() throws NoMoreWaterException
{
        if(hotWaterLevel >= 10)
        {
            hotWaterLevel -= 10;
```

```
        for(int x = 0; x < callbacks.size(); x++)
        {
                // get the callback object
                CoolerCallback cb =
                    (CoolerCallback) callbacks.itemAt(x);

                // invoke on the callback object
                cb.waterLevelChanged(
                    hotWaterLevel,
                    warmWaterLevel,
                    coldWaterLevel);
            }
        }
        else
            throw new NoMoreWaterException;
    }
```

A similar method will be employed for the `getWarmWater` and `getColdWater` functions.

Callbacks in short

In order to efficiently process invocations from multiple clients, a server should ideally set up a mechanism with which it can control how invocations are handled. Because the server does the bulk of the work, it should get to call the shots. With callbacks, we can do what corporate management has never figured out. The people who do all the work get to make all the decisions. What a novel idea!

A Java IDL Version of the Featured App

Now that we know how to create full IDL and CORBA servers along with the clients that accompany them, let's put our talents to use. The Internet Calendar Manager we discussed in previous chapters is divided into two parts: the Network client module and the Calendar server with which the module will communicate. First, we will create the client and then we will create the server. But before that we need the Interface Definition of the server itself.

Server interface

The following IDL outlines the method signatures of the remote calendar server object. The server may reside anywhere, and as we discussed earlier, can be retrieved through the Naming Service. For demonstration purposes, we'll store our calendar server in the Naming Service under the name "CALENDAR-IDL." Notice how we have enclosed our object within a module. The module will act as a holder for all of our Calendar-related objects. For example, in order to access the `AppointmentType` object from within Java, you would have to specify `CalendarIDL.AppointmentType`. As we discussed in our earlier section on language mappings, `modules` get translated into Java `packages`.

```
module CalendarIDL
{
        struct AppointmentType
        {
            string reason;
            long time;
        }

        public interface Calendar
        {
            void scheduleAppointment(
                AppointmentType appointment);

            AppointmentType[] getAppointments();
        }
}
```

Network module

As you will recall, the Network module has a simple set of methods with which we can change the server. It is instantiated by the client and takes the high-level data structures given to it by the rest of the client and sends it off to the server. Our server will then process information and maintain state. We have incorporated several methods that will enable us to access the information on the server. Here is the original code for the `NetworkModule`. Note the addition of the import statement to include all the Calendar's IDL server files. In so doing, we do not have to specify the entire package name for the Calendar's files.

```
import CalendarIDL.*;
public class NetworkModule
{
        public void scheduleAppointment(
            String reason,
            int time);

        public Vector getAppointments();
```

```
        public void initNetwork();

        public void shutdownNetwork();
}
```

We will now implement the constructor for this object. The constructor initializes the connection to the CORBA server and sets up the remote IDL object for use by the other routines. We will keep track of the remote object with the `calendarObject` variable:

```
public class NetworkModule
{
        CORBAServer calendarObject;

        NetworkModule()
        {
           // first get a handle on CORBA
           CORBA corbaInterface = new CORBA();

           // use the CORBA Naming Service to get the Calendar server
           calendarObject =
               corbaInterface.NamingService.find("CALENDAR-CORBA");
        }

        public void scheduleAppointment(
               String reason,
               int time)
        {
        }

        public Vector getAppointments()
        {
        }

        public void initNetwork()
        {
        }

        public void shutdownNetwork()
        {
        }
}
```

We now need to fill in the functionality of the network module. Because we've already initialized the remote object, we can feel free to use it and communicate with the server. In the getAppointments method, we will need to translate the array of AppointmentType objects to a Java Vector. We do this so that the rest of the application will not need to be aware of the implementation details of the server itself.

```java
public class NetworkModule
{
    CORBAServer calendarObject;

    NetworkModule()
    {
       // first get a handle on CORBA
       CORBA corbaInterface = new CORBA();

       // use the CORBA Naming Service to get the Calendar server
       calendarObject =
             corbaInterface.NamingService.find("CALENDAR-CORBA");
    }

    public void scheduleAppointment(
        String reason,
        int time)
    {
        // send the appointment to the server
        try
        {
            calendarObject.scheduleAppointment(appointment);
        }
        catch(CORBAException exc)
        {
            // error handling here
        }
    }

    public Vector getAppointments()
    {
        AppointmentType appointments[];
```

```
            // get the array of appointments from the server
            appointments = calendarObject.getAppointemnts();

            // translate the appointment array into a Java Vector
            Vector appointmentVector = new Vector();
            for(int x = 0; x < appointments.size; x++)
                appointmentVector.addElement(appointments[x]);

            // return the vector
            return appointmentVector;
        }

    public void initNetwork()
    {
        // we don't need these in Java IDL
    }

    public void shutdownNetwork()
    {
        // we don't need these in Java IDL
    }
}
```

Note how we need not implement the `initNetwork` and `shutdownNetwork` methods. In Java IDL, all of the underlying network functionality is handled for us automatically. CORBA objects are *location transparent*, meaning we don't care where or how they are implemented. Because we use the Naming Service to get to the objects, we don't have to worry about initializing connections in our client. The Object Request Broker handles all of the networking mess for us with easy-to-use programmer APIs.

Calendar server

As we have seen in our previous section on CORBA servers, implementing a server can be a tricky process. Now, we need to apply the language mapping and develop code for what the server interface is going to look like in Java. We've already shown you what the IDL for the server looks like, so here is the Java result for it. Note that we are including the Calendar objects by using the module name.

```
import corba.*;
import java.util.*;
import CalendarIDL.*;
```

```
public class CalendarImpl implements CalendarServant
{
    public void scheduleAppointment(
        String reason,
        int time
    )
    {
    }

    public AppointmentType[] getAppointments()
    {
    }
}
```

Now, we need to fill in the scheduleAppointment and getAppointments method. In scheduleAppointment, we will store our appointments transiently in a Vector. The Vector needs to be initialized in the constructor for our implementation object.

```
public class CalendarImpl implements CalendarServant
{
    Vector appointments;

    public void scheduleAppointment(
        String reason,
        int time
    )
    {
        // create an appointment
        AppointmentType appt = new AppointmentType;

        // fill the appointment
        appt.reason = reason;
        appt.time = time;

        // add it to the vector
        appointments.addElement(appt);
    }

    public AppointmentType[] getAppointments()
    {
    }
}
```

Our `getAppointments` method will return an array of `AppointmentType` variables. Unlike in our sockets implementation in Chapter 2, and unlike our subsequent implementations for RMI and JDBC in the following two chapters, here we do not need to define our own `AppointmentType`. Because we declare it in the IDL, the code for it automatically gets generated.

```java
public class CalendarImpl implements CalendarServant
{
    Vector appointments;

    public void scheduleAppointment(
        String reason,
        int time
    )
    {
        // create an appointment
        AppointmentType appt = new AppointmentType;

        // fill the appointment
        appt.reason = reason;
        appt.time = time;

        // add it to the vector
        appointments.addElement(appt);
}

    public AppointmentType[] getAppointments()
    {
        // create an array of appointments
        AppointmentType appts[] =
            new AppointmentType[appointments.size()];

        // fill the array with the contents of the vector
        for(int x = 0; x < appointments.size(); x++)
        {
            AppointmentType appt =
                (AppointmentType) appointments.elementAt(x);

            appts[x] = appt;
        }
        return appts;
    }
}
```

We must now create a server process for the servant to exist inside. We do this just as we created the server for the Cooler example earlier in this section. Inside the application main, we will initialize CORBA and rebind to a unique name in the Naming Service, in this case "CALENDAR-IDL".

```java
public class CalendarServer
{
    public static void main(
    String argv[]
    )
    {
        // the Calendar server implementation classes
        CalendarImpl calendarImpl;
        CalendarRef calendarRef;

        // the host we will connect to
        String host = "";

        try
        {
            // initialize CORBA
            CORBA corba = new CORBA();

            // create the implementation classes and
            // tie it to the ORB
            calendarImpl = new CalendarImpl();
            calendarRef = CalendarSkeleton.createRef(
                corba.getOrb(), calendarImpl);

            // now bind the objref to the proper service
            corba.rebind("CALENDAR-IDL", calendarRef);

            // now sit around and wait for invocations
            synchronized(host)
            {
                host.wait();
            }
        }
        catch (InterruptedException exc)
        {
            // error handling here
        }
    }
}
```

We will then need to register the server. You will once again need to consult the documentation for the ORB vendor you have chosen to find out how to do this. Once registered, you can run your client and never again be late for an important meeting.

"Different Vendors, Different Problems"

Because one of the biggest drawbacks to CORBA, and the main reason you will not find a CORBA implementation in this book is that there are several disparate vendors for JAVA IDL, the OMG created a complex protocol with which objects can communicate.

The Internet Inter-ORB Protocol, or IIOP (pronounced eye-op), is the "language" used by objects to exchange information. It is based on TCP/IP, as opposed to UDP, and forms a common base for all CORBA clients and servers to communicate.

You, the application programmer, will never see IIOP, and you will never know that IIOP is going under the covers. However, the Object Request Broker uses IIOP to funnel information to other ORBs. In so doing, a Visigenic ORB and an Iona ORB can talk the same language, so to speak, when communicating with one another.

So, IIOP addresses one major issue, the interoperability of objects written for different ORBs, with different CORBA implementations. However, one more major problem still exists.

CORBA applets often have serious download performance problems. Because an ORB must exist on every platform with a CORBA client or server, CORBA applets must include, as part of their implementation classes, the entire ORB. In so doing, a CORBA applet must download four hundred or so Java classes that constitute the ORB. As we discussed in our Chapter 1 section on "Performance," four hundred classes is a major data transfer as far as Java applets are concerned.

To solve this problem, the Netscape browser will include, as part of LiveConnect (which we will discuss in Chapter 10) and as part of the Netscape classes.zip file, the entire Visigenic ORB. This will allow the browser to refrain from downloading the entire ORB in a CORBA applet, creating a great performance boost for CORBA applets.

However, what if the CORBA applet was written in a non-Visigenic ORB? Well, at that point, Netscape has no choice but to download the entire ORB as it would have done without the presence of Visigenic, negating any performance boost.

While IIOP addresses interoperability on a protocol and communication level, no CORBA vendor has yet to agree on interoperability on an object source level. As of this book's publication, many of the vendors were still negotiating on the exact contents of that so-called "Java IDL" that would then be incorporated as part of the Java Developer's Kit.

Summary

CORBA is quickly becoming an industry standard. With industry giants Sun Microsystems and Netscape Communications firmly behind the technology, it may soon make an appearance in your regular programming diet. While Java begins to negate some of CORBA's difficulty, CORBA is still a long ways from being standard fare on everyone's desktop because of staunch competition from its Java-only brother, Java RMI. As we will see in the next chapter, RMI is a strong alternative to the complexity of CORBA.

CHAPTER

4

RMI and Distributed Objects

RMI Clients and Servers

Creating Dynamic Servers On-the-Fly

Understanding and Creating RMI Callbacks

Modifying the Featured Application

Java RMI: Remote Method Invocation

Java Remote Method Invocation is a simple, yet powerful, Java-based framework for distributed object design. While it shares many traits with its cousin, Java IDL, it has distinct advantages over IDL in several key areas, notably usability. Java RMI-based objects can be quickly deployed and managed across networks. While it has several shortcomings that we will discuss later, Java RMI is a fast and adequate introduction to Distributed Object Programming.

In this chapter, we will discuss the architectural decisions behind RMI and why they were made. We will also guide you through the process required to create a simple client/server system using the Remote Method Invocation mechanisms. By the end of this chapter, you should have a firm grasp of RMI along with enough fundamentals of distributed object design to help you make an informed architectural decision of your own.

Distributed Objects

Remote Method Invocation (RMI) is similar to Java IDL in many ways. However, RMI enables you to create applications that communicate with one another without the costly overhead of CORBA. A remote method invocation is a form of the Remote Procedure Call (RPC) so common in C++. Instead of creating and instantiating an object on your local machine, you create it on another machine and communicate with that object as you normally would.

So, with the advantages of the Java language, you will be able to create distributed objects that communicate with one another. Unlike CORBA, your applications must be written in Java, but that may not be a bad thing in the end. It will be difficult to re-implement your legacy applications because they must be rewritten in Java. Yet, being able to write distributed applications without expending any real effort is highly attractive. If Java is your language of choice, then RMI may be your best communication alternative.

What is RMI?

In the good ol' days of programming, all of the things you wanted to do resided in one program. If you needed a file, you simply opened it. If you needed to optimize your program, you either reduced functionality or sped it up. Lately, the notion of distributed programming has taken the industry by storm. Instead of opening a file, you open another application. Instead of reducing functionality, you farm out the work to another application and keep tabs on the process by communicating with it. Figure 4-1 illustrates the differences between local and remote object invocation.

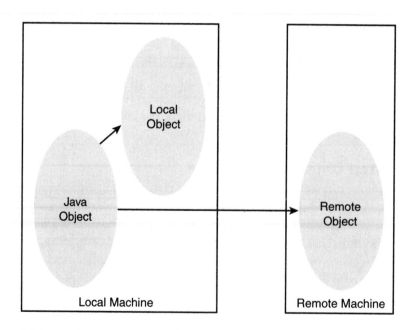

Figure 4–1 Invocations on remote objects appear the same as invocations on local objects.

Java RMI enables you to farm out work to other Java objects residing in other processes, or in other machines altogether. Not only can you execute steps in parallel using threads, but you can farm out work to other processes that will execute steps in parallel on a different machine!

Sure, many of the alternatives presented in this book enable you to do the same thing, but why would you want to do all of that work when you can let Java—the same language you've spent so much free time learning anyway—do all the work automatically? Where CORBA flaunts its language independence, RMI makes no effort to hide the fact that you are locked into a Java only solution.

How does RMI work?

When your client invokes your server, several layers of the RMI system come into play. The first, and most important to the programmer, is the stub/skeleton layer. The stubs are Java code that you fill in so that you can communicate with the other layers. For example, in Chapter 3, "Java IDL: Interface Definition Language," you saw how the IDL to Java compiler generated a bunch of code that we later filled in and used as the framework for a distributed application.

Likewise, the Java RMI system automatically enables you to use several helper functions. By inheriting from the RMI classes, your class implements the stubs or skeletons. In geek parlance, stubs are reserved for client code that you fill in, and skeletons refer to server code.

Once the stubs and skeleton layers are completed, they pass through the other two layers in the RMI system. The first of these layers is the Remote Reference layer. The remote reference layer is responsible for determining the nature of the object. Does it reside on a single machine or across a network? Is the remote object the kind of object that will be instantiated and started automatically, or is it the kind of object that must be declared and initialized beforehand? The remote reference layer handles all of these situations, and many more, without your intervention.

Finally, the transport layer is similar to a translator that takes your RMI code, turns it into TCP/IP (or whatever communication mechanism is used), and lets it fly over the network to the other end. Because the RMI system supports a technique called *object serialization*, any objects passed as parameters to a remote method, no matter how complicated, are converted into simple streams of characters that are then easily re-converted into their original object representation.

As you can see in Figure 4-2, a client that invokes a remote server first talks to its stub code, which, in turn, sends the message to the remote reference layer, which then passes it through the transport mechanism to the other machine. The other machine takes what it gets through the transport layer, re-translates into the remote reference layer representation, which passes it on to the skeleton code where the request finally makes its appearance at the remote method.

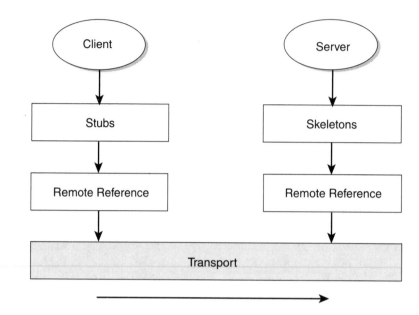

Figure 4–2 Java RMI architecture.

Stub/skeleton layer

When your client begins to invoke a server on a remote machine, the API with which you, as programmer, are concerned is the stub/skeleton code. By inheriting from the appropriate RMI class, your object obtains several RMI methods that you are required to fill in.

When the invocation is actually made, the remote object could be a replicated object. A replicated object is an object that has several instances executing at the same time. For example, a given application may have several instances of the Java String class within its threads of execution. If the String class were a remote server object, a client that invokes it should not have to worry about its various instances. The stub and skeleton layer precludes this notion of replicated objects. When you write your application and code the necessary tools to talk to a remote object, you need not concern yourself with the implementations on the remote side.

The stub/skeleton layer also abstracts you from the various transport mechanisms in the other layers. In short, the stub and skeleton layers both make sure that your program is platform independent. The system calls and routines are left for the other layers, and your code should not be tailored for one particular architecture.

Remote reference layer

The reference layer serves two purposes. First, it handles the translation from the stub and skeleton layers into native transport calls on the hosting architecture. The early version of RMI was not as platform independent as it purported to be. The problem lay in the Java Developer's Kit, and not in the RMI system itself. With the introduction of the next major revision of the JDK, the RMI system now functions properly. The RMI system is truly platform independent as it, and the Java language, was meant to be.

The reference layer also is in charge of carrying out remote reference protocols. These protocols may be point-to-point communication, i.e., local object to remote object invocations. Or, the reference protocol may refer to replicated objects. The RMI system ensures that when you invoke a remote object that happens to be replicated, all of the replicated instances will hear the same message. The replication strategy is customizable, but we refer you to the RMI System Architecture section of the RMI specification.

There is a corresponding server side reference layer that accepts the client-side instructions and re-translates them into programmer code. It ensures that the invocations are made reliably, and that the RMI system knows about any exceptions. Exceptions are thrown from this level for any problems in establishing connections, fulfilling invocation requests, or closing connections.

Basically, the reference layer is responsible for bridging the gap between programmer code and network communication. It is a go-between of data, taking what you want to do, and making sure it can be done using the network.

Transport layer

When the first miners found gold in California, they exclaimed "Eureka!" Well, Eureka! This is where the action is. While you are not able to manipulate these routines yourself, it is important to understand how the transport is implemented. From here, you will understand the limitations of RMI and be able to make an architectural decision based on them.

The transport layer is responsible for setting up connections, maintaining them, alerting applications of problems, listening for connections, and shutting them down. The transport layer consists of four components: the objects, the space between local and remote address spaces, the physical socket, and the transport protocol. Figure 4-3 illustrates a simple transport model.

The objects, or *endpoints*, are the beginning and end of an invocation. Between one object's transport endpoint to another's transport endpoint resides the entire communication mechanism on which RMI is based. The *channel* between the address spaces is in charge of upholding the connection and monitoring for signs of trouble, say the loss of an object or maybe the loss of the physical connection itself. The socket *connection* is basically the same kind of socket we saw in an earlier chapter. As we mentioned before, sockets really are the basis for all communications in Java. Finally, the transport protocol is the language in which sockets talk to one another.

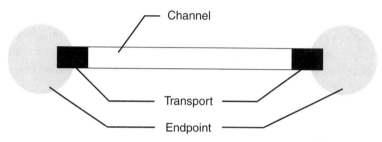
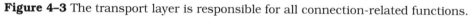

Figure 4–3 The transport layer is responsible for all connection-related functions.

Local vs. remote objects

So, what are the semantic differences between local and remote objects? All along we have stressed that at the heart of the entire system is the notion that to the client programmer, everything looks exactly like normal, non-remote Java code. In fact, even Java IDL's client applications look no different than local Java code.

Java Remote Method Invocation is quite interesting from a semantic sense. Indeed, the very idea that instantiating an object that happens to be on another network is interesting in and of itself, but to add to that the caveat that the remote object exhibits all of the properties of a local Java object adds a certain amount of usefulness to the whole matter.

What kinds of characteristics do Java objects exhibit? Well, most importantly, they are easy to implement. They are garbage-collected, meaning that once your program has no use for them, they are automatically de-referenced and their resources returned to the system. We discuss remote garbage collection in the next section.

Java objects are, of course, platform independent, as are Java RMI objects. When you make a remote method invocation in a non-Java language, chances are you must learn not only the nuances of the communication mechanism of your own machine, but that of the machine you are talking to as well. Imagine being a Solaris programmer who is trying to talk to a Windows 95 machine! It's hard enough to master Solaris inter-process communication without having to learn the esoteric Windows 95 communication layers as well!

Java RMI frees you from that morass, just as Java frees you from recompiling your code for multiple architectures. When you invoke a RMI method across different platforms, the RMI system adjusts its communication layers automatically; and because those layers are abstracted from you, the programmer, you never have to concern yourself with that confusing network code.

Garbage collection

One of the biggest advantages to Java is that there are no pointers. There is no memory to de-allocate, and you never have to deal with memory storage schemes. Java's platform independence mantra wouldn't allow it anyway, but if you were to develop for multiple platforms, you would need to be concerned with the nuances of memory management for each architecture which, like mastering multiple transport layers, is a daunting task.

Java RMI is no exception to the rule. In fact, it contains a complicated garbage collection scheme based on Modula-3's Network Objects concept of object reference counters. RMI places an object reference counter into each object. Every time another object talks to the remote object, the object reference counter is incremented, and once the object no longer needs the remote object, the counter is decremented.

There are many protective layers around the garbage collection algorithm that prevent premature object deallocation. But, most of RMI's distributed garbage collection farms off the work to the local Java Virtual Machine's garbage collection algorithm. Thus, RMI does not reinvent the wheel, so to speak.

For example, when our local object begins a conversation with a remote object, we begin to talk through the RMI system's layers. As part of the remote reference layer, our local object creates a "network" object. On the other end, at the remote machine, the remote reference layer creates another network object that converses with the remote object. The remote Virtual Machine realizes that the remote object should not be de-allocated as long as the remote network object is referring to it (see Figure 4-4). Thus, the remote object is not blown away.

Back at the local machine, when we are no longer using the remote object, the remote reference layer removes all references to the local network object. Once the local Java Virtual Machine realizes that the local network object is no longer used, it garbage collects it. As part of its `finalize` routine, the local network object sends a message to the remote network object through the reference layer that it should let go of its reference to the remote object. In so doing, the remote network object causes the remote Java Virtual Machine to garbage collect the remote object.

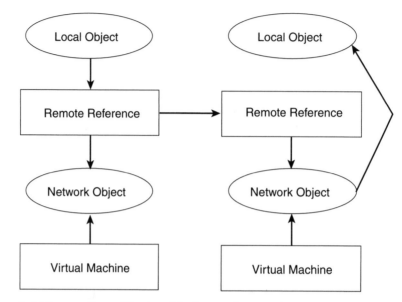

Figure 4–4 The creation of "network" objects during object communication prevents Java's garbage collection from interrupting the conversation.

Security

When you instantiate a local object from within a Java applet, security is not a concern. The applet security mechanism has already cleared your applet, and you are free to allocate and de-allocate your objects.

However, security is very much a concern for remote objects. When you try to instantiate a remote object, you must have permission to do so. The Applet class loader that is in charge of getting every class your application requires may or may not be able to instantiate the remote object. As a result, RMI in applets is limited to invoking methods on classes that are already in existence. You are not allowed to create a remote object because the applet class loader will not let you.

Applet vs. application

Currently, RMI servers must be created as Java applications. Just as in Java IDL, servers cannot be embedded within a Web page. There are several reasons why, most notably that the applet security mechanisms prevent it; but, for the time being, the RMI system does not support applet servers. The callback mechanism similar to the one we discussed in Chapter 3, "Java IDL, Interface Definition Language," can be implemented in RMI. We will discuss the callback alternative as implemented in RMI in a few sections.

Dynamic method invocations

RMI enables you to invoke a server without knowing anything about what methods are contained within the server. It's like going into a restaurant and ordering without ever seeing the menu. If you know you're in an Italian restaurant, chances are pretty good that they offer spaghetti and meatballs. Likewise, if you know what kind of server you are talking to, you can invoke it without actually knowing anything about the methods it implements.

Overview of RMI

Java's Remote Method Invocation system is a significantly easier and lighter weight approach to distributed objects than Java IDL. Contained completely within the Java language, RMI is an extension to the language itself, whereas Java IDL is a language-independent Java implementation. RMI is simple, fast, and effective for lightweight distributed systems. As your applications become more complex, Java IDL may be your best alternative.

Nevertheless, client and server programming is quite simple with RMI. As we will see in the next two sections, creating clients in RMI is a natural extension to creating Java objects.

Client

In order to create a distributed system, one of your objects must be a client, and the other must be a server. Sometimes servers can be clients as well, but in this section we will discuss the simplest case. RMI was designed with the idea that with minimal effort you will be able to create complex distributed systems with all the advantages of Java, and none of the detriments of other distributed designs. In fact, with the addition of a single line in your code, you can make an object a distributed object instead of a local one.

The beauty of RMI is that even though your code gives the illusion of normal, single-process applications, it is in fact a distributed system. When you get overloaded at work, you begin to delegate to others. Likewise, Java RMI says rather than overloading an application, why not delegate to other applications?

RMI client methodology

Let's say you call up Sears and decide to order one of those fancy toaster covers from their catalog. The operator greets you and asks for your order number. Because the client is always right, you decide to amuse yourself and annoy the poor guy taking your order. Instead of being cooperative and actually having an order number, you simply tell him that you want the "toaster oven cover with the purple polka dots and a portrait of Heath Shuler on the side."

Clearly amused, the operator goes to his catalog database and asks for the "toaster oven cover" with the appropriate description. What he gets in return is the order number and he is able to process your order.

Similarly, in RMI you have to go to a catalog of objects and ask for the object by its commonly known name. Once you have the object you can continue to process your application. The steps you need to take in order to create a client are exactly similar to those in Java IDL:

1. Get the client object from the Naming Service
2. Process the object and ready it for invocation
3. Invoke the object

RMI `Remote` classes

RMI's `Remote` class is a standard interface that you must extend from your server in order to export functionality to an RMI client. All Remote objects inherit from the `Remote` class, and your client needs to know what it's talking to. It's kind of like knowing the language you are going to talk before you converse with someone from another country.

Once your server inherits the `Remote` object, it can be instantiated upon and invoked on by remote objects. In the example in this section, we are implementing a simple RMI client that will make remote method invocations to a Java server in order to retrieve statistical data for a given NFL team. The `StatsServer` implements three functions that we will implement in our RMI servers section. We want our clients to be able to get the total running yardage, the total passing yardage, and the total number of turnovers for a team that we specify by a string. We start by including RMI in our file, and defining the client class itself.

```
package java.rmi;


public class StatsClient
{
}
```

The `Remote` classes also implement remote versions of the standard Java exceptions. Inheriting from Java's exception mechanism, `RemoteExceptions` can do everything that Java exceptions can do. The only difference between the two is that remote exceptions refer to problems with `Remote` objects rather than local Java errors.

TIP: The RemoteObject class implements the Java Object class. So, if you were to create two versions of an application, one that talks to remote objects and one that refers only to local ones; it would simply be a matter of changing the inheritance.

RMI's naming system

As we discussed earlier, the RMI system provides a simple naming system that allows you to refer to objects as special kinds of strings, rather than as geek words. In order to use a remote object, you must first retrieve it from the Registry. The Registry ensures that an object is available for use. It binds the object reference to a simple string and provides routines for accessing an object by the string under which it is stored.

In order to use the Registry, you must first start it up on your local machine. The Registry clings to a pre-defined port on your machine and funnels TCP/IP messages between clients, servers, and the Registry on that port. Embedded within the code for the RMI system is this specially assigned port, enabling the RMI system to always be able to access a running Registry. The Registry is a stand-alone Java application, so starting it is pretty simple:

```
%prompt%  java sun.rmi.registry.RegistryImpl
```

Getting an object from the Registry is actually pretty simple. You can get an object and begin invocations on it immediately by invoking one of the Registry's three functions for binding objects to strings, unbinding objects, and retrieving objects:

```
package java.rmi;

public class StatsClient
{
    StatsClient()
    {
        // get the remote object from the Registry
        Remote remoteObject = Naming.lookup("STATS-SERVER");
    }
}
```

Remote invocations

The object that is retrieved is a Remote base object. We need to transform that generic Remote object into a specific StatsServer object. In geek terms this is referred to as *narrowing*. We can narrow our Remote base object down to a StatsServer object by performing a simple cast operation, giving us access to all of the functions within the StatsServer:

```java
package java.rmi;

public class StatsClient
{
    StatsClient()
    {
        // get the remote object from the Registry
        Remote remoteObject = Naming.lookup("STATS-SERVER");

        // narrow the object down to a specific one
        StatsServer statsServerInterface;
        if(remoteObject instanceof StatsServer)
            statsServerInterface = (StatsServer) remoteObject
    }
}
```

Finally, we are ready to invoke methods on our remote server. Remember, we have three possible functions to choose from. Creating a user interface for the client is a trivial task and should be integrated into the application just as you normally would. Here, we invoke all three functions and return the data to the user on the standard output device:

```java
package java.rmi;

public class StatsClient
{
    StatsClient()
    {
        // get the remote object from the Registry
        Remote remoteObject = Naming.lookup("STATS-SERVER");

        // narrow the object down to a specific one
        StatsServer statsServerInterface;
```

```
      if(remoteObject instanceof StatsServer)
          statsServerInterface = (StatsServer) remoteObject

      // make the invocation
      System.out.println("Total yardage is: " +
statsServerInterface.getTotalRunningYardage("Redskins"));
    }
}
```

Catching exceptions

So far we have done nothing in the way of error checking. In order for our client to handle every possible contingency during a remote invocation, it needs to catch any exceptions thrown by the server. During a normal remote invocation, the exceptions can be anything from user-defined exceptions within the server to standard RMI transport exceptions. In any event, you can either catch generic Java exceptions or specific RMI ones.

RMI client invocations should catch one of seven different exceptions. The Remo-teException class is the parent class of all exceptions thrown by the RMI system. Other exceptions include Registry-thrown exceptions, such as AlreadyBoundException and NotBoundException. RMI object invocations themselves throw four kinds of exceptions:

1. StubNotFoundException
2. RMISecurityException
3. NoSuchObjectException
4. UnknownHostException

Using the standard Java methodology for adding exceptions to a program, we catch the RMI exceptions as follows:

```
package java.rmi;

public class StatsClient
{
    StatsClient()
    {
        // get the remote object from the Registry
        try
        {
```

```
        Remote remoteObject = Naming.lookup("STATS-SERVER");
    }
    catch (java.rmi.NotBoundException exc)
    {
        System.out.println("Error in lookup() " +
            exc.toString());
    }


    // narrow the object down to a specific one
    StatsServer statsServerInterface;
    if(remoteObject instanceof StatsServer)
        statsServerInterface = (StatsServer) remoteObject

    // make the invocation
    try
    {
        System.out.println("Total yardage is: " +
     statsServerInterface.getTotalRunningYardage("Redskins"));
    }
    catch (java.rmi.RemoteException exc)
    {
        System.out.println("Error in invocation " +
            exc.toString());
    }
    }
}
```

Handling security constraints

Because we dynamically load classes from the file system within our client, we must set up a corresponding Java Security Manager within our client. The client's security manager prevents the client from abusing any privileges granted by the server. For example, our server may have unrestricted access to the local file system. In order to keep the client honest and prevent it from having the same unrestricted access to the server's host, the client security manager monitors the loading process of the remote class and sets the appropriate file access permissions, as required by the client's host machine.

In our StatsServer example, our client loads the remote StatsServer and begins invocations on it. The StatsServer could very well get its data from a local file or database. In order to do so, the StatsServer would have permission to read and/or write the local file or database. To keep our client from abusing this right, we set the security manager so that the client inherits the restrictions of its machine. If the client were in a browser, it would inherit the security restrictions set in the browser. If it were a stand-alone application (as is the case in this example), it would be given the access permissions of the stand-alone application.

Adding and setting the security manager is a simple matter of inserting a line in the client. We will discuss the RMISecurityManager in the next section as we design the server for this client.

```
package java.rmi;

public class StatsClient extends Remote
{
    StatsClient()
    {
        // set the client security manager
        try
        {
            System.setSecurityManager(new RMISecurityManager());
        }
        catch (java.rmi.RMISecurityException exc)
        {
            System.out.println("Security violation " +
                exc.toString());
        }

        // get the remote object from the Registry
        try
        {
            Remote remoteObject = Naming.lookup("STATS-SERVER");
        }
        catch (java.rmi.NotBoundException exc)
        {
            System.out.println("Error in lookup() " +
                exc.toString());
        }

        // narrow the object down to a specific one
        StatsServer statsServerInterface;
        if(remoteObject instanceof StatsServer)
            statsServerInterface = (StatsServer) remoteObject
```

```
        // make the invocation
        try
        {
            System.out.println("Total yardage is: " +
         statsServerInterface.getTotalRunningYardage("Redskins"));
        }
        catch (java.rmi.RemoteException exc)
        {
            System.out.println("Error in invocation " +
                exc.toString());
        }
    }
}
```

Client overview

As you can see, designing a client in RMI is a pretty straightforward process. Once the client is finished, you must create a server to which to interface. We will do so in a moment, but we should keep in mind that the client portion of our client/server system changes most often. Therefore, we highly advise that you create your clients with a strong modular design. In so doing, you can build software components that are easily replaced. Furthermore, the user interface aspects of your application will most likely affect the client and should not play a part in server design.

Server

Servers enable other objects to connect to your local object as if they actually resided on the requesting machine. To the client nothing is different, but the server requires some added functionality to support TCP/IP processing and communication. Furthermore, a server needs to include all of the underlying garbage collection mechanisms that enable it to behave as a normal Java object that will disappear if it is no longer used.

RMI server classes

In order to get the Java tools necessary to develop an RMI server, you need to make sure your classes inherit from the RemoteServer class. The RMI system provides several different versions of the RemoteServer class, but as of now RMI gives you only the UnicastRemoteObject class.

The RemoteServer class extends RemoteObject, which gives you all of the functionality you had in a client. If your server will eventually be a client as well, you need not inherit the client code again. Furthermore, the RemoteObject superclass also makes sure that you have access to the entire RMI system. The `RemoteServer` class extends the `RemoteObject` to provide utility functions `getClientHost` and `getClientPort` that enable clients to determine the proper port to open in order to talk to your server.

The extended class `UnicastRemoteObject` is a form of a `RemoteServer`. Eventually, Java RMI will give you several different versions of communication. The Unicast server is marked by the following three characteristics:

1. The server cannot be started remotely. It must exist already and the reference lasts only for the life of the process.

2. TCP/IP is used underneath.

3. An object stream is used to pass parameters and invocations from client to server.

Once your class inherits from `UnicastRemoteObject`, you can create your server using the two constructors provided with the class. The first constructor forces you to create an object on the default port, while the other allows you to specify the port.

Creating a server interface

Like CORBA objects, RMI is driven by the notion of interfaces. As you will recall, interfaces enable you to separate the method signatures you publish to the world from the way those methods are actually implemented. For example, I can tell you that your computer comes with a mouse. You will know how to use it, how to clean it, and how to feed it cheese. In other words, all mice share a common interface. If I were then to add that you were getting a laser mouse like the ones supplied with Sun SPARC stations, you would not have to make a huge shift in thinking to use the new kind of mouse. You still know how to use it, how to clean it, and how to feed it.

In our `StatsServer` example, we need to create a simple interface with three different methods that can be invoked on it, like so:

```java
public interface StatsInterface extends Remote
{
    int getTotalRunningYardage(
        String teamName);
    int getTotalPassingYardage(
        String teamName);
    int getTotalTurnovers(
        String teamName);
}
```

Implementing a server

The interface defines the contract that you must now fulfill. In order for your client's invocation to map onto the server's actual implementation, you need to make sure that your server's methods signatures match the interface signatures exactly. Your server implementation must implement the `UnicastRemoteObject` class we spoke of earlier, as well as extend the `StatsInterface` we created:

```
import java.rmi.*;

public class StatsServer extends UnicastRemoteObject
                         implements StatsInterface
{
}
```

First we need to implement the constructor for the server. Because the server will be a stand-alone application (RMI does not yet support applet clients or servers), we need to make sure that all of our initialization is done in that constructor. RMI requires a constructor to be present. In order for the RMI system to complete its own initialization, the constructor must be invoked and must throw a RemoteException in case something goes wrong. Our constructor should also call the super class' constructor:

```
import java.rmi.*;

public class StatsServer extends UnicastRemoteObject
                         implements StatsInterface
{
    StatsServer() throws RemoteException
    {
        // call the super class' constructor
        super();
    }
}
```

Now you need to implement the three interfaces we had defined interfaces for:

```
import java.rmi.*;
public class StatsServer extends UnicastRemoteObject
                         implements StatsInterface
```

```
{
    StatsServer() throws RemoteException
    {
        // call the super class' constructor
        super();
    }
    public int getTotalRunningYardage(
        String teamName
    ) throws RemoteException
    {
        if(teamName.equals("Redskins"))
            return 432;
        else
            return 129;
    }
    … we implement the others as above …
}
```

As you create interfaces and methods, keep in mind that the methods themselves need not be concerned that they reside in an RMI server. In fact, the objects you create as RMI servers should be in line with the RMI philosophy. These are objects that could just as easily be local objects. The fact that they are remote should not affect the actual implementation of the methods themselves.

RMI `Registry` *classes*

As you can see, creating a RMI server is just as easy as creating a Java object. We define our interface, implement the interface, and now we need to publish the interfaces to the world so that any client can access and use our `StatsServer`. As we mentioned earlier, the RMI Registry keeps track of objects using a simple string. In our client we retrieved an object by the name of *STATS-SERVER*. In order for this server to be retrieved in that instance, we need to use the same string here as well.

Typically, RMI Registry procedures are implemented in the main routine of your stand-alone application. In the future, when RMI supports applets as well, these procedures will be placed in the init method:

```
import java.rmi.*;

public class StatsServer extends UnicastRemoteObject
                         implements StatsInterface
{
```

```
StatsServer() throws RemoteException
{
    // call the super class' constructor
    super();
}

public int getTotalRunningYardage(
    String teamName
) throws RemoteException
{
    if(teamName.equals("Redskins")
        return 432;
    else
        return 129;
}

… we implement the others as above …

public static void main(
    String args[]
)
{
    // create a local instance of our object
    StatsServer statsServer = new StatsServer();

    // put the local instance into the Registry
    Naming.rebind("STATS-SERVER", statsServer);
}
}
```

RMI server security constraints

As we discussed when we designed the client for this object, we need to specify a security manager. The manager we implemented in the client is the Java RMISecurityManager.

NOTE: The RMISecurityManager should be used when the server requires *minimal* security restrictions. If you require a security system to provide more robust access control, feel free to substitute your favorite security manager in its place.

In any event, the security manager should be set with the `System` class' `setSe-curityManager` method. If you do not specify a security manager, then the RMI system loads only those classes specified in the Java `CLASSPATH` environment variable.

ALERT: RMI uses the `CLASSPATH` as a default security manager to prevent unexpected and potentially dangerous results from RMI objects.

Adding a security manager is as simple as it was with the client. Remember, the client's security manager prevents downloaded objects from modifying the local file system. The server's security manager prevents the server from doing harm to the host machine. This kind of control is not necessarily meant to control the server itself, but to prevent any *client* from using the server in a malicious manner.

```java
import java.rmi.*;

public class StatsServer extends UnicastRemoteObject
                    implements StatsInterface
{
    StatsServer() throws RemoteException
    {
        // call the super class' constructor
        super();
    }

    public int getTotalRunningYardage(
        String teamName
    ) throws RemoteException
    {
        if(teamName.equals("Redskins")
            return 432;
        else
            return 129;
    }

    … we implement the others as above …

    public static void main(
        String args[]
```

```
)
{
    // set the security manager
    try
    {
        System.setSecurityManager(new RMISecurityManager());
    }
    catch (java.rmi.RMISecurityException exc)
    {
        System.out.println("Security violation " +
            exc.toString());
    }

    // create a local instance of our object
    StatsServer statsServer = new StatsServer();

    // put the local instance into the Registry
    Naming.rebind("STATS-SERVER", statsServer);
}
}
```

Generating stubs and skeletons

Once the interface is completed, you need to generate stubs and skeleton code. Stubs are sort of like backup quarterbacks. They stand in for the starter when he is not available. Sometimes the actual Java object could reside in another virtual machine. Stub code is generated to stand in for the remote class that cannot be accessed in order to provide a successful compile. The RMI system provides an RMI Compiler (`rmic`) that takes your generated interface class and produces stub code on its behalf:

```
%prompt%   javac StatsInterface.java
%prompt%   javac StatsServer.java
%prompt%   rmic StatsServer
```

Note how this is radically different from Java IDL! In Java IDL, we generated stubs and skeletons based on the IDL file, then we created the server code. In RMI, we create the server code, then generate the supporting stubs and skeletons. Once the stub code is compiled and linked in, your RMI application may be completed and installed in the Registry. Once the RMI application resides in the Registry, it is available for the client to invoke as we did in the previous section.

Once the stubs and skeletons are completed, you must start the RMI Registry by hand. Unlike Java IDL, RMI objects are not started automatically upon invocation. Therefore, because the RMI Registry is an RMI object in its own right, it must be started by hand:

```
%prompt%  java sun.rmi.registry.RegistryImpl
```

Once the Registry is started, the server can be started and will be able to store itself in the Registry. If the server is available through the Registry, it can be invoked upon by the client.

```
%prompt%  java StatsServer
```

Note once again how this is radically different from Java IDL. Not only must the Registry be started, but so must the server. Later on when we compare Java IDL and Java RMI more thoroughly, we will discover that this kind of location independence and automatic startup is vital to mission critical applications. For now, take note of the differences as you formulate the alternative more suited for your applications.

NOTE: As you can see, creating an RMI server is not a difficult task. In fact, it is amazingly similar to Java IDL in many respects. This is not by accident. Both Java IDL and Java RMI share the same lineage within Sun Microsystems. The architects of RMI and the brains behind IDL both come from the same distributed object projects, and as a result have created Java-based distributed object systems that share the same characteristics.

Server overview

So now that we can create servers in RMI, we can publish services to the rest of the world. Clients anywhere can use our servers as if they were remote objects. But, what if we wanted every client to use a different instance of the remote server? If we used our current paradigm, we would have to make sure our clients created their own server somewhere else. But, we want them to use the same server process remotely, just use different instances of the server itself. We can accomplish this with the notion of factories. Factories enable clients to create servers on-the-fly, all of them contained within the factory's process. That way, if two clients are banging on the same kind of server, what one does won't affect the execution of the other.

RMI Dynamic Server Creation

In the previous sections, we created a server and the client that invokes it. Unfortunately, in order for the client to use the server, the server has to be up and running beforehand. Because it implements the `UnicastRemoteObject`, the RMI system does not allow you to start up the server from the client. As a result, you are severely limited in the number and kinds of things you can do with RMI. This is where creating a dynamic server can be quite useful.

The factory solution

Using a few additional techniques, you can trick RMI into creating a server for you on-the-fly. With dynamic server creation, you will be able to create multiple instances of remote objects and interact with them. In a normal local class, you can instantiate several different objects of the same class. In fact, you are limited only by your machine memory in what you can do.

In a distributed object world, you need to create a distributed constructor to create and manage remote objects for you. In geek terms, these distributed constructors are referred to as *object factories*. Factories create objects for you and manage their existence. They are essentially servers just like those we created in the previous section, except that they have exactly one method associated with them. Factories typically implement a "create an object" method that is then passed back to the calling function to use as a normal server. The object is created on-the-fly, and the client is told from where to get it (see Figure 4-5).

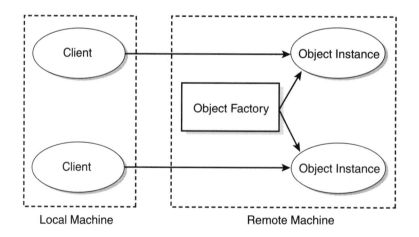

Figure 4–5 Clients can go to factories to create objects for them dynamically.

Just as in the previous section, the factory is a standard RMI server with a well-known name in the Registry. You get and invoke it just as you normally would, but instead of using it as your remote object instance, you simply use it to create a remote object instance that you invoke as you normally would.

In our `StatsServer` example, suppose we wanted a different `StatsServer` for each NFL team. Each server would have to deal only with requests for a certain team and would not be overloaded by requests from all the clients requesting information. If a server received a request for a team it did not support, we could throw an exception and notify the requesting client that the team is not available. See Figure 4-6 for a depiction of clients going through factories to get to servers.

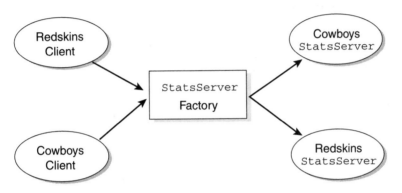

Figure 4–6 Clients can go to factories to get the proper server.

Creating a factory

The objective here is to create an RMI server whose entire job is to create other RMI servers dynamically. So, the RMI Factory server must have one method that returns an object reference and creates the server that the reference points to.

So, we need to create a new interface in the same manner as we created the `StatsInterface` from the previous section, as well as modify the `StatsInterface` not to accept a team name. Remember, a `StatsServer` will exist for each team, rendering useless the need to pass in a team name when requesting statistics.

```
public interface StatsInterface extends Remote
{
    int getTotalRunningYardage() throws RemoteException;
    int getTotalPassingYardage() throws RemoteException;
    int getTotalTurnovers() throws RemoteException;
}
```

```
// this belongs in a separate file!
public interface StatsServerFactoryInterface extends Remote
{
    StatsInterface getStatsServer(
        String teamName);
}
```

Notice how our `getStatsServer` method returns an instance of the `StatsInterface` we modified. The get method also passes in a teamName. It is our intention that the server instance will act on that team name and load the appropriate statistics for that team name.

Implementing the object server

The original `StatsServers` were designed to return data when given a team name. Our new methodology calls for a server for each team. Thus, the constructor for the `StatsServer` instances should set the team name. In a more general sense, we are handling much of the specificity required by the server from within the factory. If your server, regardless of its purpose, required specific information to initialize, count on it being set from within the constructor.

What follows is the modified server code, taking into account the initialization of the team data from within the constructor. The constructor will be called by the factory's create function when this server is instantiated.

```
import java.rmi.*;

public class StatsServer extends UnicastRemoteObject
                         implements StatsServerInterface
{
    String teamName;

    StatsServer(
        String teamName
    ) throws RemoteException
    {
        // call the super class' constructor
        super();

        // set the local team name variable
        this.teamName = teamName;
    }
```

```
    public int getTotalRunningYardage() throws RemoteException
    {
        if(teamName.equals("Redskins")
            return 432;
        else
            return 129;
    }


    … we implement the others as above …

}
```

Notice how we removed the main function. It is not needed here because this particular kind of server will never be a stand-alone application. Instead, the factory will act as the stand-alone application, and this object will always be dynamic. The factory is in charge of instantiating this object from within its own process space when it told to do so by an invocation on the getStatsServer method.

Implementing a factory

Implementing the factory is similar to implementing the server in the previous section. We merely create the factory implementation code, making sure to instantiate and pass back a StatsServer object when the getStatsServer method is called:

```
public class StatsServerFactory extends UnicastRemoteObject
                        implements StatsServerInterface
{
    StatsServerFactory() throws RemoteException
    {
        // call the super class' constructor
        super();
    }

    public StatsServer getStatsServer(
        String teamName
    )
    {

        StatsServer localServer = new StatsServer(teamName);

        return localServer;
    }

}
```

Notice how the teamName is passed to the object constructor as we coded previously. With this kind of factory/server implementation, you could create several different StatsServer implementations from within your clients, all referring to their own specific team. Note that the factory's get method as it is implemented now does not keep track of the objects that it creates. It merely instantiates and passes back an object. If you needed to keep track of every individual object in a Vector or HashTable, you should be able to do so with no problem. In the getStatsServer method, you simply need to store the object in your storage mechanism, then pass it back to the client.

Invoking a factory

From within your client, creating and using a factory shouldn't be any more difficult than when you had to do the same thing with the RMI client in that section of this chapter. In fact, because we've done most of the work, let's simply modify the old client below:

```java
package java.rmi;

public class StatsClient extends Remote
{
    StatsClient()
    {
        // set the client security manager
        try
        {
            System.setSecurityManager(new RMISecurityManager());
        }
        catch (java.rmi.RMISecurityException exc)
        {
            System.out.println("Security violation " +
                exc.toString());
        }

        // get the remote factory object from the Registry
        try
        {
            Remote remoteObject =
                Naming.lookup("STATS-SERVER-FACTORY");
        }
        catch (java.rmi.NotBoundException exc)
        {
```

```
            System.out.println("Error in lookup() " +
                exc.toString());
        }


        // narrow the object down to a specific one
        StatsServerFactory statsServerFactory;
        if(remoteObject instanceof StatsServerFactory)
            statsServerFactory = (StatsServerFactory) remoteObject

        // now get a reference to the StatsServer object
        // this object will be a pure REDSKINS object
        StatsServer statsServerInterface;
        try
        {
            statsServerInterface =
                statsServerFactory.getStatsServer("Redskins");
        }
        catch (java.rmi.RemoteException exc)
        {
            System.out.println("Error in invocation " +
                exc.toString());
        }

        // make the invocation
        try
        {
            System.out.println("Total yardage is: " +
                statsServerInterface.getTotalRunningYardage());
        }
        catch (java.rmi.RemoteException exc)
        {
            System.out.println("Error in invocation " +
                exc.toString());
        }
    }
}
```

Clearly the methodology is to get the factory and use it to create and invoke on remote objects. Notice how we initialize the StatsServer to a **Redskins** object and invoke the usual routines on the StatsServer object, not the StatsServerFactory object.

Dynamic server overview

Dynamic servers give us great flexibility in our remote object systems. Clients can truly execute on remote objects as if they were local objects. They can have complete control over how a server gets started and the parameters with which it runs. This enables them to run more efficiently, safely, and reliably. Another way we can improve the performance of client/server systems in RMI is with callbacks. As we discussed in Chapter 3 on Java IDL, callbacks give servers the ability to control how and when clients make invocations on them.

Callbacks

When we last spoke of callbacks, we used them as a means to get around the limitation of having no servers within an applet. It enabled us to create a method that would allow a C++ object to invoke our Java applet embedded inside a Web page. While we sacrificed by not having control over the initialization or startup of the callback applet as we would have had with a CORBA server, we were satisfied that our applet would be able to act as the recipient of data.

Java RMI has similar limitations with its servers. Unfortunately, a Java RMI server cannot be embedded within a Web page, so we have to implement similar callback mechanisms inside our servers and clients.

Why callbacks?

Let's say that clients of our `StatsServers` wanted to display new data as they arrived to the server. Rather than routinely pinging the server for information and creating a network backlog, we would like our client to change its on-screen state information only when the server has new information to report.

Just as we used the callback mechanism in Java IDL to support this kind of dynamic update, we will implement a server-driven event mechanism that will enable our client to passively update live information. Our solution should be scaleable, meaning that it should work just as efficiently for a few clients as it should for several thousand clients. It should be easy to implement, and it should solve the problem without hassle to the client programmer.

Creating the callback

Because our callback object essentially will be an RMI object, we need to create a new client interface. As you can see in the following code, we need to create a method that the server will invoke when it senses a change in its information.

In order to setup this client interface, we must create a new public interface file similar to the ones we created for the `StatsServer` itself:

```
public interface StatsCallbackInterface
{
    void statsChanged(
        String teamName,
        int passingYards,
        int rushingYards,
        int turnovers);
}
```

We also must modify the StatsServer itself so that it can register for these call-backs. Remember, we need to tell the server that it has to send us information back when it gets a change. In order to do so, we have to send it an object on which it can invoke the callback. Because our client will implement the StatsCallbackInterface object, we should pass an object of that type to the registration function:

```
// new file…
public interface StatsServerInterface extends Remote
{
    int getTotalRunningYardage(
        String teamName);
    int getTotalPassingYardage(
        String teamName);
    int getTotalTurnovers(
        String teamName);

    void addCallback(
        StatsCallbackInterface statsCallbackObject);
}
```

Implementing the callback client

Now that we have created the proper interfaces to our callback client and changed the server to use callbacks, we need to modify the client appropriately so that it will register for a callback as the first step in its own initialization phase. Remember, whenever the server gets changed, the client makes a call to the statsChanged function, so we need to add that function to our client class. In addition, we need to make sure the client implements the StatsCallback-Interface interface, otherwise it will not be able to send itself to the server and be registered for an update.

```
package java.rmi;

public class StatsClient extends StatsCallbackInterface
{
    public void statsChanged(
        String teamName,
        int passingYards,
        int rushingYards,
        int turnovers
    )
    {
    }

    StatsClient()
    {
        ... same as before ...
    }
}
```

Filling in the callback method

Now, we need to do something with the information we receive when a callback is invoked. For now, we'll write our results to the standard output device, but keep in mind that we could just as easily have a user interface handle our display routines.

```
package java.rmi;

public class StatsClient extends StatsCallbackInterface
{
    public void statsChanged(
        String teamName,
        int passingYards,
        int rushingYards,
        int turnovers
    )
    {
        System.out.println("Received dynamic update: ");
        System.out.println("Yards passing: " + passingYards);
        System.out.println("Yards rushing: " + rushingYards);
        System.out.println("Turnovers: " + turnovers);
    }
```

```
    StatsClient()
    {
        … same as before …
    }
}
```

Registering callbacks

Once we've completed the callback method itself and modified all of the interfaces, we need to have the client add itself to the server's callback list. The server
then will be able to go down the list whenever it gets a change and invoke the
statsChanged method on all of the clients. However, the server will not be
aware of the client unless the client registers itself for updates.

```
package java.rmi;

public class StatsClient extends Remote
{
    public void statsChanged(
        String teamName,
        int passingYards,
        int rushingYards,
        int turnovers
    )
    {
        System.out.println("Received dynamic update: ");
        System.out.println("Yards passing: " + passingYards);
        System.out.println("Yards rushing: " + rushingYards);
        System.out.println("Turnovers: " + turnovers);
    }

    StatsClient()
    {
        // set the client security manager
        try
        {
            System.setSecurityManager(new RMISecurityManager());
        }
        catch (java.rmi.RMISecurityException exc)
        {
            System.out.println("Security violation " +
                exc.toString());
        }
    }
```

```
    // get the remote object from the Registry
    try
    {
        Remote remoteObject = Naming.lookup("STATS-SERVER");
    }
    catch (java.rmi.NotBoundException exc)
    {
      System.out.println("Error in lookup() " +
          exc.toString());
    }

    // narrow the object down to a specific one
    StatsServer statsServerInterface;
    if(remoteObject instanceof StatsServer)
        statsServerInterface = (StatsServer) remoteObject

    // register the callback right here
    try
    {
        statsServerInterface.addCallback(this);
    }
    catch (java.rmi.RemoteException exc)
    {
        System.out.println("Error in lookup() " +
            exc.toString());
    }
  }
}
```

TIP: Note how we removed the initial invocation on the server from the previous listing. With callbacks added, we do not have to go to the server to get information, the server will come to us to give us information. Wouldn't it be nice if the BMW dealer came to you to give you a car instead of the usual slimy way they do things now?

We must now modify the server to add the callback to its list. Like Santa Claus, it checks to see if everything is naughty or nice and make sure you are signed up for your gift, in this case a series of updates to the server. Our server keeps track of each callback object in a vector so that it is easy to traverse the list when the time comes to provide an update.

```java
import java.rmi.*;

public class StatsServer extends UnicastRemoteObject
                        implements StatsServerInterface
{
    // the list of callback objects
    Vector callbackObjects;

    StatsServer() throws RemoteException
    {
        // call the super class' constructor
        super();
    }

    public void addCallback(
        StatsCallbackInterface statsCallbackObject
    )
    {
        // store the callback object into the vector
        callbackObjects.addElement(statsCallbackObject);
    }

    public int getTotalRunningYardage(
        String teamName
    )
    {

        if(teamName.equals("Redskins")
            return 432;
        else
            return 129;
    }

    … we implement the others as above …

    public static void main(
        String args[]
    )
    {
        // set the security manager
```

```
            try
            {
                System.setSecurityManager(new RMISecurityManager());
            }
            catch (java.rmi.RMISecurityException exc)
            {
                System.out.println("Security violation " +
                    exc.toString());
            }

            // create a local instance of our object
            StatsServer statsServer = new StatsServer();

            // put the local instance into the Registry
            Naming.rebind("STATS-SERVER", statsServer);
        }
    }
```

Invoking callbacks

Note that our server in its current state does not have any methods with which it will accept changes in the information it sends back. Your servers more than likely will include a method or similar to setPassingYards. We have created a fake setPassingYards method, which follows, that gets the team name and the passing yardage for that team as a parameter. See how we actually invoke the callbacks from within this function:

```
import java.rmi.*;

public class StatsServer extends UnicastRemoteObject
                         implements StatsServerInterface
{
    // the list of callback objects
    Vector callbackObjects;

    StatsServer() throws RemoteException
    {
        // call the super class' constructor
        super();
    }
```

```
public void addCallback(
    StatsCallbackInterface statsCallbackObject
)
{
    // store the callback object into the vector
    callbackObjects.addElement(statsCallbackObject);
}

public void setPassingYards(
    String teamName,
    int passingYards
)
{
    // do everything that needs to be done to set the variable
    // internally…

    // now go down the vector and invoke on
    // each callback object
    for(int x = 0; x < callbackObjects.size(); x++)
    {
        // convert the vector Object to a callback object
        StatsCallbackInterface callback =
        (StatsCallbackInterface) callbackObjects.elementAt(x);

        // invoke the callback
        callback.statsChanged(teamName, passingYards,
            rushingYards, turnovers);
    }
}

public int getTotalRunningYardage(
    String teamName
)
{
    if(teamName.equals("Redskins")
        return 432;
    else
        return 129;
}
```

```
… we implement the others as above …

public static void main(
    String args[]
)
{
    // set the security manager
    try
    {
        System.setSecurityManager(new RMISecurityManager());
    }
    catch (java.rmi.RMISecurityException exc)
    {
        System.out.println("Security violation " +
            exc.toString());
    }

    // create a local instance of our object
    StatsServer statsServer = new StatsServer();

    // put the local instance into the Registry
    Naming.rebind("STATS-SERVER", statsServer);
}
}
```

Callbacks in short

Callbacks are important tools for developers of high availability servers. Because servers can easily be inundated with invocations from clients, the logical step is to defer those invocations until a time that is both convenient and proper. By setting up callbacks, you can engineer your server to process and accept invocations more efficiently by enabling servers to make invocations when they are ready.

With a suite of tools that enable us to create simple clients and servers to more advanced factory servers and callback servers, we can go about implementing our calendar application once again. With sockets, we were able to define our own application messaging system. With Java IDL, we could just as easily have used a legacy server written in another language ages ago. Now, with Java RMI we will find that creating a server for our featured application is just as easy as creating a regular Java object.

A Java RMI Version of the Featured App

As we have seen in the past few sections, the methodology for creating RMI clients and servers is very similar to that of Java IDL. The big difference, however, is that Java RMI is written completely in Java with nothing resembling the IDL. The advantage to Java-only systems is the language itself. Java's simplicity and gentle learning curve gives RMI itself an appearance of simplicity. Java-centric applications do not, however, have the advantages of Java IDL, namely language independence and implementation hiding.

We will start by first rewriting the public interface for our server. Once that step is complete, we can go about writing clients to talk to the interface and server that will subsequently implement the interface. The RMI system is easy, and finishing the Internet Calendar Server using it is equally so.

RMI interface

Remember, our interface must extend the RMI system's `Remote` classes. As we discussed earlier, the `Remote` classes provide the functionality for our server interface to talk to the remote Reference layer of the RMI system. Without this kind of "translator" we would never be able to receive invocations within our server. So, following the instructions we outlined earlier, we must declare our interface as follows:

```
public interface CalendarServerInterface extends Remote
{
    public void scheduleAppointment(
        AppointmentType appointment);

    AppointmentType[] getAppointments();
}
```

Note how the interface uses the `AppointmentType` object, which is nowhere to be seen. We must declare that object in Java ourselves and place it inside its own public class. The `AppointmentType` object will be a stand-alone Java object in its own right, but we must implement it so that we can use the data structure:

```
public class AppointmentType
{
    String reason;
    int time;
}
```

> **NOTE:** We do not need any methods within the class because it will do nothing but contain our information. We could very easily create functions to store and retrieve the data values, but that would amount to unnecessary overhead in this case.

RMI client

Once our interface has been defined, we can create our client and then talk to the server. Remember, we will simply reimplement the `NetworkModule` class so that we can have a seamless interaction with the rest of the Calendar application. After all, we are changing only this module, we never want to touch any other parts of the code.

```java
public class NetworkModule
{
    public void scheduleAppointment(
        String reason,
        int time);

    public Vector getAppointments();

    public void initNetwork();

    public void shutdownNetwork();
}
```

Our client will first initialize the RMI system in its `NetworkModule` constructor. The constructor not only will get the RMI system but also it will initialize the remote object variable. When we retrieve the remote object from the RMI Naming server, we will also have to narrow it down to a specific `CalendarServer` object.

```java
public class NetworkModule
{
    CalendarServer calendarObject;

    NetworkModule()
    {
        // first get a handle on the object
        Remote remoteObject = Naming.find("CALENDAR-RMI");
```

```
        // narrow to an CalendarServer
        if(remoteObject instanceof CalendarServer)
            calendarObject =
                (CalendarServer) remoteObject;
    }

    public void scheduleAppointment(
        String reason,
        int time)
    {
    }

    public Vector getAppointments()
    {
    }

    public void initNetwork()
    {
    }

    public void shutdownNetwork()
    {
    }
}
```

Once we have completed the constructor information, then we must fill in the rest of the methods. Once again we need to translate the array of `AppointmentType` variables into a Java `Vector`. The rest of our application does not need to know how we are storing the appointments, just that they can retrieve the appointments at will.

```
public class NetworkModule
{
    CalendarServer calendarObject;

    NetworkModule()
    {
        // first get a handle on the object
        Remote remoteObject = Naming.find("CALENDAR-RMI");
```

```java
        // narrow to an CalendarServer
        if(remoteObject instanceof CalendarServer)
            calendarObject =
                (CalendarServer) remoteObject;
}

public void scheduleAppointment(
    String reason,
    int time)
{

    AppointmentType appointment = new AppointmentType();

    // first create the appointment
    appointment.reason = reason;
    appointment.time = time;

    // now send the appointment to the server
    calendarObject.scheduleAppointment(reason, time);
}

public Vector getAppointments()
{
    // the variable to store all of our appointments in
    AppointmentType appointments[];

    // now get the appointments
    appointments = calendarObject.getAppointments();

    // translate into a vector
    Vector appointmentVector = new Vector();
    for(int x = 0; x < appointments.size; x++)
        appointmentVector.addItem(appointments[x]);

    // return the vector
    return appointmentVector;
}

public void initNetwork()
{
}
```

```
    public void shutdownNetwork()
    {
    }
}
```

Once again, we do not have to initialize the network because the RMI system handles all of the underlying mechanisms for us. RMI objects, similar to Java IDL objects, are location transparent. We do not care where or how these objects are implemented, only that they are available for our use. The network sockets, protocols, and connections are handled for us by the RMI system and we therefore need not concern ourselves with them.

Now we must set our security mechanism so that the client application we have created will have access to the server. Later on, our server will set its security manager so that clients cannot access the local machine on which the server is hosted. Here, we conform our security manager to that of the server so that we can have access in the first place:

```
public class NetworkModule
{
    CalendarServer calendarObject;

    NetworkModule()
    {
        // set the security manager
        try
        {
            System.setSecurityManager(new RMISecurityManager());
        }
        catch(java.rmi.RMISecurityException exc)
        {
            … error handling…
        }

        // first get a handle on the object
        Remote remoteObject = Naming.find("CALENDAR-RMI");

        // narrow to an CalendarServer
        if(remoteObject instanceof CalendarServer)
            calendarObject =
                (CalendarServer) remoteObject;
    }
```

```java
public void scheduleAppointment(
    String reason,
    int time)
{
    AppointmentType appointment = new AppointmentType();

    // first create the appointment
    appointment.reason = reason;
    appointment.time = time;

    // now send the appointment to the server
    calendarObject.scheduleAppointment(reason, time);
}

public Vector getAppointments()
{
    // the variable to store all of our appointments in
    AppointmentType appointments[];

    // now get the appointments
    appointments = calendarObject.getAppointments();

    // translate into a vector
    Vector appointmentVector = new Vector();
    for(int x = 0; x < appointments.size; x++)
        appointmentVector.addItem(appointments[x]);

    // return the vector
    return appointmentVector;
}

public void initNetwork()
{
}

public void shutdownNetwork()
{
}
}
```

RMI server

The server we create will need to inherit from the interface we defined earlier. We will then implement each method in the server, starting with the constructor. The constructor will establish the object's presence on the RMI system and ready it for invocations:

```
public class CalendarServer extends UnicastRemoteObject
                            implements CalendarServerInterface
{
    CalendarServer() throws RemoteException
    {
        // call the super class' constructor
        super();
    }

    public void scheduleAppointment(
        AppointmentType appointment
    )
    {
    }

    public AppointmentType[] getAppointments()
    {
    }
}
```

We must now fill in the methods of our server so that we can process information. As with the previous implementations of the server, we will not concern ourselves with the specifics of how the data will be stored. Rather, we will leave those implementation details for later.

```
public class CalendarServer extends UnicastRemoteObject
                            implements CalendarServerInterface
{
    CalendarServer() throws RemoteException
    {
        // call the super class' constructor
        super();
    }
```

```
public void scheduleAppointment(
    AppointmentType appointment
)
{
    // store the appointment in a list somewhere
    … store it …
}


public AppointmentType[] getAppointments()
{
    // initialize the appointment list
    AppointmentType appointments[] =
        new AppointmentType[numAppointments];

    // get all of the appointments from the storage mechanism
    for(int x = 0; x < numAppointments; x++)
        appointments[x] = appointmentList[x];
}
}
```

Because RMI servers are Java applications, we must add a main function to our class. The main function will not only launch the application code, it will also bind our application to the Naming server under a given name. The name we used in the client section was "CALENDAR-RMI," so that is the name under which we must store our server:

```
public class CalendarServer extends UnicastRemoteObject
                            implements CalendarServerInterface
{
    CalendarServer() throws RemoteException
    {
        // call the super class' constructor
        super();
    }

    public void scheduleAppointment(
        AppointmentType appointment
    )
    {
```

```
        // store the appointment in a list somewhere
        … store it …
    }


    public AppointmentType[] getAppointments()
    {
        // initialize the appointment list
        AppointmentType appointments[] =
            new AppointmentType[numAppointments];

        // get all of the appointments from the storage mechanism
        for(int x = 0; x < numAppointments; x++)
            appointments[x] = appointmentList[x];
    }

    public static void main(
        String args[]
    )
    {
        // create the local instance of the CalendarServer
        CalendarServer svr = new CalendarServer();

        // out the local instance into the Naming server
        Naming.rebind("CALENDAR-RMI", svr);
    }
}
```

Now, we need to set our security manager so that we can limit the access of the client to our host machine. Even though our application is rather innocuous, we don't want harmful clients to come along and maliciously wound our host machine. This is the Java security mechanism at its best:

```
public class CalendarServer extends UnicastRemoteObject
                            implements CalendarServerInterface
{
    CalendarServer() throws RemoteException
    {
        // call the super class' constructor
        super();
    }
```

```java
public void scheduleAppointment(
    AppointmentType appointment
)
{
    // store the appointment in a list somewhere
    … store it …
}

public AppointmentType[] getAppointments()
{
    // initialize the appointment list
    AppointmentType appointments[] =
        new AppointmentType[numAppointments];

    // get all of the appointments from the storage mechanism
    for(int x = 0; x < numAppointments; x++)
        appointments[x] = appointmentList[x];
}

public static void main(
    String args[]
)
{
    // set the security manager
    try
    {
        System.setSecurityManager(new RMISecurityManager());
    }
    catch(java.rmi.RMISecurityException exc)
    {
        … error handling …
    }

    // create the local instance of the CalendarServer
    CalendarServer svr = new CalendarServer();

    // out the local instance into the Naming server
    Naming.rebind("CALENDAR-RMI", svr);
}
}
```

We must now generate the skeleton and stub code. Remember, the RMI system provides an RMI compiler, `rmic`, which we can use to generate those stubs from Java class files. Unlike the `idltojava` compiler supplied with Java IDL, Java RMI's compiler generates its skeleton code from precompiled Java classes:

```
%prompt%   javac InternetCalendarServerInterface.java
%prompt%   javac CalendarServer.java
%prompt%   rmic CalendarServer
```

Summary

Java RMI is a powerful alternative to Java IDL. Because they share the same lineage, and therefore much of the same functionality, they are often confused and are most definitely competitors. In this chapter, we have shown the biggest advantage to RMI: it is Java. Because Java IDL requires knowledge of CORBA as well as its own Interface Definition Language, it can be difficult at times. Meanwhile, because it has sacrificed some of the overhead of CORBA such as automatic activation and language independence, Java RMI provides an effective, yet simple, distributed object platform.

The next chapter outlines the means necessary to attach your existing client/server applications, be they written in sockets, Java IDL, or Java RMI, to large databases using only the Java language. Java Database Connectivity is a very important tool for plugging Java into existing data stores with low overhead and great simplicity.

CHAPTER
5

How JDBC Works

Database Management, the Old Way

Getting Information from a Database

Putting Information into a Database

A Database Project in Java

Java
Database
Connectivity

Today, nearly all companies choose to store their vast quantities of information in large repositories of data. These databases are vital to the dissemination of information via the Internet. Java, as the anointed Internet language, answers the need to connect information storage to application servers using the Java Database Connectivity framework.

As we will see in these next few chapters, JDBC is a core set of APIs that enables Java applications to connect to industry standard and proprietary database management systems. Using JDBC, your applications can retrieve and store information using Structured Query Language statements as well as a database engine itself. Included in this chapter is a brief introduction to SQL and its merits.

Inside JDBC

As the Java revolution moves on, there remains an extraordinarily large camp of people who require access to legacy systems and legacy databases in particular. While Java IDL provides a robust set of Java objects to connect legacy applications with the Internet applications of today, a coherent methodology for accessing databases directly from within a Java object is lacking.

Java Database Connectivity was created for just such a case. Knowing full well that there are a plethora of databases in existence today, the architectural challenge for JDBC was to provide a simple front-end interface for connecting with even the most complex of databases. To the programmer, the interface to a database should be the same regardless of the kind of database to which you want to connect.

Database drivers

In the desktop world, a driver enables a particular piece of hardware to interface with the rest of the machine. Similarly, a database driver gives JDBC a means to communicate with a database. Perhaps written in some form of native code but usually written in Java itself, the database drivers available for JDBC are wide and varied, addressing several different kinds of databases.

Typically, the JDBC core API is available for users to download and use as a development tool. Then, the programmer has to acquire one of the many database drivers that fits the database best. With the API and driver, the application has the tools necessary to exchange information between Java objects and databases.

The guidelines for creating the JDBC architecture all center on one very important characteristic: simplicity. Databases are complex beasts, and companies that rely on them generally have an army of personnel ready to administer and program them. As a result, transferring that complexity to Java via JDBC would violate the ethos of the language. Therefore, the JDBC architects developed the specification with the idea that database access would not require advanced degrees and years of training to accomplish.

The DriverManager object

At the heart of JDBC lies the `DriverManager`. Once a driver is installed, you need to load it into your Java object by using the `DriverManager`. It groups drivers together so that multiple databases can be accessed from within the same Java object. It provides a common interface to a JDBC `Driver` object without having to delve into the internals of the database itself.

The `Driver` is responsible for creating and implementing the `Connection`, `Statement`, and `ResultSet` objects for the specific database, and the `Driver-Manager` then is able to acquire those object implementations for itself. In so doing, applications that are written using the `DriverManager` are isolated from the implementation details of databases, as well as from future enhancements and changes to the implementation itself, as you can see in Figure 5-1.

Database `connection` interface

The `Connection` object is responsible for establishing the link between the Database Management System and the Java application. By abstracting it from the `DriverManager`, the `Driver` can isolate the database from specific parts of the implementation. It also enables the programmer to select the proper driver for the required application.

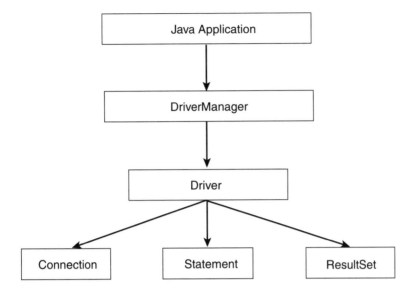

Figure 5–1 The Driver abstracts the Connection, Statement, and ResultSet objects from the application.

The `Connection.getConnection` method accepts a URL that enables the JDBC object to use different drivers depending on the situation, isolates applets from connection-related information, and gives the application a means by which to specify the specific database to which it should connect. The URL takes the form of `jdbc:<subprotocol>:<subname>`. The subprotocol is a kind of connectivity to the database, along the lines of ODBC, which we shall discuss in a moment. The subname depends on the subprotocol but usually allows you to configure the database that the application will look at.

Database `statement` **object**

A `Statement` envelops a query written in the Server Query Language and enables the JDBC object to compose a series of steps to look up information in a database. Using a `Connection`, the `Statement` can be forwarded to the database and obtain a `ResultSet`.

`ResultSet` **access control**

A `ResultSet` is a container for a series of rows and columns acquired from a `Statement` call. Using the `ResultSet`'s iterator routines, the JDBC object can step through each row in the result set. Individual column fields can be retrieved using the get methods within the `ResultSet`. Columns may be specified by their field name or by their index.

JDBC and ODBC

In many ways, Open Database Connectivity (ODBC) was a precursor to all that JDBC is intended to accomplish. It adequately abstracts the boring tedium of databases, and the proprietary APIs to those databases, from the application programmer, it ties many different kinds of databases together so that you only have to create one source file to access them, and it is fairly ubiquitous. Recognizing the relative acceptance of ODBC technology, JDBC offers a JDBC-to-ODBC driver that can be had for free from various Web sites.

NOTE: Because of copyright restrictions, we will be unable to supply these drivers on the CD-ROM, but you may visit the JDBC page on the JavaSoft Web site at `java.sun.com/jdbc` and get the latest information and pointers to them.

With this special bridge, JDBC applications can talk to the same database access engine as non-Java applications. Furthermore, integrating JDBC into your existing business process can be done fairly easily because the bridge ensures that no additional work is required to enable Java Database Connectivity.

As you can see, the JDBC application communicates with the database using the same existing OLE or COM protocol. Furthermore, any administration issues associated with the database are negligible because the existing administration strategy is still applicable. Application programmers need know only that the ODBC bridge will be used and should not tailor their application to it.

Installing the ODBC driver for Windows 95 will be discussed in the next section. Because it is a Microsoft product, the process is easy, but the reliability is in doubt. Keep in mind that most mission-critical applications are run using heavy-duty, perhaps even workstation-based databases. While these databases are expensive and difficult to administer, they are oodles more reliable than the Microsoft solution. In any event, we will show you how to write applications tailored for Microsoft because the general computing populace, and more importantly the audience of this book, will not necessarily have access to huge database servers.

JDBC in general

Java Database Connectivity encapsulates the functionality of databases and abstracts that information from the end-user or application programmer. Creating simple JDBC applications requires only minor knowledge of databases, but more complex applications may require intensive training in database administration and programming. For that reason, we have chosen several simple and fun examples to display the power of a Java solution that will more likely than not be used by mission-critical applications.

Databases and SQL

Databases are storage mechanisms for vast quantities of data. An entire segment of the computer industry is devoted to database administration, perhaps hinting that databases are not only complex and difficult, but are best left to professionals. Because of this level of difficulty and of our desire to get you started in linking Java to databases, we have chosen to implement a widely available, easily administered, and simply installed database. Microsoft Access can be purchased at your local software retailer. If you want to get started, it's a good place to start. From there, you can move on to more complex databases such as Oracle and Sybase.

In this section, we intend to introduce and create a simple database. In the next section, you will create a simple Java client that accesses the database and gets information from it. We suggest that further exploration into JDBC be preceded by a serious investigation into SQL. The Structured Query Language enables you to create powerful instructions to access databases. Once you grasp SQL, you will be able to understand the reasoning and theories behind JDBC.

Creating an Access database

We will need to first start Microsoft Access so that we can create a database to talk to. This is an important step, but one that those who either do not have access to or who do not wish to use Microsoft's database can tailor for their own database. After starting Access:

1. Select "Database Wizard" so Access will help you create a database.

2. We are going to create a "Blank Database" so select that icon.

3. Name the database and then you will get a series of tabbed folders. Go to "Tables" and click on "New".

4. You will get a spreadsheet-like view in which you can enter your data.

5. Enter your data as shown in Figure 5-2 and then select "Save" to store the table to the database. Name your table **PresidentialCandidate.**

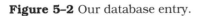

	ID	Candidate	Percentage	Electoral
	1	Clinton	49	379
	2	Dole	42	159
	3	Perot	8	0
*				

Figure 5-2 Our database entry.

As you can see in Figure 5-2, we entered the important statistics from the last Presidential election. The percentage is stored as a whole number, not as a decimal. This allows the application to determine how it will represent the information. We also store the electoral votes that each candidate received.

Simple SQL

Now we must create a series of queries for this database so that we can access them from JDBC in Chapter 6, 'The Java Web Server.' To do so, we need to know a little bit of SQL. This is by no means intended to be the end-all and be-all of SQL tutorials. This is a Java book, and as such we will minimize our discussion of SQL.

The Holy Grail of SQL instructions is the `Select` call. `Select` enables you to pull out specific portions of a database table. Alongside the `Select` call, you must specify both the database table `From` which you want the information and the filter for the information. So, when you **Select From** a table, **Where** the parameters match your requirements, you get a result back.

The `Where` statement may contain what is known as a conditional. A conditional enables you to further tailor the match parameters for a database query. In a moment, we will query a database table for all the Presidential candidates who received electoral votes in the 1996 election. From a field of three candidates, we will end up with two. Big party politics aside, our query will return a result based on the parameters we specify.

In theory, that result always will be a database table of its own. For example, given the following table of Presidential election results, and the accompanying SQL statement, we will receive a table in return (see Figure 5-3).

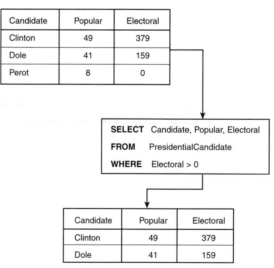

Figure 5–3 SQL statements can be made to return entire tables.

This table is sort of like a local variable. It disappears from memory if we don't use it right away. We could just as easily include this SQL statement within another SQL statement and achieve predictable results. These are called subqueries, and are another powerful tool of which SQL programmers can take advantage.

The beauty of SQL is its simplicity. Obviously, a language of such great importance has several nuances that database experts have long known, but it is still fairly easy to start writing SQL statements, as we will discover in this chapter.

Generating SQL

In order to create the necessary queries for our Access data, we must do the following steps. This will let us call these "super queries" rather than being forced to specify SQL in our Java code. There are advantages and disadvantages to this approach, which we will discuss in a moment.

1. Select the "Queries" tab in the main database view.
2. Select "New,"
3. Select "Design View,"
4. Immediately select "Close" in the "Show Table" view
5. Go to the "Query" menu and select "SQL Specific" and then "Union."

Now we are presented with a little text input area in which we can enter our query. Using the limited amount of information we have just learned, we must create three queries, one for each candidate, that will retrieve the important statistics for us. We have shown the ClintonQuery in Figure 5-4, and you can see what your database will look like when all three queries are completed.

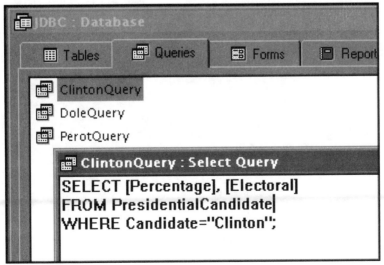

Figure 5–4 Getting stats on Bill Clinton from the database.

Note that we have limited the amount of queries. You could just as easily create more complex queries, and if you know SQL pretty well we encourage you to do so. Otherwise, it is probably best to get this "proof of concept" example down pat before proceeding.

Introduction to the ODBC driver

Once the database is completed, we must make it available via the database server. To do so, we must edit the ODBC Control Panel. The ODBC Control Panel assigns our database to the driver, allowing invocations on the database to pass through the driver right into the database. Unless the database is made public to the ODBC driver, this cannot happen because the system will not know about the database's existence.

To assign the database to the driver, select the driver Control Panel. The Control Panel should have been installed with Access. If it is not there, check your Microsoft Access installation instructions. Inside the Control Panel, select "MS Access 7.0" and "Select" the proper database from within the Setup dialog box (see Figure 5-5).

Figure 5–5 Starting the ODBC driver.

Once completed, the ODBC driver will be aware of the database you have created and await invocations on it. As long as the incoming queries specify the "PresidentialCandidate" database, they will be dispatched to the database and from there to our SQL queries.

Summary

ODBC is a proprietary database management protocol. It enables you to access information on databases from within Microsoft Windows. Once ODBC is set up on our machine, we can get information from the database by creating Java applications that interface to it.

Retrieving information

At first glance, you probably wonder where the "server" chapter for this section is. Well, we created it when we created our database! The beauty of JDBC clients is that they link directly with databases. In geek terms, this is referred to as a "two-tier" model in which the client is the first tier and the database itself is the second tier. So far we have promoted the three-tier model in which clients do nothing but look good and interface with servers. The servers contain all of the business logic and the databases only store data.

In JDBC and the two-tier model, the client contains all of the business logic and is responsible for contacting and accessing the database. Our JDBC client uses SQL queries to contact our Microsoft Access database. The downside to this is the complexity of the client and the scalability of the system. With potentially hundreds of clients banging on the same database, the database could get overloaded. With a three-tier model, the database is queried by only one application—the server—and the server is responsible (and is more capable) of handling the hundreds of simultaneous requests.

In any event, we will present you with a more thorough look at the advantages and disadvantages of the two- and three-tier models in Chapter 12, "Making an Architectural Decision." In this section, we show you how to go to a database and get information. In the next section, we will show you how to put information into the database.

Creating the user interface

Our user interface should be simple and elegant. Once again, we don't want to confuse people with what we are trying to do. We will create a button for each candidate. Upon activation of the button, the client will execute SQL statements on the server and get information. Then it will display the information in the text fields provided. See Figure 5-6 for a sample GUI.

Figure 5–6 Sample GUI for the Presidential election application.

The user interface will enable us to underscore the simplicity of JDBC. We have seen how it can handle the most complex of cases, but here we once again keep our examples fun and easy.

As we proceed, we will show you how to implement the two important functions in this application. The `PresidentialElection` application's constructor and its corresponding `action` method will initialize and invoke the database, respectively.

```
public class PresidentialElection
{
    Button clintonButton;
    Button doleButton;
    Button perotButton;

    TextField popularField;
    TextField electoralField;

    PresidentialElection()
    {
        // create the user interface here
    }

    public boolean action(
        Event evt,
        Object obj
    )
    {
        if(evt.target == clintonButton)
```

```
        {
        }
        else if(evt.target == doleButton)
        {
        }
        else if(evt.target == perotButton)
        {
        }
    }
}
```

As we saw in Chapter 3, "Java IDL: Interface Definition Language," the integration of the user interface and simple Java applications with our complex network aware components is pretty easy. All we have to do now is fill in the constructor and the `action` methods.

Database security

Because we are writing an application, handling our own security is not a requirement. However, if we wanted to write an applet, once again we would need to use a `SecurityManager` to set our access to the host database. Because Java applets are able to connect only to their host machine, our security manager is required to make sure we have access to the database on the host machine. By setting the security manager, you can check to see if you have access to the database before a query is executed. Keep in mind, the security manager deals with security as it relates to Java. Database access security is handled through the instantiation of the `Connection` object.

Using the JDBC driver

As we discussed earlier, we must include the JDBC driver in our application. To do so, we obtain a `Connection` object from the `DriverManager`. The `Driver-Manager` takes a URL and translates it into a handle for an actual database. Then we can invoke our SQL statements on the database and retrieve information. From the `Connection` object, we can retrieve `Statement`, `PreparedStatement`, and `CallableStatement` objects to help us format our SQL queries.

As JDBC gains more acceptance, database vendors will provide drivers for Java applications to use to contact their database. Often, there will be some overlap between these different drivers. Choosing the proper driver can be a difficult task, but JDBC enables you to create a colon separated list of drivers through which JDBC will search for the first available driver.

Here, we will use the standard ODBC driver included with JDBC. This will enable us to connect to ODBC databases such as the Microsoft Access database we just created. So long as our ODBC driver has been set up to await this kind of query, this will succeed. We will need to load the specific class for the database "manually."

```java
import java.sql.*;

public class PresidentialElection
{
    Button clintonButton;
    Button doleButton;
    Button perotButton;

    TextField popularField;
    TextField electoralField;

    // the connection to the database
    Connection dbConnection;

    PresidentialElection()
    {
        // create the user interface here

        // create the URL representation of our Database
        String url = "jdbc:odbc:PresidentialCandidate";

        // load the database driver
        Class.forName("sun.jdbc.odbc.JdbcOdbcDriver");

        // make the connection to the database
        dbConnection = DriverManager.getConnection(
            url, "username" "password");
    }

    public boolean action(
        Event evt,
        Object obj
    )
    {
        if(evt.target == clintonButton)
```

```
        {
        }
        else if(evt.target == doleButton)
        {
        }
        else if(evt.target == perotButton)
        {
        }
    }
}
```

After we created the URL representation for our database, we needed to connect to the database itself. Once that is done our application is linked to the database and can make invocations at will.

Creating queries

Now, we must fill in the action method so that we can make the query on the database. Here, instead of specifying SQL in the executeQuery instruction, we will execute the queries we created within our database itself. This enables us to create central queries within the database that other applications can use. It not only makes life easier for the database programmer, but it eliminates errors and streamlines the query process.

```
import java.sql.*;

public class PresidentialElection
{
    Button clintonButton;
    Button doleButton;
    Button perotButton;

    TextField popularField;
    TextField electoralField;

    PresidentialElection()
    {
        // create the user interface here

        // create the URL representation of our Database
        String url = "jdbc:odbc:PresidentialCandidate";
```

```
    // load the database driver
    Class.forName("sun.jdbc.odbc.JdbcOdbcDriver");

    // make the connection to the database
    Connection connection = DriverManager.getConnection(
        url, "username" "password");
}


public boolean action(
    Event evt,
    Object obj
)
{
    if(evt.target == clintonButton)
    {
        // create the statement
        Statement statement =
            dbConnection.createStatement();

        // get the result
        ResultSet result = statement.executeQuery(
            "ClintonQuery");

        // walk through the result for the information
        while(result.next())
        {
            int popular = result.getInt(1);
            int electoral = result.getInt(2);

            popularField.setText("Clinton " + popular);
            electoralField.setText("Clinton " + electoral);
        }
    }
    else if(evt.target == doleButton)
    {
        ... similar routines ...
    }
    else if(evt.target == perotButton)
    {
```

```
         … similar routines …
     }
  }
}
```

In place of "`ClintonQuery`," we could just as easily have included the entire SQL statement as it appears in Microsoft Access. As mentioned, we choose not to because of the simplicity of storing central queries on the database itself. Furthermore, the Perot and Dole queries are invoked similarly.

Database and SQL overview

Once we are able to interface with the database, we should be able to put information in it. Databases are not static entities. They are ever-changing, and in keeping with that trait, Java provides some pretty cool tools to get to databases and change the data stored therein.

Storing information

JDBC also gives you a means to store information in a table. Once again, this is done using standard Structured Query Language statements. By using SQL, JDBC makes sure that its own learning curve is pretty small. JDBC gives you much flexibility in creating statements, as we have seen in Chapter 4, "Java RMI, Remote Method Invocation."

Let's say that suddenly we discover that Bill Clinton is really Daffy Duck! The seven hundred-thousand people who wrote in "Daffy Duck" on their ballot as their choice for President of the United States really voted for Bill Clinton. As a result, the percentage by which Bill Clinton won the 1996 election changed. We need to create a JDBC query to modify the percentage.

Creating the connection

The first thing we must do is create the connection as we did before. We will also add a button to change the percentage of votes for Bill Clinton. We could with a slight bit more complication and effort create a more customizable change area. It could have text fields for each entry and a submit button. Using the data in the text field, we could change the data in the table. For now, however, that is more complex than is needed.

```
public class PresidentialElection
{
    Button clintonButton;
    Button doleButton;
    Button perotButton;
    Button changeButton;
```

```
TextField popularField;
TextField electoralField;

PresidentialElection()
{
    // create the user interface here

    // create the URL representation of our Database
    String url = "jdbc:odbc:PresidentialCandidate";

    // load the database driver
    Class.forName("sun.jdbc.odbc.JdbcOdbcDriver");

    // make the connection to the database
    Connection connection = DriverManager.getConnection(
        url, "username" "password");
}

public boolean action(
    Event evt,
    Object obj
)
{
    if(evt.target == clintonButton)
    {
        ... same as before ...
    }
    else if(evt.target == doleButton)
    {
        ... same as before ...
    }
    else if(evt.target == perotButton)
    {
        ... same as before ...
    }
    else if(evt.target == changeButton)
    {
    }
}
}
```

We also needed to insert event handling information for the new button. As you can see, there is no change between the connection for retrieving information and the connection here for setting the information.

Forming a statement

The burden, in JDBC, is placed on the formation of statements. As database programmers expect, there is no need to learn anything new or confusing. Java is treated as nothing more than a container for an SQL statement. The SQL statements we create here as well as when we stored information are nothing fancy, nothing special, and no more interesting than a normal SQL statement.

In order to change the information in a database we need to use the SQL Update statement. We must specify a column and row to change. But, instead of encapsulating the SQL statement with a regular JDBC Statement, instead we will use a PreparedStatement. PreparedStatements give you the ability to insert parameters within the statement itself. The following example contains two parameters, popularvote and candidate:

```
UPDATE PresidentialCandidate
SET popularvote = ?
WHERE candidate = ?
```

The popularvote field is marked as field number one while candidate is field number two. To set the fields, we use the set methods supplied with JDBC along with the number of the field you want to change: setInt, setString, etc. To define the fields, use the question mark.

Now we can create a PreparedStatement. Note, however, that in this chapter we are not using pre-created queries as we did in Chapter 4, "Java RMI, Remote Method Invocation." Instead, we will create the query directly from JDBC. As we discussed earlier either approach is completely acceptable. The choice is not one of effort, but rather of programming approach. If your business makes heavy use of pre-created queries, obviously you will choose to invoke them from JDBC. If database interaction is not as important, then there is really no need to define queries ahead of time.

```
public class PresidentialElection
{
    Button clintonButton;
    Button doleButton;
    Button perotButton;
    Button changeButton;
```

```java
TextField popularField;
TextField electoralField;

PresidentialElection()
{
    // create the user interface here

    // create the URL representation of our Database
    String url = "jdbc:odbc:PresidentialCandidate";

    // load the database driver
    Class.forName("sun.jdbc.odbc.JdbcOdbcDriver");

    // make the connection to the database
    Connection connection = DriverManager.getConnection(
        url, "username" "password");
}

public boolean action(
    Event evt,
    Object obj
)
{
    if(evt.target == clintonButton)
    {
        … same as before …
    }
    else if(evt.target == doleButton)
    {
        … same as before …
    }
    else if(evt.target == perotButton)
    {
        … same as before …
    }
    else if(evt.target == changeButton)
    {
```

```
        // create the statement
    PreparedStatement pstate =
        connection.prepareStatement(
            "UPDATE PresidentialCandidate " +
            "SET popularvote = ? " +
            "WHERE candidate = ?");

        // set the parameters for the statement
    pstate.setInt(1, 50);
    pstate.setString(2, "Clinton");

        // execute the statement
    pstate.executeUpdate();
        }
    }
}
```

Now that we can create a simple system of clients that change information in a database, we can try to create a client for our featured application that will store and retrieve its information from a similar database. By creating this purely two-tier model, you can compare it with the three-tier applications we created for Sockets, Java IDL, and Java RMI in the previous three chapters.

A JDBC version of the featured app

As we have seen in the previous sections, creating a JDBC interface to a database is fairly easy. The difficult parts involve setting up the database and installing the driver. While we won't discuss the finer points of drivers or database administration, we will create the database as well as the interface to it.

Creating the database

Once again, we will create the database and associated queries using Microsoft Access as shown in Figure 5-7. As before, our decision to use Access is due largely to its ubiquity and ease of use. We want you to be able to create interfaces to databases quickly and easily, and Microsoft Access provides a simple means to do so. As with all third-party products, if you require assistance with Access, contact Microsoft. In any event, if you have access to Sybase, Oracle, or another database, feel free to use it. You should not have to modify the code, but you will have to install a driver for the database you plan to use.

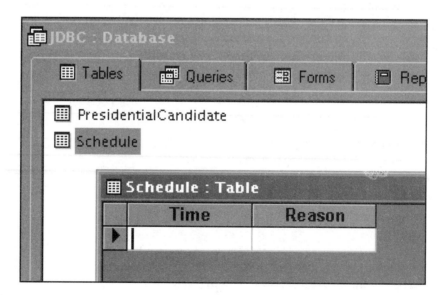

Figure 5–7 Our new database.

We will store our appointments in the database using two keys, the reason for the appointment and the time of the appointment. This conforms to the interface to the Network module. In a moment we will discuss how to map the network module to the database. For now, take a look at the Access table in Figure 5-8.

Figure 5–8 Table for our appointments.

We must create a query within the database to get appointments for us. Figure 5-9 shows you what that query looks like. You can create it by following the steps we described earlier when we created a query for the `PresidentialElection` database. We will not create a query for scheduling appointments because we want to use a `PreparedStatement` like we did when we stored the `Presiden-tialElection` information earlier.

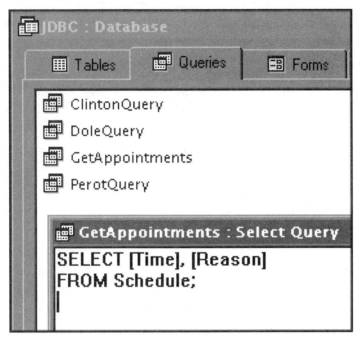

Figure 5–9 GetAppointments query.

Mapping the network module to database queries

Now we need to connect the network module to the database. Remember, a driver must be installed for the database. Without it the database access queries cannot function. Our network module's interface looks like this:

```
public class NetworkModule
{
    public void scheduleAppointment(
        String reason,
        int time);

    public Vector getAppointments();
```

```
    public void initNetwork();

    public void shutdownNetwork();
}
```

Obviously, we will map the `scheduleAppointment` method to a `Prepared-Statement` query, but we will map the `getAppointment` method to the `GetAppointments` query. We will pass our constructor's code directly to the `initNetwork` method, and we must close our connection to the database, the `shutdownNetwork` method is the logical place to include that code.

Developing the client

Now we must fill in the code for the network module. Doing so is just as simple as before. Let's first take a look at the network module's code without the modifications. We must incorporate the JDBC classes as well as the classes for the driver.

```
import java.sql.*;

public class NetworkModule
{
    NetworkModule()
    {
    }

    public void scheduleAppointment(
        String reason,
        int time)
    {
    }

    public Vector getAppointments()
    {
    }

    public void initNetwork()
    {
    }

    public void shutdownNetwork()
    {
    }
}
```

Once our client is ready, we must fill in the information for each function. First we will schedule appointments using the `scheduleAppointment` query that we created earlier. Essentially, the network module acts as a pass-through from the rest of the application directly to the database. Normally, we would try to incorporate some kind of middleman to handle the pass-through from our GUI to the database, but for simplicity's sake we will not develop a three-tier application here. In the future, if you desire a three-tier application, your middle-tier server would make these calls.

Establishing the connection

First we must create the connection to the database and link our network module to it. This ensures we have a clear path to the database. Any errors here should be caught and thrown back. We also must make sure to load the database driver manually by specifying its entire class name.

```java
import java.sql.*;

public class NetworkModule
{
    // the connection to the database
    Connection dbConnection;

    NetworkModule()
    {
        // init the network
        initNetwork();
    }

    public void scheduleAppointment(
        String reason,
        int time)
    {
    }

    public Vector getAppointments()
    {
    }

    public void initNetwork()
    {
        // create the URL representation of our Database
        String url = "jdbc:odbc:Schedule";
```

```
        // load the database driver
        Class.forName("sun.jdbc.odbc.JdbcOdbcDriver");

        // make the connection to the database
        dbConnection = DriverManager.getConnection(
            url, "username" "password");
    }

    public void shutdownNetwork()
    {
    }
}
```

Making an SQL Invocation

Invoking the database is relatively straightforward and not unlike our earlier
invocation of the Presidential Election database. Here, we substitute our own
invocation. The difference in this invocation, however, is that we will retrieve a
complex type from the SQL query. As a result, we must translate the complex type
into the Vector that is expected as a return value for the GetAppointments
invocation.

```
import java.sql.*;

public class NetworkModule
{
    // the connection to the database
    Connection dbConnection;

    NetworkModule()
    {
        // init the network
        initNetwork();
    }

    public void scheduleAppointment(
        String reason,
        int time)
    {
    }
```

```java
public Vector getAppointments()
{
    // create the statement
    Statement statement = dbConnection.createStatement();

    // get the result
    ResultSet result = statement.executeQuery(
        "GetAppointments");

    // walk through the result for the information we need
    while(result.next())
    {
    }
}

public void initNetwork()
{
    // create the URL representation of our Database
    String url = "jdbc:odbc:localhost";

    // load the database driver
    Class.forName("sun.jdbc.odbc.JdbcOdbcDriver");

    // make the connection to the database
    dbConnection = DriverManager.getConnection(
        url, "username" "password");
}

public void shutdownNetwork()
{
}
}
```

Notice how the current invocation steps through the ResultSet and makes it into a Vector. When your applications need to handle more complex results from an SQL query, you will need to do much of the same.

Invoking SQL to make a change

Now we must implement the Java side to our setAppointment operation. Our setAppointment query assigns a new entry into the database.

```
public void scheduleAppointment(
    String reason,
    int time)
{
}
```

We must first take the reason and time variables and translate them into an SQL statement. Unlike our previous database modification example, here we must insert an element, not simply change an existing one. To do so, we need to use the SQL `Insert` statement.

```
INSERT INTO Schedule
VALUES (1, 'Meet with marketing');
```

We will once again use the PreparedStatement object to put together a statement.

```
public void scheduleAppointment(
    String reason,
    int time)
{

    PreparedStatement pstate =
        connection.prepareStatement(
            "INSERT INTO Schedule " +
            "VALUES (?, ?)");

    // set the parameters for the statement
    pstate.setInt(1, 1);
    pstate.setString(2, "Meet with marketing");

    // execute the statement
    pstate.executeUpdate();
}
```

Shutting down the connection

In JDBC, unlike RMI or IDL, we must close the connection to our database. This ensures that the Database Management System has sufficient connections for other applications to connect to it. For high-availability databases, this is quite an important characteristic. The database must be available at all times, and even though our connection disappears when the application shuts down, we must still publish an interface to the database connection that will allow us to eliminate it.

```
public void shutdownNetwork()
{
}
```

Summary

Databases are storage mechanisms designed to enable you to warehouse vast quantities of data. By linking Java applications to them, you can create programs that are instantly useful. Today, there are hundreds of applications that interface with databases using outdated, archaic applications. Combined with a proven communication mechanism like IDL or RMI, JDBC can help you to access and manipulate that information.

But, developing applications in IDL or RMI can lead to interesting quandaries. With IDL, the client side must have an ORB running locally. With RMI, the server must always be running. Perhaps a fast, easy middle ground is required.

Web servers provide the logical extension to sockets that allow everyday people access to databases. What if a Web server was created that was fully programmable using Java?   In the next chapter we will discuss a Web server written entirely in Java that enables programmable extensions, called *servlets*, that can work with both RMI or IDL and take the place of those more advanced communication mechanisms.

PART III

Advanced Java Networking

Using the foundation laid out in Part II, Advanced Java Networking focuses on two technologies for more robust inter-application communication. The Java Web Server is an HTTP server written entirely in Java. In conjunction with the other technologies mentioned in Part II, the Java Web Server can help servers become more than application servers, adding full World Wide Web information publishing functionality as well. Beans, though not exactly an example of networked applications, allows applications to be built as reusable components that exchange information with one another and with remote processes. A special chapter on some of the other Java initiatives that are worth noting is also included.

Chapter 6: The Java Web Server
Chapter 7: Java Beans
Chapter 8: The Networked Java World

CHAPTER
6

What Is an HTTP Server?

Applets on the Server Side!

Say Goodbye to CGI-BIN

Serving More than Web Content

The Java
Web Server

What if your normal Web server was capable of providing dynamic network content? If it could go out and connect to other distributed objects, using solutions from earlier in this book, it would be able to funnel information to a client without the client even once knowing of the machinery behind the scenes. So far we have discussed alternatives that have brought networked computing to the client side while creating specific client applications to accept that information. With the Java Web Server, a servlet, in essence a server side applet, can funnel information back to a web browser as a standard HTML file. The browser needs not know anything about object design, internal machinery, or even what a servlet is.

In this chapter, we will explain the basic functionality of an HTTP server, followed by a brief tutorial on servlets and how to modify servlets to be an object server, like CORBA or RMI, at the same time. The Java Web Server and the servlet architecture is an exciting use of the Java language that we have come to know and love. The examples in this chapter are designed to bring that excitement and fun back to you.

Inside an HTTP Server

As we will see in a moment, Java Web Server is nothing more than an enhanced web server product. The fact that it is written in Java does not distinguish it from Microsoft's own BackOffice web server or Netscape's Commerce Server. Java Web Server provides dynamic content without having to employ the cumbersome tools that we have seen thus far.

But, what is an HTTP server anyway? What does it do, and what purpose does it serve?

Web server architecture

At its most bare bones and most basic level, an HTTP server simply listens for messages and returns results. It does so by clinging to the pre-designated HTTP port and awaiting requests. Often, these requests are formatted along the lines of "GET filename." When presented with such a request, the HTTP server will grab the appropriate file and return it to the calling client. While the general public will admit it has nary a clue as to what "client/server computing" is, the reality is that they have been doing it all along.

The portion of the Web server that listens for file requests is called an HTTP daemon. A daemon, as we discussed in a Chapter 1 section on threads, is a special process whose entire role is to hang around with no distinct startup time and no distinct shutdown time. It has a specific role that it plays, in this case to fetch files and return them across a network, but does so without any special hoopla. Often times, the Web server will handle multiple requests simultaneously (see Figure 6-1).

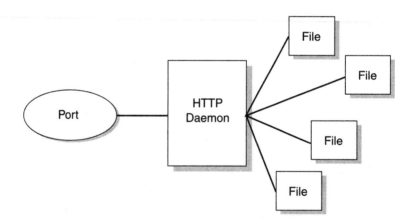

Figure 6-1 Web servers handle requests for multiple files.

Once the daemon gets a request, it will go and get the file and return it to the requester. As we discussed in our chapter on sockets, this is a pipe, or two-way connection between the client and the server.

Using a Web server

Today, we use a Web browser to get static document content. The server gets a request from the browser, finds the file it is looking for, and returns it to the calling browser. This is the way the Web works today.

More than likely, the Web will shift to more dynamic data. Data (essentially HTML files) today is created beforehand, placed on a server, and downloaded by clients. Eventually, the Web will move to a point where the data is never created beforehand, but generated on-the-fly. It will facilitate small, efficient programs that create dynamic content for you, and help to prevent the timely distribution of data. How many times have you gone to a Web page and found the link unattached or the file outdated? With dynamic data, you can assure that the file is generated today rather than five, maybe six months ago.

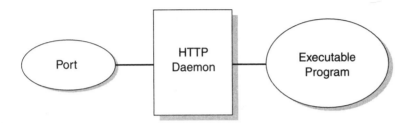

Figure 6–2 The World Wide Web moves to executable content.

As you can see in Figure 6-2, the shift to executable rather than static content on the web is actually pretty easy to do. The next few sections will outline the Java answer to this particular Web server question.

Advanced Web server features

The Web servers of the present also incorporate several advanced features such as security, performance enhancements, and administration. Security is discussed in detail in Chapter 11, "Java and Security," and, indeed, much of the Java security concerns that have cropped up over the last year or so stem from concerns over the Web server itself. Will Secure Electronic Transactions actually work over the Web? These are issues that will be dealt with by the Web server community far before they are incorporated into Java itself.

Performance enhancements are created due largely to smarter multi-threaded environments, faster hardware, and more capable network connections. Often, performance tuning of a Web server is done by spawning a thread for every HTTP request.

Finally, network administration is an issue in and of itself, but Web network administration embodies more than that of its traditional father. Network administration deals largely with local area networks. With Web servers, the network administration issues are expanded on a wider scale, over Wide Area Networks. What happens when machines fail, or when HTTP servers get overloaded? As advances in hardware failover technology and Java Network Management are unveiled, the Web administration will continue to get easier, but at the same time more complex.

HTTP Server overview

The HTTP server is the most common means normal people use to harness the power of the Internet. But even the tried and true HTTP server is moving away from the simplicity of serving static data. The Web as a whole is moving toward executable content. Servlets give us a way to program the server side of an HTTP connection. Today, we have several alternatives ranging from Web browsers to FTP clients that allow us to plug in to the network. What's been lacking is the server side connection to that interactive content.

Servlets

Until now, an HTTP server has functioned solely to provide the client with documents. The documents, usually written in HTML, perhaps with embedded Shockwave or Java functionality, have been statically created days, weeks, even months before the client actually fetched it. If you want to create dynamic document content, you must use the Common Gateway Interface. CGI scripts were a hack designed to provide two-way communication via the World Wide Web. Servlets replace the need for CGI scripts, and give you a much cleaner, more robust alternative.

What is a servlet?

Servlets are Java applications that reside on the server side of an HTTP server. More likely than not you created several Java objects designed to be used by the client. Typically, these Java objects are restricted by security constraints that challenge your ability to use files and networks on a whim. Servlets are not subject to artificial security restrictions and enable you to extend the easy nature of Java programming to the server side of an HTTP connection (see Figure 6-3).

Servlets can be used to create dynamic HTML documents. The documents generated by a servlet can contain data gleaned from other sources, including remote objects, databases, and flat files. As we will see in a later section, servlets also can be integrated with your existing RMI or IDL servers. Furthermore, the investment of time required to learn servlet programming is negligible because knowing Java automatically ensures that you will "know" servlets.

So, why don't we just use RMI? Normal Java objects have well-defined public interfaces that can be used by a variety of clients, including Web pages, other applets, even CORBA servers. These Java objects are conventional objects that are instantiated every time one is needed. In the end, if you create an object, you very well could have five or six copies hanging out there being used by object requesters.

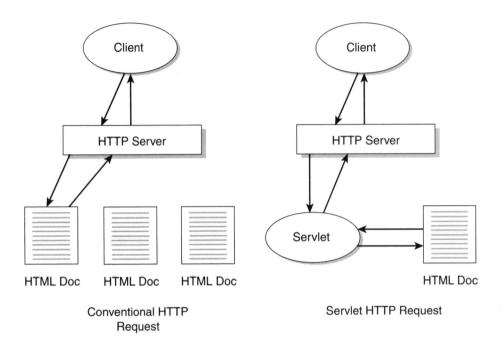

Figure 6–3 Servlets create documents on-the-fly rather than getting documents that were already there.

Servlets, on the other hand, have no defined interfaces. They are faceless Java objects. The Java Web Server simply maps a request onto a servlet, passing it the entire URL call. The servlet then does what it is programmed to do and generates dynamic content. Servlets cannot have an interface as we know it. Instead, all of its functionality is restricted to one function within its class hierarchy.

The Servlet API

The Servlet API maps each servlet to a specific HTTP request. The Java Web Server is responsible for taking the mapping and invoking the proper servlet. Servlets can be initialized, invoked, and destroyed depending on the request. The Java Web Server makes sure the servlet carries out its instructions correctly.

Furthermore, because servlets are implemented in Java, they are platform independent and architecture neutral. As with normal Java objects, servlets require a valid Java Virtual Machine to be present on the machine on which it runs. In addition, the servlet requires a valid Java Web Server that is capable of routing requests properly.

ALERT: The java.servlet package is a set of APIs that is in a constant state of flux. Because the Java revolution is so new, and because the standards in this corner of the computer science world are never fully baked, much of what we write about today is obsolete tomorrow. In light of this, we will outline only those APIs that we deem will not be changed. Nevertheless, we may be proven wrong on several counts, but that's life in this brave new world.

The Servlet interface shown in Figure 6-4 should be implemented by objects that want to be dynamic information providers. In the diagram in Figure 6-4, those objects that provide the functionality defined in the Servlet interface are capable of handling ServletRequests.

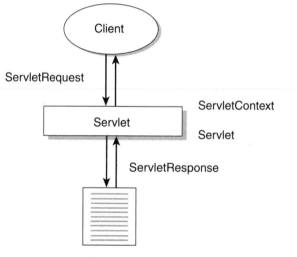

Figure 6–4 The Servlet class hierarchy gives you easy access to input and output streams for dynamic documents.

The ServletRequest object contains the entire HTTP request passed to the servlet by the Java Web Server. The ServletRequest is also capable of extracting parameters from the HTTP request itself. For example, the following URL contains four elements:

```
http://prashantiscool.com/prashant.html?heath
```

First, the request defines the kind of protocol that is used. Here, we use the hypertext transfer protocol. The HTTP request is fairly ubiquitous on the Web these days, but as new protocols such as the Internet Inter-ORB Protocol (IIOP) become more prevalent, this portion of the request will become more and more important.

We then see the domain name for the request. In this instance, we access the Web site `prashantiscool.com`, presumably to send generous cash donations to one of the authors of this book. Obviously, this portion of the address varies widely from places such as the boring `www.microsoft.com` to the exciting `www.sun.com`.

Finally, we access the document and its parameters. The Java Web Server maps the `prashant.html` document request to a servlet, passing the parameter `heath` as part of the `ServletRequest` data structure. Keep in mind that the physical document `prashant.html` does not actually exist; it will be generated on-the-fly by the servlet.

Responses are sent back to the requesting client via the `ServletResponse` object. The Java Web Server translates the `ServletResponse` object into a dynamic document of some kind. We will see later how we can generate dynamic applets, but we will still pass the data back through a `ServletResponse` instance.

Why not CGI scripts?

CGI scripts are language independent. They can be written in everything from C++ to PERL or AWK. Scripts implementing the Common Gateway Interface simply pass environment variables to one another all the while generating dynamic documents. They can provide a ton of functionality, as we have seen with the explosive growth of the Web. Certainly without CGI scripts the Web could never have been a two-way form of communication that was readily accepted by the general public.

CGI scripts have two major drawbacks, however. First, they suffer from horrible performance numbers. They are turtle slow and are not scaleable. Multiple CGI requests on the same server end up creating new processes for each request. The end result is that CGI processes do not cooperate with one another as threaded applications would, and instead hog system resources slowing not only the scripts themselves but the HTTP server that hosts it as well.

CGI scripts are also completely platform dependent. While the language with which they are written can vary, they cannot be transported from a Windows machine to a Macintosh. They are written once, and used in one place.

The Java Web Server provides an alternative to this morass. Because they are written in Java, servlets are platform independent. They can be moved between machines with ease and without recompiling. Servlets also can take advantage of clever threading mechanisms and provide fast turnaround and efficient processing of data.

Servlets overview

These days, HTTP servers are commodities to be had in much the same way as a pair of Nike Air Jordans. You can get HTTP servers from Netscape, from Microsoft, even for free via the World Wide Web. Companies whose sole product is a Web server are doomed to failure. In an effort to provide a new kind of Web server to the Web surfing public, Sun Microsystems has created the Java Web Server architecture.

Java Web Server generates dynamic documents through normal protocol requests. The dynamic documents are created by Java objects known as servlets. As we will see in the next two sections, Servlets are both easy and fun to write. Without much effort, you can create a dynamic document server that will render your CGI scripting techniques of the past obsolete.

Dynamic Documents

We spoke earlier about the Java Web Server translating document requests into servlet calls that, in turn, create and pass back a document corresponding to the request. The servlet must be capable of accepting different parameters from the client and also be able to formulate a response quickly and efficiently. By using servlets, we would not have to create those documents days, weeks, perhaps even months in advance. Rather, we simply create a program that, given a set of parameters, can generate a document at the moment of the request. In so doing, we generate up-to-the-minute information without resorting to software hacks like CGI scripts.

Creating the servlet

All servlets need to inherit from the `GenericServlet` base class. The base class creates all of the functionality required to map Java Web Server requests onto a physical servlet process. The servlet process is started automatically by the server if it isn't yet running. Any subsequent requests on the servlet process either can be queued until the servlet is ready to process it or another servlet can be started up to process it. These are administrative tasks that we will discuss in a moment.

Meanwhile, we need to implement the servlet architecture to retain a request, process data, and send documents back. Let's say we want to create a shrine for the greatest vegetable of all time, the pumpkin. Since ancient times, pumpkins have provided nourishment and low-calorie, low-fat food for the masses. From roasted pumpkin seeds to delicious and healthy pumpkin pie, the pumpkin has been an integral part of human history for generations.

When our server receives a request for the document `pumpkin.html` we tell it to call the servlet. The servlet then generates a dynamic document for a delicious pumpkin recipe. Later on, we will allow the client to determine which recipe it wants to see, but for now we return a random pumpkin recipe.

We start by creating the `PumpkinServlet` object that extends the `Generic-Servlet` base class. As we mentioned before, the `GenericServlet` base class is required for all servlets and implements the underlying HTTP to servlet mechanisms.

```
public class PumpkinServlet extends GenericServlet
{
}
```

Handling Java Web Server requests

Every object that inherits from the `GenericServlet` base class must implement the `service` function. The `service` function has two parameters, a `ServletRequest` object and a `ServletResponse` object and can throw one of two exceptions, either the `ServletException` or an `IOException`. The `ServletRequest` object gives us information about the request sent to us, particularly what kinds of parameters we are receiving. In this simplest of cases, we are not dealing with parameters, but we will in a moment. The response object enables us to set the proper stream to which we can write our dynamic document.

```
public class PumpkinServlet extends GenericServlet
{
    public void service(
        ServletRequest servletRequest,
        ServletResponse servletResponse
    ) throws ServletException, IOException
    {
    }
}
```

Setting headers and defining content

Once we implement the service function, we can fill in the details. We must set our response parameters first. In order for the Java Web Server to pass back a dynamic document, we need to tell it what kind of document we are sending back. Is this a Quicktime movie or an HTML file? In browser parlance, the type of file is specified by the *Content Type*. If you were to start Netscape or Internet Explorer and play around with the settings, you could farm off content types to different helper applications. For example, all .mov Quicktime files sent to a particular browser could end up starting a Quicktime Movie Player and start the animation. In much the same way, we need to specify what kind of document we are sending back by setting the content type.

```java
public class PumpkinServlet extends GenericServlet
{
    public void service(
        ServletRequest servletRequest,
        ServletResponse servletResponse
    ) throws ServletException, IOException
    {
        // set up the response
        servletResponse.setContentType("text/html");
    }
}
```

Creating the document

Now, we need a standard output stream to which we can write our dynamic document. As we discussed in our first chapter on "Advanced Java," streams are wonderful things that have numerous purposes. Here we take a regular response object and obtain an output stream for it:

```java
public class PumpkinServlet extends GenericServlet
{
    public void service(
        ServletRequest servletRequest,
        ServletResponse servletResponse
    ) throws ServletException, IOException
    {
        // set up the response
        servletResponse.setContentType("text/html");

        // get the dynamic document's output stream
        OutputStream docOutput = new OutputStream(
            servletResponse.getOutputStream());
    }
}
```

In order to send information back to the client, we must create an `HtmlPage` object that will handle much of our HTML formatting. Now, our dynamic document can be generated simply by writing to the HTML page. By setting the headers and obtaining the output stream from the response object, we sent our information directly back to the Java Web Server:

```
public class PumpkinServlet extends GenericServlet
{
    public void service(
        ServletRequest servletRequest,
        ServletResponse servletResponse
    ) throws ServletException, IOException
    {
        // set up the response
        servletResponse.setContentType("text/html");

        // get the dynamic document's output stream
        OutputStream docOutput = new OutputStream(
            servletResponse.getOutputStream());

        // generate an HTML page
        HtmlPage dynamicPage = new HtmlPage("Pumpkin Seeds");

        // write the document
        dynamicPage.add("<NL>");
        dynamicPage.add("  <LI>Get seeds");
        dynamicPage.add("  <LI>Stick in Oven");
        dynamicPage.add("  <LI>Don't burn");
        dynamicPage.add("</NL>");
    }
}
```

Accepting parameters

Let's say we want to offer two different pumpkin recipes to our client. One is for pumpkin pie, the other is for the pumpkin seeds we wrote previously. The `ServletRequest` object stores all of the parameters sent by the client and enables us to know how we should respond. Using the `getParameter` method of the `ServletRequest` object, you can get the value for the parameter you specify. In so doing, you can adjust your processing to provide the proper output for the given request.

Our client must be able to request one of the following two documents:

```
http://<machine>/pumpkin.html?recipe=seeds
http://<machine>/pumpkin.html?recipe=pie
```

The first thing we need to do is acquire the parameters from the servlet's request object. The `ServletRequest` object contains it as part of its object definition and also provides a helper method to access the parameter itself. Once we get the table of parameters, we can parse the table and get the required parameter value:

```java
public class PumpkinServlet extends GenericServlet
{
    public void service(
        ServletRequest servletRequest,
        ServletResponse servletResponse
    ) throws ServletException, IOException
    {
        // parse the request and get the parameters
        String recipeType =
            servletRequest.getParameter("recipe");

        // set up the response
        servletResponse.setContentType("text/html");

        // get the dynamic document's output stream
        OutputStream docOutput = new OutputStream(
            servletResponse.getOutputStream());

        // write the document
        dynamicPage.add("<NL>");
        dynamicPage.add("  <LI>Get seeds");
        dynamicPage.add("  <LI>Stick in Oven");
        dynamicPage.add("  <LI>Don't burn");
        dynamicPage.add("</NL>");
    }
}
```

Now that we know which recipe the client wants, we can add the logic to route the proper recipe back as a dynamic document:

```java
public class PumpkinServlet extends GenericServlet
{
    public void service(
        ServletRequest servletRequest,
        ServletResponse servletResponse
    ) throws ServletException, IOException
    {
        // parse the request and get the parameters
        String recipeType =
            servletRequest.getParameter("recipe");

        // set up the response
        servletResponse.setContentType("text/html");

        // get the dynamic document's output stream
        OutputStream docOutput = new OutputStream(
            servletResponse.getOutputStream());

        // write the document
        if(recipeType.equals("seeds"))
        {
            // do all of the HtmlPage stuff for the seed
        }
        else if(recipeType.equals("pie"))
        {
            // do all of the HtmlPage stuff for the pie
        }
    }
}
```

Information from outside sources

What if we wanted our servlet to go and get a recipe from a database of recipes? Instead of hard coding the recipe into the servlet, we could go to a flat file or database, read in the recipe, format it for HTML, and pass it back as a dynamic document. With applets this would be virtually impossible because of Java security restrictions. However, servlets are restricted only by the file system on which they reside. Therefore, if we make the database or flat file available to the servlet, we enable the servlet to talk to the file, get the recipe, and pass it back as an HTML file.

Let's say we have a recipe for a pumpkin-flavored margarita located on our local disk, already in HTML format. We want to get that file, and return it to the requester. We should setup our return document first exactly as we have before. We then need to open and echo the file to our docOutput stream:

```java
public class PumpkinServlet extends GenericServlet
{
    public void service(
        ServletRequest servletRequest,
        ServletResponse servletResponse
    ) throws ServletException, IOException
    {
        // parse the request and get the parameters
        String recipeType =
            servletRequest.getParameter("recipe");

        // set up the response
        servletResponse.setContentType("text/html");

        // get the dynamic document's output stream
        OutputStream docOutput = new OutputStream(
            servletResponse.getOutputStream());

        // write the document
        if(recipeType.equals("seeds"))
        {
            // do all of the docOutput stuff for the seed
        }
        else if(recipeType.equals("pie"))
        {
            // do all of the docOutput stuff for the pie
        }
        else if(recipeType.equals("margarita"))
        {
            // first open the file
            FileInputStream margaritaFile =
                new FileInputStream("margarita");
```

```
        // now read the file line by line, echoing each line
        // to the HtmlPage
        while(margaritaFile != null)
        {
            Byte newByte = margaritaFile.getByte();
            …send the information to the HtmlPage…
        }
    }


    }
}
```

Making network calls

Let's suppose for a second that we have a CORBA server that is sitting out on the Internet and accepting recipes of all kinds from the general Web surfing public. Our pumpkin recipe servlet should be able to hook up to the CORBA server and get information from it as well.

Now suppose we have another recipe for a delicious pumpkin milkshake. This recipe is stored as a CORBA object. We need to retrieve the text containing the recipe from the object, known in the CORBA Naming Service as "MILKSHAKE," and stick it in our docOutput variable so that it can be returned to the HTTP client. We must first initialize the docOutput variable, content type, and Servlet-Response objects. Afterward, we may add our CORBA client code much as we did our file code in the previous section:

```
…
        else if(recipeType.equals("milkshake"))
        {
            // first create the CORBA object
            CORBA corbaObjects = new CORBA();
            MilkshakeServer milkshakeServer =
                corbaObjects.NamingService.find("MILKSHAKE");

            // now get the recipe from the object
            String recipe = milkshakeServer.getRecipe();

            // form an HTML document out of the result
            … do the HtmlPage stuff here …
        }
…
```

Servlet administration

So far we've created three different servlets, compiled them, and made sure they worked. Now, we need to make the Java Web Server aware of each servlet. Remember, normal HTTP requests come in from the clients, talk to the Java Web Server, and are then routed to a servlet if necessary. The Java Web Server administration tools shown in Figure 6-5 allow you to configure the Java Web Server itself as well as add new servlets on-the-fly. The key is to map each servlet onto an HTML file. When the client requests that HTML file, the Java Web Server automatically routes the request to a servlet.

Sections	Servlet Loading		
Log Out	**Servlet Name**	**Class Name**	**Class Loca**
Basic Configuration	proxy	sun.server.http.ProxyServlet	local
Proxy Configuration	bboard	BBoardServlet	local
Server Tuning	counter	Counter	local
Proxy Cache	fun	FunServlet	local
Virtual Hosts	simpleformservlet	SimpleFormServlet	local
Users			
Groups			
Access Control	Servlet Name:	pumpkin	
Resource Protection			
File Aliasing	Class Name:	PumpkinServlet	
Log Configuration	Class Location:	servlet/pumpkin/src/	
Servlet Aliasing			
Servlet Loading	Arguments:		
Mime Section	Load at Startup:	○ Yes ⊙ No	
Site Certificate			
		Add Delete	

Figure 6–5 Java Web Server administration tools.

By specifying the name of your servlet as it will appear to the browser and the Java class for the servlet, you can map the HTML file request that your Java Web Server will receive directly into your servlet. You might also want to specify the physical location of the servlet as well as the arguments upon startup. Servlets that can be loaded at startup are typically those servlets that are always active. Our pumpkin servlet is active only upon invocation. Servlets, like CORBA objects, can be activated automatically upon invocation, or, like RMI objects, can be activated "manually" (in reality, by the Web server itself, not by hand like RMI) upon startup.

ALERT: Because of the fluidity of the Java Web Server project, the screen grab in Figure 6-5 may not match the latest product. However, the functionality will remain the same.

Form servlets

The HTML syntax provides for several different kinds of checkboxes, buttons, and text fields inside of which you can enter data and pass it to a CGI script. Because Java Web Server is the long-awaited liberation from CGI, it needs to have mechanisms that support the passing of information from an HTML form to the servlet itself. One of the few additional modules supplied with the basic architecture is a `FormServlet`. The `FormServlet` provides a simple means to supply parameters to a servlet from a form.

Dynamic documents overview

Now we've shown how servlets can be made to create documents dynamically and supplant the universal acceptance of a Web browser. What if we were able to take the power of IDL or RMI solutions and bring them to the Web as well? Servlets allow us to merge the server-side programming ability of the Java Web server with the widespread acceptance of tools such as CORBA or Java RMI.

Multi-Purpose Servers

What we've created so far is the Java code for a dynamic HTTP server. As we've seen, the server routes requests from normal HTTP clients to Java servlets that return HTTP-conformant requests. We've also created several Java servers that promote the distributed object paradigm. What if we were able to create a Java server that was a servlet at the same time that it was a CORBA server?

What servlets give you is the ability to access your servers in many different ways. Today, if a business is a CORBA shop and chooses to implement all of their distributed processing using an ORB, they will often have to create another component altogether to allow web-based clients to access their data. In the three-tier model, this means that the middle tier has several objects, all handling multiple types of requests and translating them into data storage and retrieval actions.

By incorporating a servlet alongside a CORBA or RMI server, the server can accept web requests directly. Once again, the determination of which approach you may wish to take could end up being a philosophical one. By splitting the

Web server component from the distributed object server as shown in Figure 6-6, you can achieve a highly modular middle tier. If the Web server has a bug, you can swap in a new servlet without affecting the rest of the system.

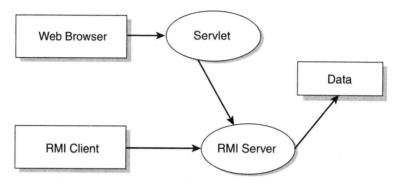

Figure 6–6 Servlets calling RMI objects directly.

However, if performance and a fast development cycle are at a premium, combining the servlet with the object server (see Figure 6-7) may be an excellent solution. By keeping redundancy to a limit you can speed up the time it takes to deploy a new server. Administration of your combined object system may be easier simply because there are fewer parts that can go wrong.

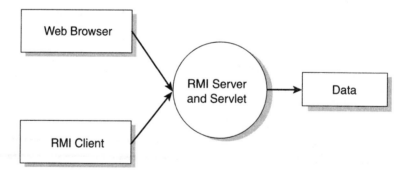
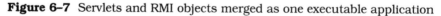

Figure 6–7 Servlets and RMI objects merged as one executable application

Client invocations

The actual client invocations on a multi-purpose server could be from either a Java Web Server via HTTP requests, or from a CORBA client itself. The CORBA client could invoke on a servlet that is simultaneously accepting HTTP requests. The beauty of this is that the servlet is a CORBA object in a CORBA namespace. Because of this, the servlet can provide fast turnaround for dynamic documents based on its own internal CORBA state. Whereas splitting the servlet from the server would force the servlet to make an additional CORBA invocation, combining them saves the expense of needless CORBA communication.

Server architecture

Actually designing the CORBA servlet is pretty simple. We will use the pumpkin example from the previous section and wrap a CORBA object around it. The IDL for the CORBA portion of our server is as follows:

```
interface PumpkinServer
{
    string getRecipe(
        string recipeType);
}
```

Notice how we can specify the type of recipe we want just as if it were sent via the HTTP request. Once the IDL is created, we generate code as we did in Chapter 3, "Java IDL: Interface Definition Language," namely the Skeleton and associated helper classes. We will then need to create the implementation file as follows:

```
public class PumpkinServerImpl implements PumpkinServerServant
{
    public PumpkinServerImpl()
    {
    }

    public String getRecipe(
        String recipeType
    )
    {
        getRecipeFor(recipeType);
    }
}
```

With the implementation completed, we need to modify the PumpkinServlet object to incorporate the CORBA functionality. We do so in the init method of the servlet. This allows us to ready the CORBA mechanisms to send and receive invocations.

```
public class PumpkinServlet extends GenericServlet
{
    public void init()
```

```
    {
        // link up with the ORB
        corba = new CORBA();

        // create the servant class
        PumpkinServerImpl pumpkinImpl = new PumpkinServerImpl();

        // create the container class
        pumpkinRef = PumpkinServerSkeleton.createRef(
            corba.getORB(), pumpkinImpl);

        // bind this server to the Naming Service
        corba.rebind("Pumpkin", pumpkinRef);
    }

    public void service(
        ServletRequest servletRequest,
        ServletResponse servletResponse
    ) throws ServletException, IOException
    {
        … same as before …
    }
}
```

What we have now is a working servlet that is accessible via the Web page as well as a working CORBA server that is ready to be invoked upon by other CORBA clients. While the same thing could be accomplished as in Chapter 3, the functionality of the CORBA server is provided in the `PumpkinServerImpl` object, while the `PumpkinServlet` object merely starts the `PumpkinServerImpl` object up and gives it a container in which to reside.

Summary

Servlets are a fantastic way to bring the ease of use and power of the Java language to the Web servers that are so ubiquitous today. Rather than creating a hacked solution that adds complexity to your existing software development process, why not merge the Web server with Java? The Java Web Server is a Web server in its own right, meaning that the ability to access static documents is definitely not lost. However, with a little additional work, you can create executable content for your Web pages and begin to truly harness the power of the Internet by making it a place where applications are run, not simply downloaded.

Once you create these fancy communication objects, you need a way to package them together and publish them to the world. In so doing, you can reuse your own work as well as let others take a look at your brilliance. Java provides a great means to put objects together with its Beans technology. Beans allows you to group objects under one umbrella and distribute them to others.

CHAPTER 7

Component Models

Java Beans

Using Beans

ActiveX Technologies

OpenDoc

Java Beans

Java Beans, ActiveX, and OpenDoc support the notion of an application component model. A component model enables several different kinds of programmer parts to work together. In the Internet world, we refer to everything from Java applets to parts that directly interface to databases or desktop applications as components that we can reuse. By developing reusable components, you can preserve the effort you place into software development by packaging them in modules that you can publish to others.

A "Bean" is a component made up of several other objects. By putting them all in one place, with a well-defined interface to the group, you can give them out to others to reuse. Someday soon, rather than creating a clock application for your Java applications, you will grab a clock "bean" and simply shove it in your application. Beans brings object-oriented programming and Java into the next big wave of computing: components.

Component Models

As an example of a component model, think of your car, which is a complex machine with several different parts. Because it relies on each of these parts in order to function properly as a car, it requires a component model to enable the engine, brakes, turn signals, and cup holders to work together. Without a component model, your car would be a disorganized collection of things that vaguely accomplish a task. The automotive geniuses behind the BMW Z3 convertible surely understood the interaction between the different design elements of the car.

For example, to add a convertible top, they had to improve the body of the car itself in order to increase the stability of the vehicle. In much the same manner, Beans applications take into account the needs of each component (see Figure 7-1).

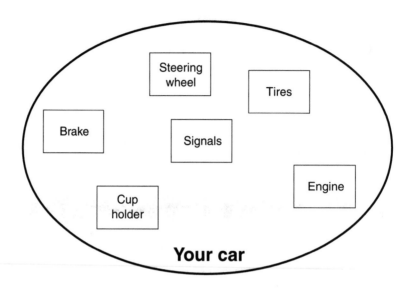

Figure 7–1 Your car is composed of several different components. Your car, in turn, is a component that can be reused by others.

Component models are not necessarily examples of network programming. Instead, component models provide a means to assemble several networked components under one umbrella. One of the components in a large application may be a network component in charge of talking to remote objects. When you group it with other non-networked objects, that one component makes all of the components networked.

The competition

Microsoft's ActiveX and Sun's Java Beans are component models competing for Internet parts. Today, the Abstract Window Toolkit includes a static component model that promotes interaction between parts within the same applet or application. The AWT does not address the issue of multiple different kinds of Internet parts within the same page. Instead it defines interaction between AWT components only within an applet or application.

Apple Computer is a late entry into the Internet Component Model sweepstakes. Apple's OpenDoc technology eventually will be folded directly into Java Beans, so in the end two component models will arise and compete. Apple and Sun's collaboration extends to all aspects of network computing. Their alliance brings the power of Sun's Solaris Operating System, clearly superior to Windows NT, to the ease-of-use and application base of the Apple Macintosh. As the two platforms begin to interoperate seamlessly, the component model that drives their respective applications will become more and more important to the efficiency with which they network.

In this chapter, we discuss component models with Java Beans. We devote a later section to the differences between ActiveX, OpenDoc, and Beans. Eventually, one component model will emerge, but for now we concentrate on Beans. As the owner and progenitor of the Java language, Sun Microsystems has a competitive edge over Microsoft in the Internet arena. While Microsoft will continue to dominate the desktop, new Java technology will emerge the fastest and the most reliably from Sun.

Overview of Beans Component Model

In conceptual terms, a component model is a definition of how different parts interact with one another within one granular space. Translating the big picture definition into Java APIs is a more difficult task. A component model becomes both an overall architectural plan as well individual APIs that enable programmers to realize the vision.

Every component, referred to as a "Bean," should provide each of five different services designed to promote interaction between one another:

1. Interface Publishing
2. Event Handling
3. Persistence
4. Layout
5. Builder Support

Interface publishing

In order to enable one Bean to make another Bean do something, the Beans must have a published and pre-defined set of routines. When several Beans join together, they form a *Java Beans application*. In order for a Bean application to function properly, its constituent Beans must be able to communicate with one another.

The component Beans must publish their interfaces to the container Bean application so that any Bean within the application can acquire a reference to a component. Other components may then invoke the Bean and use it as it were intended. For example, if we were to create a Java Beans application to catalog all of our toys, we would create several individual Beans then link them together. One of the Beans may talk to a database that keeps track of our toys, another Bean may display and handle a user interface. In order for the user interface Bean to get to the database, it must use the database Bean. The database Bean must publish an interface to itself in order for it to be used.

Event handling

In the AWT, you can create a user interface with a button and a text area. When the button gets an event, it can trigger a consequential event in the text area. The end result is that the event is handled and passed onto another object.

Similarly, Beans must be able to pass events to one another. Beans applications need not be unified under one user interface. In fact, a Beans application may have several different applets contained within it, all of which have their own user interface. When something happens in one applet, the other applets may want to know. In our toy catalog example, we want to have two different applets. One applet lists every toy, the other displays a picture of each toy. If you select "Buzz Lightyear Action Figure" from the list, the list sends a message to the display applet to show a picture of the toy. We can model our Beans application to use each applet and unify them.

In much the same way, Beans components can be made to talk to one another and trigger events in each other. The powerful component model on top of which Beans was developed promotes the idea of object separation. Remember, you are really creating separate objects that could exist in their own right without a Beans container. The fact that you are combining each of these separate applets under one roof says a great deal about the highly object-oriented nature of the Java language.

Persistence

As we discussed in our Chapter 1 section on Object Serialization, persistence of objects is a very important topic. Persistence moves us from a session-based paradigm in which objects are started, exist for a little while, and then disappear, to a lifecycle-based paradigm in which objects are started and exist for a little while. This time, however, instead of the object disappearing off the face of the silicon, it is saved, restored, and allowed to exist again afterwards. Java Beans supports persistence primarily through object serialization. You may, however, attach a JDBC application to your Bean and store your Bean on a database. Just as with serialization, Java Beans will let you handle your own persistence if you choose not to take advantage of its own brand of object storage.

Layout

Earlier we spoke of Beans applications whose components each have their own distinct user interfaces. The Beans framework provides a set of routines to effectively lay out the various parts so that they don't step on one another. The layout mechanisms also allow the sharing of resources. Let's say your two different user interfaces both used a fancy picture button. You could share the picture button class across each component, saving download time and improving the efficiency of your application. Beans applications assist a great deal in improving the performance of large applications.

The Beans layout mechanisms allow you to position your Beans in rectangular areas. The programmer is left to decide whether the regions overlap or maintain a discrete layout space. Beans makes no effort to provide a complex layout manager, choosing instead to implement the standard Java managers.

Builder support

One other area in which you might want to invest significant design time is in builder support. Chances are that your Bean could be reused by other programmers who desire to take advantage of your hard work. Packaging your Beans in such a way that GUI builder applications can access them may be beneficial to you.

A GUI builder could obtain a catalog of methods used by your Bean application, as well as the proper means to access each individual Bean. That way, the builder can graphically represent the Beans application, and provide connections into the application from outside. The end result is that your Beans application could be used by another application.

Distributed Beans

Because Beans are written in Java, they are fully portable and can take complete advantage of the write-once-run-anywhere principle. Furthermore, Java Beans ensure that no matter how small your constituent components, it will not in any way overburden them. This allows full distribution of applets and applications wrapped in Java Beans containers. You will not have to make trade-off decisions on whether to use Beans or not and you will have complete freedom to use Java Beans.

Java Beans also does not interfere with the communication mechanisms we described earlier in this book. It exists peacefully alongside both Java IDL and Java RMI. Just because your applications want to communicate with the network does not mean Java Beans is off-limits to you.

Why use Beans?

If you've ever tried to create a series of applications on a single Web page, no doubt you've discovered the limitations of the applets themselves. Your applets cannot communicate with one another, and an event in one cannot trigger an event in another. Java Beans proposes a solution to that limitation. Beans at its essence is nothing more than a giant Tupperware container for applets and applications. By sticking all of your applets within the same container, you can effectively have them communicate freely, so long as they do not leave the container.

But, Beans adds several more capabilities than does a simple container class, many of which we've discussed in this section. Java Beans is Java; Java Beans is easy; Java Beans is fun. Most importantly, however, Java Beans is a flexible way to group Java applets and applications under a unified umbrella. We can only wish the United Nations could work as well!

So, What's the difference?

Java Beans is a flexible, platform independent alternative to ActiveX technologies from Microsoft. While Microsoft claims platform independence, they do so solely for client applications. Currently, only Microsoft's Internet Explorer supports ActiveX. As such, Microsoft has made IE available for a multitude of platforms, beginning with Windows 95 and Windows NT. Nevertheless, the server-side components of ActiveX can run only on Windows servers.

One thing is clear: *Java Beans allows server-side components on any platform, ActiveX does not.*

Once again, Microsoft has proposed what it calls an "open" solution, but it turns out to be a Microsoft-specific solution. This is contrary to the spirit of the Internet, and Microsoft will be called on it. Java Beans is the alternative, and it isn't a bad one at that.

In addition, because ActiveX controls are nothing but Windows binaries that have free reign over the local machine, it is quite simple to mask a virus or other pernicious programs inside it. To make matters even worse, ActiveX controls are dowloaded automatically by Internet Explorer, so there's a chance that you won't even know that one is being sent over the wire to your computer. To counteract this, Microsoft has proposed a technology called Authenticode that will allow you to pre-determine from which sites you will accept ActiveX controls. However, as we will see in Chapter 11, computer security is never a guarantee.

On the other hand, Java Beans that are assembled to form an applet are still restricted by the Java "sandbox" that prevents it from accessing any files on the local machine. Because of this restriction, Java Beans can be regarded as a secure technology.

Java Beans

Java Beans provides a ton of functionality at a very little price. When you use the Java-endorsed component model, you are ensured a language compliant implementation that does nothing to violate the spirit of the Java language. The same security model, application interaction model, and event model are used throughout Java Beans.

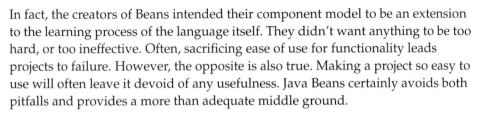
In fact, the creators of Beans intended their component model to be an extension to the learning process of the language itself. They didn't want anything to be too hard, or too ineffective. Often, sacrificing ease of use for functionality leads projects to failure. However, the opposite is also true. Making a project so easy to use will often leave it devoid of any usefulness. Java Beans certainly avoids both pitfalls and provides a more than adequate middle ground.

Component interaction

As you can see in Figure 7-2, a given Java Bean supports three levels of interaction. Each Bean exhibits certain properties, can be invoked by several methods, and can, in turn, trigger events in other beans. It is this component interaction model that lends Beans its great flexibility. Simply by publishing the APIs for itself, a given Bean can tell every other Bean about its properties and methods, and trigger events based on other published APIs and invocations on its own method library.

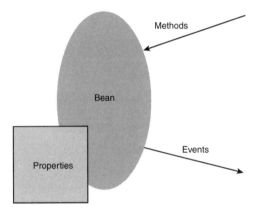

Figure 7–2 Each Java Bean supports three interaction levels: properties, methods, and events.

Properties are discussed in detail a bit later, but they are essentially the internal representation of a Bean. Imagine that you have a giant vase filled with an assortment of roses, baby's breath, and ferns. Your vase is the Bean in this instance, because it contains other elements. Does your Bean keep track of every kind of flower in a vase? How many of each flower is in a vase? Properties are the basic quality of a Java Bean, and in our case every flower within the vase itself.

Methods are those things that can be done to a Bean. Can you add flowers or remove flowers from a vase? Can your vase also be filled with water? In that case, water is a property, and filling the water is a method, or something that is done to one of the properties.

Let's say your flowers smell beautiful! They give off a wonderful scent that every-one appreciates. These are events triggered by the vase and pushed out to the rest of the Beans within the same component model.

Network communication

A key element of effective distributed design is deciding where to split the local computation and the remote computation. When we created the Internet Calendar Manager discussed in the previous chapters, we had to determine where we were going to split the local processing of appointments from the remote storage of the appointments. We decided to create the Network module that would handle that situation for us. The module receives raw data from the network and translates it into usable data structures for the rest of the application (see Figure 7-3).

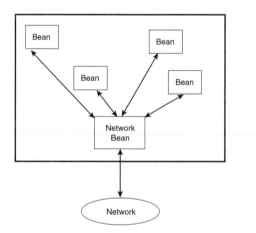

Figure 7–3 A set of Beans can use a network Bean to connect to the network.

We recommend that Java Beans be used in much the same way for networked communication. Create a Bean whose sole purpose is to funnel information to and from remote processes. With this kind of modular design, your Bean can act as a go-between to network resources, saving precious computation cycles.

As of now, the Java Bean product road map calls for Java IDL, Java RMI, and JDBC support. Further revisions of the Beans specification will implement other network mechanisms as they are created. We have chosen to implement the Java IDL version of the featured application for this chapter.

 TIP: Recent partnerships between JavaSoft and Apple Computer lends Beans the ability to link documents created in Apple's OpenDoc standard to a Java Bean. In this manner, Java Beans will be able to manipulate network document resources in much the same manner as it can now talk to standard network sockets, RMI, IDL, and OLE components.

User interface issues

Java Beans was designed with the idea that they can be integrated very easily into GUI builders. GUI builders need access to each component that they play with, so the Beans APIs were designed accordingly. Every standard Bean supports the notion of *introspection*. Each Bean can be looked into, in much the same way we could look into a window (see Figure 7-4). We don't see the whole picture, and we certainly don't see what exactly is going on, but we can see a snapshot of what is possible. Introspection enables us to see the APIs for a given Bean, and more importantly, for an application builder of some kind to plug into the Bean and hook other components to it.

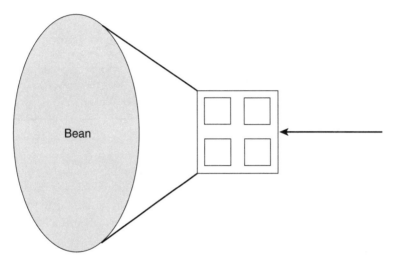

Figure 7–4 The notion of introspection supported by each standard Bean enables GUI builders to see inside the Bean and access components needed.

TIP: Beans also supports Uniform Data Transfer (UDT) between components. The UDT mechanism alluded to in the Beans specification declares that data can be transferred between Beans in a variety of easy-to-implement ways. Choosing between Drag-and-Drop, Cut-and-Paste, Keyboard, and other methods is a matter of Bean implementation.

Java Beans also supports the notion of GUI merging. With GUI merging, child Beans can percolate their user interface properties up to the parent. In so doing, the parent Bean can set up a consistent look and feel for a GUI, and child Beans can add components to the GUI. The classic example is with a menu bar. The parent Bean can provide the general appearance of the bar, while its child Beans can add entries to the bar (File, Edit, View, and so forth) This way, the child Bean has total and complete control over what a GUI is, while the parent sets a general policy for what it will look like.

Persistence

Beans should also be able to save their internal properties between invocations. For example, if we were to instantiate a Bean, change its state, then shut the Bean down, in some instances we want the data we changed to return when the Bean is started up again. This is referred to as a *persistent state;* in other words, the values are not reinitialized every time.

TIP: Persistence can be implemented in several ways, but in the end you have the choice between automatic, Bean-provided persistence, or managing your own persistence. When you manage your own persistence, more than likely you will want to do so using the network. Your Bean can store its internal properties on a remote database, and you can access and store the changes using JDBC. Or, you may want to use RMI or IDL to handle your storage techniques.

Events

Java Beans provides an AWT-friendly event notification mechanism. If an event is triggered in your Bean, you should be able to pass that event on to other Beans in your component model. Sometimes events will come in over a network, and in these cases you should handle them as if they were coming from a local Bean.

Properties

Because Beans are nothing more than Java classes, you can create whatever member variables you desire. Furthermore, Beans can contain other Beans within them. In our earlier vase of flowers example, our vase bean could very easily be contained within a "living room" Bean, which could be contained within a "house" Bean, which could be contained within…well, you get the picture.

Beans in a nutshell

Beans enable you to harness the power of object-oriented programming and take it to a new level. Instead of publishing libraries of classes, you can now publish entire objects that can be used, abused, imported, delegated, or whatever you choose to do with them. Beans could just as easily be applications in their own right, but instead are there to help you.

This book only glosses the surface of what Beans can do for you. Trust us, there will be much, much more written on this fascinating and exciting topic. To whet your appetite, however, let's create a simple Bean that models our National Pastime.

Using Java Beans

The basic principle underlying Bean development is that you create the constituent parts just as you normally would. Every applet, every document, every component in the Beans application should be developed, tested, and ready by the time you get to the Beans stage. Once the components are available, you can use one of two methods to bring them together. As we mentioned earlier in this chapter, the Beans specification calls for easy manipulation of a Bean by a GUI builder. The GUI builder can connect beans together using a simple drag-and-drop type interface. We will discuss that scenario in a moment.

Creating a Java Beans application

Before a Java Beans application can be developed and deployed, you must first understand the underlying principles of the Beans. Every application consists of the various components as well as two critical base objects that handle the flow and storage of information.

Events are exchanged among Beans through the `EventListener` and `Event-Source` objects. The `EventListener` object is created to look for certain kinds of events within the application. Each Bean creates a listener for itself if it wants to receive events. In essence, it *subscribes* to a list of specific events. A Bean may also create for itself an `EventSource` to create and *publish* events for other Beans within the application. Figure 7-5 shows how events can be triggered between beans.

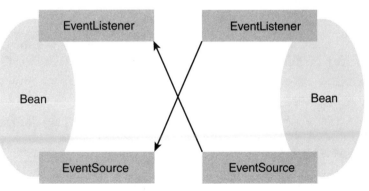

Figure 7-5 An EventSource can trigger events to EventListeners tuned in to the proper event

A simple example

If we were going to model a baseball game, we would first need to create a container for the whole game to fit inside. For simplicity's sake, we will include only a pitcher and a catcher. Our pitcher object will throw an event, similar to a baseball, and the catcher object will catch the event later on.

Our baseball game must be configured to listen for events fired by the pitcher. We will have to create an interface called `PitchListener` for the pitches to be sent to. The `PitchListener` object is a user-created extension to the AWT standard `EventListener` object. We simply add a method called `throwPitch` to the `PitchListener`. Our `BaseballGame` object will implement `throwPitch`, but we will define the `PitchListener` interface here and implement the `throwPitch` method when we are ready to connect all of our beans.

```
public interface PitchListener extends EventListener
{
    public void throwPitch(
        String pitch);
}
```

We must then create a `BaseballGame` object that will listen to all of the other objects, and fire the events that it catches to each of its constituent components. In order for it to listen in on the other objects, it must implement the `PitchListener` base class.

```
public class BaseballGame extends Applet implements PitchListener
{
    Pitcher pitcher;
    Catcher catcher;
}
```

Now, the `Pitcher` and `Catcher` must be created within the `BaseballGame` applet. We will do this as we normally would for any other Java object.

```
public class BaseballGame extends Applet implements PitchListener
{
    Pitcher pitcher;
    Catcher catcher;

    BaseballGame()
    {
```

```
    // set our layout
    setLayout(new GridLayout(2, 1));

    // create the pitcher
    pitcher = new Pitcher();
    add(pitcher);

    // create the catcher
    catcher = new Catcher();
    add(catcher);
    }
}
```

Finally, we must add the BaseballGame object as a listener of the Pitcher object. Remember, in our simple game of catch, the pitcher is going to fire events and the catcher is going to do nothing but receive them.

```
public class BaseballGame extends Applet implements PitchListener
{
    Pitcher pitcher;
    Catcher catcher;

    BaseballGame()
    {
        // set our layout
        setLayout(new GridLayout(2, 1));

        // create the pitcher
        pitcher = new Pitcher();
        add(pitcher);

        // create the catcher
        catcher = new Catcher();
        add(catcher);

        // add the game as a listener to the pitcher
        pitcher.addListener(this);
    }
}
```

Instantiating components

You create the `EventSource` and `EventListener` objects within a component object much as you would a `String` or `Hashtable`. They are merely member variables within the object. The difference is that they are fully capable of talking outside the component to the Java Beans container application. So, our constructor for the `Pitcher` object will initialize the data as well as create the event objects:

```java
public class Pitcher implements Serializable
{
    private Vector myListeners;

    private Button fastball;
    private Button curveball;
    private Button slider;

    Pitcher()
    {
        // set our layout
        setLayout(new GridLayout(1, 3));

        // initialize the buttons
        fastball = new Button("fastball");
        add(fastball);
        curveball = new Button("curveball");
        add(curveball);
        slider = new Button("slider");
        add(slider);

        // create the listener vector
        myListeners = new Vector();
    }
}
```

The pitcher must implement methods to add and remove listeners.

```java
public class Pitcher implements Serializable
{
    private Vector myListeners;
```

```
    private Button fastball;
    private Button curveball;
    private Button slider;

    Pitcher()
    {
        // set our layout
        setLayout(new GridLayout(1, 3));

        // initialize the buttons
        fastball = new Button("fastball");
        add(fastball);
        curveball = new Button("curveball");
        add(curveball);
        slider = new Button("slider");
        add(slider);

        // create the listener vector
        myListeners = new Vector();
    }

    public void addListener(
        PitchListener listener
    )
    {
        myListeners.addElement(listeners);
    }

    public void removeListener(
        PitchListener listener
    )
    {
        myListeners.removeElement(listeners);
    }
}
```

And finally, we must add code from within our event handler to pass the event back up to all of our listener objects. Remember, our listener is a PitchListener object, and we need to cast our vector result to it.

```java
public class Pitcher implements Serializable
{
    private Vector myListeners;

    private Button fastball;
    private Button curveball;
    private Button slider;

    Pitcher()
    {
        // set our layout
        setLayout(new GridLayout(1, 3));

        // initialize the buttons
        fastball = new Button("fastball");
        add(fastball);
        curveball = new Button("curveball");
        add(curveball);
        slider = new Button("slider");
        add(slider);

        // create the listener vector
        myListeners = new Vector();
    }

    public void addListener(
        PitchListener listener
    )
    {
        myListeners.addElement(listeners);
    }

    public void removeListener(
        PitchListener listener
    )
    {
        myListeners.removeElement(listeners);
    }
    public boolean action(
        Event evt,
        Object obj
```

```
    )
    {
        // do this only for button events
        if(evt.target instanceof Button)
        {
            // create a pitch to throw based on the button pressed
            String p = new String((String) obj);

            // go through each vector and push the event up
            for(int x = 0; x < myListeners.size(); x++)
            {
                PitchListener listener =
                    (PitchListener) myListeners.elementAt(x);

                listener.throwPitch(p);
            }
        }
    }
}
```

The catcher object is nothing more than a normal Java object. It need not implement any special Beans code. Rather, the listener will push events onto the catcher as if they were normal button events. The catcher will then respond to them accordingly.

```
public class Catcher extends Panel
{
    TextArea pitchArea;

    Catcher()
    {
        // set our layout
        setLayout(new GridLayout(1, 1));

        // create the area where the catcher tells us what he got
        pitchArea = new TextArea();
        add(pitchArea);
    }

    public void catchPitch(
        String pitch
```

```
    )
    {
        pitchArea.addText("And the pitch is a ... " + pitch);
    }
}
```

When the listener calls the catcher's `catchPitch` method, the catcher can then do something with it. Our hierarchical structure could very easily be implemented without the Beans infrastructure. But, once again, this is the beauty of Beans as opposed to ActiveX or OpenDoc. *Java Beans is Java.*

Connecting Beans events

Now that we've created a BaseballGame container, `Catcher` bean, and `Pitcher` bean, we need to connect them so that events fired by the `Pitcher` are caught by the `BaseballGame` and passed down to the `Catcher`. In fact, we need only call `catchPitch` on our `Catcher` instance within the `BaseballGame` object:

```
public class BaseballGame extends Applet implements PitchListener
{
    Pitcher pitcher;
    Catcher catcher;

    BaseballGame()
    {
        // set our layout
        setLayout(new GridLayout(2, 1));

        // create the pitcher
        pitcher = new Pitcher();
        add(pitcher);

        // create the catcher
        catcher = new Catcher();
        add(catcher);

        // add the game as a listener to the pitcher
        pitcher.addListener(this);
    }

    public void throwPitch(
        String newPitch
```

```
    )
    {
        // tell the catcher to catch my pitch
        catcher.catchPitch(newPitch);
    }
}
```

So in the end, we have three networked components talking to one another using the Java Beans infrastructure, as shown in Figure 7-6.

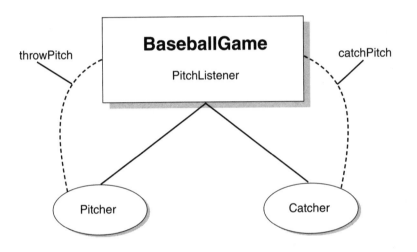

Figure 7–6 Component interaction is simple using the Java Beans infrastructure.

Bean introspection

As we have mentioned, introspection is the ability of your Bean to be probed from another outside, or introspecting, class. The introspecting class surveys the contents of your Bean and keeps track of what services are available within it. After introspecting a Bean, the outside class can then go about creating its own methods to interface with your Bean. Typically, introspection will occur on behalf of object builders that will know nothing about the implementation of a Bean, only being able to survey its internals.

These GUI builders could have a suite of Beans already existing locally. It can then allow you to create your own Bean by tying in the functionality of other Beans. This can be displayed graphically. GUI builders that take full advantage of Beans introspection will soon be available. In addition, the Bean Developer's Kit will include all the tools and Java classes necessary to develop your own Beans and Beans-based applications.

Summary

The magical world of Java Beans is only the beginning of the "component race." As corporations look to streamline the all-important software development process, they will look more and more to the theories of object-oriented programming and component models. Java Beans is but one of the many component models seeking the hearts and minds of Software Engineers and their bosses. Not to be left out of the software development race, Microsoft has its own answer, which is highlighted in the next section.

ActiveX

Let's say you want to create a Web page with your company's sales figures on it. Your sales department maintains all of its information in a Microsoft Excel spreadsheet. Rather than creating a graph in some kind of paint program and putting a GIF on your Web page, you want to do something dynamic, something that requires no additional effort on your part. If you remember anything from this book, remember that anything and everything is possible in the Internet era.

What is ActiveX?

ActiveX isn't exactly a new product from Microsoft. In fact, it's been around for several years under different monikers and within different parts of the Microsoft Corporation's organizational structure. ActiveX controls, for example, are nothing more than Visual Basic's OCX controls. Nevertheless, the hype and hoopla surrounding ActiveX's "introduction" is very new, and is causing quite a stir within the Internet community.

Today, you more than likely fiddle with your Microsoft Word documents, saving them on your local disk. You create and link in some Excel spreadsheets to illustrate points within your Word documents. You might even link the whole shebang into a PowerPoint presentation. This is called Object Linking and Embedding, or OLE. The object part refers to each component of your presentation, everything from the Word document to the Excel spreadsheet. Objects are linked into other Microsoft products and embedded within the documents, presentations, spreadsheets, or databases that you create. This model is illustrated in Figure 7-7.

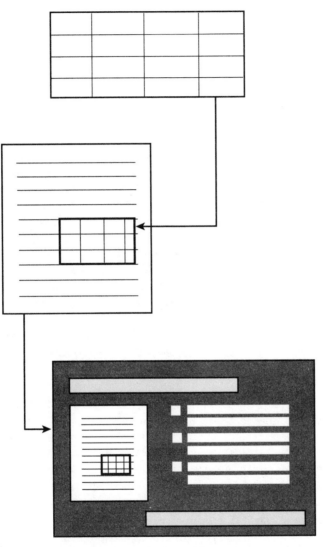

Figure 7–7 Today, you can link various Microsoft components into one "package" using Object Linking and Embedding, or OLE.

ActiveX takes everything one step further. Let's get back to our original proposal. Our fictitious company wants to stick the data within the spreadsheet onto the Web without any effort. ActiveX let's you link and embed objects into *Web pages*. Whoa! As shown in Figure 7-8, your Web page will now display spreadsheets, graphs, and data created within Excel. The actual living, breathing spreadsheet is inside your Web browser! Pretty cool, huh?

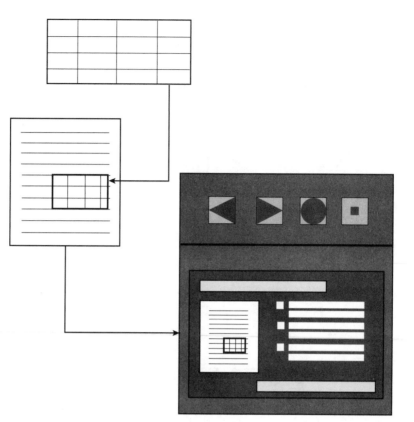

Figure 7–8 ActiveX does for Web pages what OLE did for desktop applications.

Well, there's one catch. This only works on Microsoft Windows machines. Yes, for better or worse, the operating system from Redmond is required to view ActiveX documents. Moreover, ActiveX works only within Microsoft's own proprietary browser, Internet Explorer. Granted, Microsoft provides an ActiveX plugin for its arch rival, Netscape Navigator, but you can't really expect them to put the same effort and functionality into a Netscape version, can you?

To make things even more Redmond-centric, ActiveX documents that embed Microsoft objects do so in a pretty clever manner. The object that is inside the Web page is quite literally an Excel spreadsheet. It's just a tad bit smaller than a usual Excel spreadsheet. Because that Excel object is a real Excel spreadsheet, it actually uses the Microsoft Excel executable program to drive it. This means that in order to see the object, you must have Microsoft Excel installed on your system so that the Web browser can use the Excel executable. That's right, go out and buy some more Microsoft software. Hmmm.

The Microsoft "vision"

Clearly, Microsoft wants to rule the world. But Microsoft isn't as big as it is because of its operating system. No, the name of the operating system game is *applications*. Without useful, cost-effective, time-saving applications, an operating system would be worthless. Ask IBM. OS/2 is a great operating system, mostly stable, more so than Windows ever has been. But, OS/2 has absolutely minimal applications. Windows 95 has more applications than you can count. Everyone, from weekend hacker to mega-corporation, develops applications for Windows 95 first.

Microsoft doesn't only make an operating system, it makes countless applications for the operating system. Applications created by Microsoft, ranging from Microsoft Word to Monster Truck Madness, are guaranteed to run under Windows. In the end, Microsoft Windows sells 40 million copies not because it is some kind of cultural phenomenon on par with Metallica, but because it creates applications that people want to buy. After all, given the choice between a text editor and Microsoft Word, any moonlighting Java author would choose Word in a heartbeat.

So, Microsoft does not want to lose its grip on its application monopoly. With that in mind, they brought us ActiveX—a means to embed its several applications directly within the Internet. Thus, Microsoft's vision seems to be to make money using the Internet by selling more and more copies of its applications.

ActiveX controls

An ActiveX control is a component in the same sense that a Java Bean is. Where we created Java Beans to enable different parts of a dynamic document to talk and work with one another seamlessly, we can use ActiveX controls. Both Beans and ActiveX communicate with OLE, enabling Java Beans to do the same fancy document editing that ActiveX allows. Nevertheless, with Java Beans six months behind ActiveX, Microsoft finally has what it has wanted for the past year: the chance to be *ahead* in the Internet race.

With ActiveX, your controls are free to make several computations so long as it resides within an ActiveX *container*. A container is the boundary of the ActiveX control. Each control needs a parent OLE component. Microsoft's Internet Explorer serves as an ActiveX container. With Microsoft's plugin, Netscape Navigator also acts as an ActiveX container.

Once the ActiveX control is contained, it can begin to go about its work in the same way that a Java Bean does. For example, I could have several ActiveX controls embedded within the same Web page. One could be a Java applet, one could be a spreadsheet, and another could be an ActiveX button. The spreadsheet and button could be made to talk the OLE protocol, enabling each of them to compute and exchange data as they wish. The Java applet could gather the information and, because it is fully capable of talking TCP/IP, send the information across the Internet.

ActiveX controls can also start the applications that created them. For example, we created a spreadsheet using OLE, then stuck it inside an ActiveX control. When you view the ActiveX control inside your Web page, or directly on your ActiveX-enabled desktop, the native application will literally be running within the confines of the control.

ActiveX and Java

Part of the hype surrounding ActiveX concerns the future of Java. Anyone who has ever used the language (and we assume that because you are reading this book, you fall in that category) will agree that it is easy, fun, and exciting to finally enjoy programming again. The alternatives of the past (namely C++ and C) were frustrating, difficult, and involved a very steep learning curve. When Java came around with its promise to make computers fun and easy again, most people jumped on the bandwagon instantly.

Sun, in a rare stroke of marketing brilliance, made Java freely available to anyone who wanted it. As a result, in the course of the past few years, Java has become the de facto Internet programming language. ActiveX is not a programming language, it is a component model. Therefore, ActiveX does not threaten Java, it actually improves it! While it may seem illogical that Microsoft may improve a Sun product, it brings credibility to a language perceived by intellectuals as a "toy language."

ActiveX and Java form a very unusual partnership, kind of like the Redskins and the Cowboys merging to form one team. Nevertheless, ActiveX and Java are complimentary technologies. When Java Beans begins to get a foothold, then we'll see the real battle take place.

Summary

ActiveX and Java Beans will compete toe-to-toe for a space on every developer's platform. While Microsoft locks you into the Windows environment, Beans is an open, more flexible Java-based alternative. While the "big two" of Microsoft and Sun Microsystems fight it out, an old war horse also wants to enter the component model sweepstakes. Apple has their own plans for component models, and with a typical Apple focus on usability, it, too, is worthy of mention.

OpenDoc and CyberDog

Remember Apple Computer? The same folks that brought you the Macintosh, then squandered their innovation, nearly went out of business, almost formed "SunApple" with Sun Microsystems, and now claims that they are still on the edge of computing has created what amounts to OLE's biggest competitor on the desktop. OpenDoc is another Internet component model, enabling you to contain several different kinds of documents on a Web page.

OpenDoc ships with all Macintosh systems, meaning Apple corners the market on a whopping eight percent of the desktop computing population. Yet, despite its sparse presence, OpenDoc is an innovative, exciting component model. Apple then used OpenDoc to create Cyberdog, a tool embedded within the Macintosh Operating System (MacOS). Cyberdog brings dynamic Internet documents to your Macintosh environment. For example, your ClarisWorks document on "The Pitfalls and Perils of Fishing in the Sahara" could not only embed an Internet Web site on the Sahara Desert within it, but also live video on your experiences while fishing in the Sahara. Note that you will now be able to prove that you caught that 50-foot bass.

OpenDoc components

So far, we've discussed ActiveX and Java Beans. OpenDoc is another flavor of the same brand of component models. Where OLE is to the Windows environment, OpenDoc exists to counter for the Macintosh. OpenDoc is a means to contain several documents on the Macintosh, integrate seamless messaging between those documents and applications, and by that token tie in the Internet to a document.

While third-party OpenDoc components are sparse and not yet available, the fact remains that OpenDoc is sort of like CORBA, an open standard going up against the proprietary and inferior OLE. As of today, CORBA is losing big to OLE simply because of the application base for OLE controls. Remember, what we are talking about are software components that can be linked and brought together to form an application.

Imagine you were to build your own word processor. Let's say that all you really need is a text edit region, a spell checker, and a bunch of file controls to save and load that file. Why go out and buy a $200 word processor from Microsoft when you can create one on your own. Simply go to a Web site, select a text edit component you like, select a spell checker for your language (Pig Latin, the future of conversation), and select a set of file controls for your platform. Click on "Purchase," and voila! You have yourself a downloadable word processor that you made all by yourself using OpenDoc, OLE, or CORBA.

In the end, this could be the future of software development. Moving from a product-based industry to a service-based industry is a theory that is not without its detractors. Microsoft likes to believe (and they may well be correct) that the consumer really does want a $200 word processor chock full of features. OpenDoc and CORBA proponents believe this is nonsense. Someone, somewhere will win, and the answer may be a hybrid of the two camps.

In any event, the nature of OpenDoc as a competitor to OLE is something worth noting. Eventually, OpenDoc and CORBA may form an unholy alliance to unseat OLE. OpenDoc components that are CORBA-aware could quite simply be the most important thing that could happen to propel the software industry into the service paradigm.

Cyberdog

The engineers at Apple recognized that OpenDoc is nothing without an application that uses it. Cyberdog takes OpenDoc one step further. Cyberdog is analogous to Java Beans and ActiveX in that it takes the component model, in this case OpenDoc, and morphs it into a ready-for-the-Internet component model.

Let's say you are modifying a document in an OpenDoc-enabled word processor such as ClarisWorks. From within Claris you can drag and drop Web sites. What you get is not an icon or a static symbol of the Web site, but a real, live, connected-to-the-Net Web site within your application. To understand what this means, step out of our current state of Web browsing. Today, we surf the Web and edit files in an entirely different location. Why can't Web sites be editable, and why can't our documents be Web sites?

Cyberdog enables you to take surfing the Web to new heights by embedding Web sites and Internet content (which could just as easily be a film clip from a remote server, an audio file from your best friend's computer, or even a live Chat session with the creator of the Lava Lamp) directly into your applications and documents.

Summary

The software war taking place between Apple, Sun, and Microsoft is one that can only benefit consumers. We, the programmer, will be able to build distributed object systems that adhere to an accepted component model. Our software users can benefit because their applications are developed faster, more reliably, using what is essentially Commercial Off The Shelf (COTS) parts. After all, Ford doesn't build a brand new battery for every model car it puts out. Why should software developers have to redo their work every time?

Now that we've explored the nuances of Java networking, component models, and the Java language, it's time to check out what else is going on in the world of Java. These are some of the esoteric, hilarious, off the wall, surprisingly useful applications being developed in this brave new world.

CHAPTER 8

What Others Are Up To!

Where Do We Go From Here?

The Networked
Java World

Much of what we have discussed in this book is of the "how to" genre. In this chapter, we take a different approach: From the "that's how" perspective, we take a good look at what else is going on out there.

Marimba, Inc. (`http://www.marimba.com/`) was formed about a year ago by some of the original architects of the Java language. Led by Kim Polese, the marketing genius who made Java "free" to the general public, they have put together a product that just may make the Web accessible to folks who don't know, or want to know, what "http colon slash slash" really is. Other companies, like Active Software and Netscape, are building entire frameworks for advanced networking with the Internet. Sometimes, these projects branch off the subject of Java, but all of them have a profound impact on the Internet, and therefore also on Java.

Finally, we will also discuss two Java initiatives that we have chosen to highlight briefly. Both of these special Java communication mechanisms address the issue of bringing legacy systems written prior to the Java revolution in other non-Java languages into the fold of your newer "Java-tized" applications.

Marimba

Bongo and Castanet are Marimba's two main products. Castanet is one of the hottest networking products to arrive in the Java revolution. It works quite simply. First, your client computer downloads something called a Castanet *tuner*. The tuner resides on your client machine and is always ready to accept transmissions or to send information back to a server. On the server side, the Castanet component is called a *transmitter*. The transmitter sends information back to your client applications. Client applications are referred to as *channels* and are developed with Bongo (see Figure 8-1). Do you get where we're going with this?

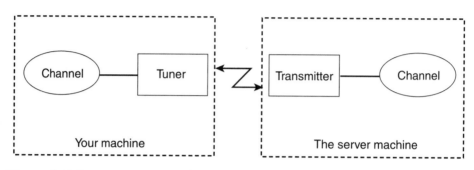

Figure 8-1 Castanet tuners and transmitters enable you to view channels.

Let's take a look at how our television operates. First, we install the television in our living room. Built into the television is a tuner that takes information from a transmitter across town and displays that information as channels. Do you have to know anything at all about how the transmitter works, how the television operates, or how the pixels get drawn on the screen? Nope, you just sit down with a Diet Coke in one hand, the clicker in the other, and surf the airwaves.

Castanet brings the television paradigm to the Internet. Now, instead of beer and chips during a football game, you can snack on Jolt and donuts whilst surfing the Net! All you have to do to experience this revolution in Internet transmission is visit the Marimba Web site at `http://www.marimba.com/` and download the tuner for your client. Then, sit back, relax, and surf to your heart's content!

How does it work?

Castanet is inherently language independent. It works on files, not application executables. Thus, when you download a new channel, it can be written in any language, and the tuner will simply execute it regardless. However, because Java is the only language with sufficient security to prevent the downloading of malicious files, Marimba has chosen to implement only Java at this time. As we mentioned, Castanet is composed of three major parts: the transmitter, the tuner, and channels.

Transmitter

Transmitters are streamlined additions to regular HTTP servers. As we discussed in Chapter 6, "The Java Web Server," HTTP servers do nothing more than serve static content. Transmitters are sort of like the Java Web Server in that they can serve dynamic content to Web clients. They are passive communicators, meaning they do not actively seek clients to download to; rather, they are contacted by tuners wishing to download channels. When transmitters are contacted by tuners, they make channels available for downloading.

One of the cool things about transmitters is that they can receive feedback from channels. Today, when you turn on "The Price is Right," you can ogle the Craftsman table saw on which the contestant is bidding. If the channel were able to sense your response, it could send that information back to the tuner, which would funnel the information to the transmitter. The transmitter could then tweak the data it sends to the channel so that you can get a close up of the table saw.

NOTE: It is important to note that channels are entirely capable of remaining anonymous and not sending feedback (imagine the security holes that would creep up if you weren't able to! Big Brother would be watching constantly!).

Tuner

A tuner resides on your client machine and funnels the data feed from the transmitter to the channel (and vice versa as we discussed in the last section). Tuners do nothing more than act as middleman between channels and transmitters. Furthermore, because channels use tuners, channel programmers need not build network code of their own. Rather, they simply write their application to send and receive information from the tuner, and everything else is handled for them.

Channels

Channels are application executable programs that contain the tools necessary to act on data. Once channels are installed on your local machine, they can extract information from transmitters via the tuner. Furthermore, the channel can get information from a local source. The local source should then be able to plug directly into the local tuner and funnel information to the channel. No additional programming of the channel would be necessary to use a local source of information as opposed to a networked source.

Channels are also dynamically updated by a method Marimba refers to as "differential updating." Differential updating is accomplished using a table called an *index* that keeps track of the data files that compose a channel. When a channel is found to be out of data, the index of the local channel is compared to the index of the remote channel, and only the files that have been changed are downloaded. Today, when you download an applet that has changed since the last time you downloaded it, the entire applet gets downloaded, wasting time and network resources. With differential updating, channels are kept up-to-date without sacrificing network performance.

Channels are created using Bongo, Marimba's GUI-based channel builder. Using Bongo, you can design and layout your channel and include all the necessary functionality to make the channel not only function as a Castanet channel, but as a regular Java application or applet as well.

Repeaters

Transmitters can also be configured as something called a repeater. A repeater is merely a transmitter that also acts as a tuner. For example, if our transmitter were to be notified of an updated channel by another transmitter, it would be acting as a tuner. The repeater would get an update from the "parent" transmitter that a channel has changed and then download the changed portion automatically as all tuners do. In so doing, a repeater can cascade the changes in a channel down through a hierarchical system of repeaters.

Firewalls and proxies

As we will discuss in Chapter 10, "Java Hardware," security is of the utmost concern for Internet programmers. Indeed, without an adequate answer to the question of whether or not our computer systems are safe from intruders, the Internet will never truly become the place we all hope it will be. Firewalls protect computer systems from probing outsiders. They constrict, limit, and sometimes eliminate access to data from sources outside the firewall. Firewalls are intrusive, powerful beasts that are sort of like the bouncer at your favorite nightclub. Without the proper identification, you'll never get in.

Firewalls provide interesting dilemmas for programmers. Our clients can get out of the firewall to get information, but the server on the other end can never penetrate the firewall to get the information to the client. As a result, proxies are needed. Proxies are the ID you need to present to the bouncer to get in and dance the night away. They can tag the client's initial request and allow the response to get back in. Marimba's products support proxies and firewalls so that you can connect to transmitters outside a firewall and receive information back via the proxy.

Castanet vs. Java IDL and Java RMI

Where does Castanet fit into this book? Is it a replacement for Java IDL or Java RMI? The answer, surprisingly, is quite possibly yes. Why would you want to program clients and services in Java IDL and Java RMI when you could simply use a GUI tool to build those clients? A long time ago, we all programmed in BASIC on a text screen. Microsoft then figured out that people really just want to drag and drop components and create a GUI and build applications from there. Thus, Visual Basic was born.

Today, we spend much of our time building Java applications "by hand" rather than designing and architecting solutions. Java IDL and Java RMI are still invaluable tools on the server side, enabling you to publish vast quantities of information. Indeed, an IDL or RMI server could very easily provide the data feed on which channels depend (see Figure 8-2).

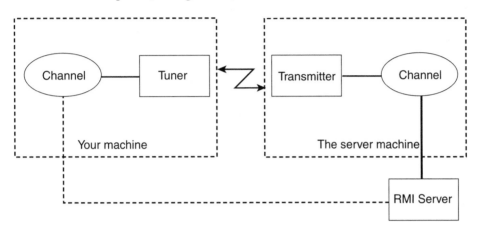

Figure 8-2 Castanet can use IDL or RMI servers.

This book and the topics we have chosen are not obviated by Castanet or Bongo. Rather, because of Marimba, Java is now fully capable of providing rich, dynamic, unlimited content to clients using the servers and services we build using IDL, RMI, Sockets, or Beans.

Why Castanet?

Netscape's Marc Andreesen refers to Castanet as one of the most important advances in the Java revolution. The reason is perhaps not as obvious as it should be. By using Castanet tuners, transmitters, and channels, Internet content providers ranging from the obvious, such as MTV, to the not-so-obvious, like an ordinary chiropractor's office, can generate dynamic content that is both easy and fast to download. The dynamic content can be streaming audio and video, thus making the channel-tuner-transmitter motif even more obvious, or it can simply give information on specific medical advances, techniques, or appointments as they change. Regardless, the Castanet system can be used to keep a person's computer up-to-date with the latest software, or it can even facilitate advertising and sales in an easier, more targeted fashion.

Castanet is in its infancy, but, like its Java progenitor, is growing fast. Several companies with visions of dynamic multimedia dancing in their heads are quickly flocking to the technology. If you require an easily accessible, dynamically downloadable stream of information, perhaps Castanet is your answer.

NOTE: You can learn more about Castanet by reading Laura Lemay's *Official Marimba Guide to Castanet* published by SamsNet. Those of you more interested in Bongo can pick up another SamsNet title, the *Official Marimba Guide to Bongo* by Danny Goodman.

Where Marimba succeeds in bringing the notion of the Web to mass market consumers with channels and tuners, Active Software shores up the intranet side for large-scale corporations. Already in use in several key corporations, ActiveWeb enables businesses to connect their back-end data stores directly to the Internet using Java. Built on top of CORBA, ActiveWeb may be an answer for your business' information publishing needs.

Active Software

Corporations today are discovering the power and wealth of the Internet. The challenge is to bring that same power and flexibility to the corporate desktop and the intranet. Active Software (`http://www.activesw.com/`) was formed to address the issue of bringing existing applications directly to the World Wide Web. ActiveWeb is designed to funnel information between legacy applications, the Internet, and the corporate intranet.

How ActiveWeb works

ActiveWeb is based on a component called the *information broker.* The Active Information Broker acts as a middleman for requests between providers and consumers of information. It works on the principle of a *publish and subscribe* system. When applications want to disseminate information to the world, they publish it to the broker. When they want to get information, they subscribe to the broker (see Figure 8-3).

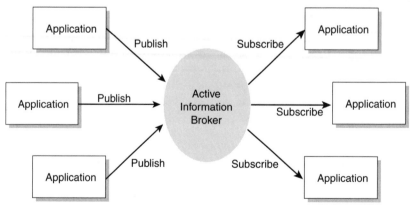

Figure 8-3 ActiveWeb is a publish and subscribe system.

Now, several Active Information Brokers can be set up so that each broker is publishing and subscribing to one another. That way, when an application on one broker publishes information, the broker can funnel it to other brokers whose subscribers may want the information.

Publish and subscribe systems

The Active Information Broker is the nexus of the publish and subscribe system put forth by Active Software. It keeps track of not only who is a subscriber and who is a publisher, but also the kinds of information that the publisher is publishing or that the subscriber wishes to receive. The publisher generally sends an event of some kind and the information broker examines it and routes it to every appropriate subscriber. The subscriber, meanwhile, has setup what is, in essence, a callback with the broker so that it can be notified whenever an event it is interested in has arrived.

Another kind of delivery system that is also covered by the information broker is the "ask and you shall receive" method (which we are familiar with as the tried-and-true client/server methods we have implemented everywhere else in this book). To accomplish such a thing within the publish and subscribe framework, the receiving application publishes an event, and immediately subscribes to the response event. The application that is subscribed to that particular publish event then immediately responds by publishing the response event to which the original receiver has already subscribed (see Figure 8-4).

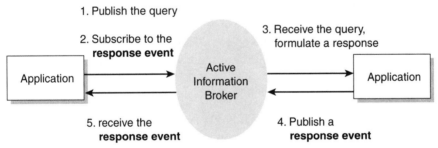
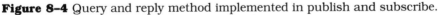

Figure 8-4 Query and reply method implemented in publish and subscribe.

As you can see, ActiveWeb is a flexible, powerful, scaleable environment for connecting your legacy systems to the Internet.

Firewalls and security

ActiveWeb also addresses concerns over security by letting you place an Active Information Broker outside the firewall and making it cooperate with the Web server. In so doing, the information broker can then open a single port and allow outsiders to access information inside the firewall through a controlled, secure location on the firewall.

Integrating legacy systems and databases

The Active Information Broker enables you to connect applications to existing databases by using a database adapter. Currently, adapters are available for Sybase, Oracle, and a few other relational database vendors. Adding additional vendors is simply a matter of creating another adapter. Contact Active Software if you require access to other databases not currently supported.

Database adapters act by taking events from the publish and subscribe system and translating them into SQL queries on databases. As we discussed in Chapter 5, "Java Database Connectivity," SQL is a powerful language for communicating with databases. ActiveWeb eliminates the need for you to create those queries by hand through a robust set of tools that will not only enable you to create queries on databases, but will also enable you to build an entire object system from the client all the way down to the server.

ActiveWeb and Java

ActiveWeb is much, much more than simply Java networking. We have given you a taste of what Active Software is up to simply because we feel they are on to something in this network revolution. All ActiveWeb applications can be written in Java, giving you the true power and flexibility you need to actually program the Internet.

ActiveWeb vs. IDL and RMI

As we mentioned, ActiveWeb is built on top of CORBA. However, it provides much more than CORBA by introducing an entire framework for object systems. The information broker is quite similar to the ORB, and its ability to navigate firewalls, the Internet, and the intranet without any unnecessary training makes it worth investigating. If you are sold on the CORBA or RMI philosophy of abstracting the network from the average programmer, then ActiveWeb may very well be worth investigating.

Netscape

Netscape essentially ushered in the Internet era when it made the power of the Internet available for mass market consumers. Information on demand, ease of use, the network on our desktop are but a few things brought to us thanks to Netscape Navigator. But, Navigator and Netscape in general is at a crossroads. While Netscape reaped all the rewards and benefits of the era it launched, it also woke up industry giant and startup-killer Microsoft. As the folks at Apple and IBM will attest, when Microsoft plays the game, they play for keeps.

As Microsoft integrates the Web directly into Windows, Netscape faces a quandary: Continue its line of Navigator products and eventually be eclipsed by Internet Explorer, or lead the Internet revolution in a direction away from Microsoft. Given the choice of life or death, Netscape chose life and announced its Open Network Environment (ONE).

What is Netscape ONE?

Netscape ONE is not necessarily a product, but rather is a set of foundation classes on which to build applications. Using ONE, you can build a series of applications for both the client and server side that are instantly connected. Using HTML files as a platform, ONE embeds clients and applications directly into a Web page, just as we currently put applets in a page. ONE is not something new, but rather an *open standard* for doing so.

Just as with Java IDL and Java RMI, ONE enables you to split processing across a network by integrating a series of servers that can be easily plugged into the Netscape Web server. In so doing, ONE's embedded clients can communicate across the network and you, the consumer, can experience the distributed computing paradigm that we have espoused throughout this book.

So why even bother learning RMI or IDL? Because using RMI or IDL servers, you too can build ONE back-end applications. In fact, Netscape wholeheartedly embraces the Object Management Group's Internet Inter-ORB Protocol used throughout CORBA. Thus, ONE servers are, essentially, CORBA servers, and ONE clients are, essentially, CORBA clients. Why not just call it CORBA? Because ONE is much more than CORBA. It includes support for Netscape's Secure Socket Layer (SSL), mail protocols, and other Internet protocols. Netscape's partnership with Visigenic software ensures that CORBA servers and IIOP-compliant services will be available for ONE developers to use as they see fit.

Netscape ONE and Java

Unlike ActiveX, which is highly Windows and Microsoft-centric, ONE makes an effort to limit the extent to which applications must rely on an operating system by using Java as its language of choice on both the client and the server sides. Java servers written using ONE will communicate via the IIOP protocol and allow CORBA and ONE clients alike to connect to them (see Figure 8-5).

ONE also claims full platform independence through the Java language. Yet, Netscape expressed reservations over Java's performance and, in parallel, incorporated JIT compilers into its full line of products. Thus, Java and ONE form a unique, fast, powerful combination. Netscape also realized that some developers prefer not to use Java, and introduced LiveConnect as a component of ONE. LiveConnect enables Java libraries and objects to be called from C++ or C objects. In so doing, ONE not only can embrace non-Java developers, but can help Java developers to incorporate existing libraries written pre-Java in C or C++, or even IIOP servers on remote hosts.

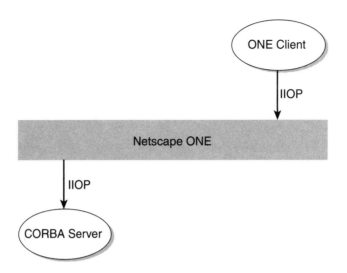

Figure 8-5 ONE clients can connect via the ONE framework to CORBA servers.

Now that these companies and others like them have blazed a trail for Java programmers to begin networking applications, you can get some ideas of where to take your business from here. Perhaps ActiveWeb is all you need, or maybe you want to develop your own intranet system. Regardless of your intention, this book should help get you started. But, this book is limited in its scope. There are several Java communication technologies out there that we haven't even begun to explore. One of these is mentioned in the following section. We urge you to contact the people in charge if you feel any of these alternatives may be able to help you.

ICE-T

Once you overlook the ridiculous name (Interprise Computing Environment Toolkit—Don't ask what an Interprise is), Sun Microsystems' ICE-T makes a whole lot of sense. ICE-T is an asynchronous messaging system that enables your Java clients to talk to C or C++ servers. By enabling your Java Web applications to connect and contact your existing legacy systems, ICE-T delivers on its promise.

How does it work?

ICE-T is based on asynchronous communication, which enables clients to send a message to a server, and then go about its business. With synchronous communication, clients that make invocations block until the invocation returns. Imagine calling a very long remote function and having to wait around until it finishes. With ICE-T, you can build Java clients that connect to C++ servers in a safe manner. If the C++ server were to freeze up (presumably because of a memory problem), then the Java portion will not flake out.

ICE-T also includes several C and C++ libraries that handle the Java interaction on the server side. Therefore, when your Java clients contact the C++ server, it can use a message format that is already agreed upon. ICE-T also includes source code builders for those who don't want to program in icky old C++. Furthermore, ICE-T is "high level" enough that you don't really have to know what sockets are and how they work to use it.

ICE-T and Java

As we discussed throughout this book, the biggest problem facing software architects today is how to integrate their existing legacy applications with the Web. ICE-T provides a nice, tight framework for your Java applications to tie directly into C and C++ servers. Yes, you can build your own version of ICE-T by having Java talk to a socket that is read on the other end by a C++ application. In fact, underneath the covers, this is exactly how ICE-T operates. But, ICE-T also gives you a standardized message format that will enable you to talk to other ICE-T servers, or enable others to write clients that talk to your ICE-T servers.

In this book, we have constantly berated C++ as archaic, difficult, and error prone. But, as we go about our daily programming lives, we sometimes happen upon instances in which C or C++ is the only solution. For all its strengths, Java is still interpreted, and always will be. If you need to interface with a specific platform directly and with great speed, you may need to use C. In order to ready those applications for the Web, you can use ICE-T to funnel the information from the C or C++ server back to the Java client on the Web.

Summary

There are many more Java initiatives floating around many other companies. Microsoft surely has something up its sleeve, and IBM isn't fooling around either. Several tools companies are putting together more Java networking components every day. This is the fun part of the Java revolution. Every day something new comes out, some company has found the new "killer Java app."

As you attempt to stay on top of these new and exciting products, try to determine where their roots are. If they are a derivative of Java IDL, examine how well they implement their product on top of IDL and CORBA. If they make native method calls, try to determine how or if sockets are used. Once you understand the fundamentals we have shown you, then you can begin to make intelligent decisions about the products that will arise as the Java Revolution speeds on.

No matter what technology you implement, if your application system is large enough, you will need a way to manage your objects. Using the Java Management API (JMAPI), you can set up your normal and networked Java objects to be integrated into a framework that enables network managers to check, modify, and terminate runtime characteristics of your distributed system. The JMAPI is written in Java, uses RMI underneath, can help you keep track of how your objects are run, and is discussed in the next chapter.

Java Networking Information

This part concentrates on some of the additional information that may be of use to application developers. JMAPI, the Management API for Java, is a set of objects that allow the easy construction of Java servers capable of being administered from afar. Java Hardware concerns the new Java operating system and hardware derivatives associated with it. Security addresses some of the topics of security and safety in Java applications as well as the issues of Internet security in general. The final chapter goes through the various alternatives presented in this book with a frank and honest discussion of why and when a specific technology should be used.

Chapter 9: JMAPI: Java Management API
Chapter 10: Java Hardware
Chapter 11: Java and Security
Chapter 12: Making an Architectural Decision

CHAPTER 9

Managing Networks of Computers

Introducing Management to Clients and Servers

JMAPI: Java Management API

The Java Management API is a heavy-duty implementation of the Solstice suite of network management tools that come bundled with Sun Microsystems' Solaris operating system. While JMAPI does not require Solaris, it can help you to bring the power of Solstice to your operating environment. Your Java objects can be ensured of some semblance of stability if you provide a means by which your applications can be monitored by a "neutral third party." If your applications go down, JMAPI can help you bring them back up. At the heart of networked communication is the need for the reliability that JMAPI can help provide.

In this chapter, we cover network management, and show you how to introduce a management scheme for your clients and servers. Also, we touch briefly on how and when to manage your objects. The concept of network management is discussed in short, with emphasis on the needs of a management API and how those needs are met by JMAPI.

What is Network Management?

At first glance, a book about Java networking does not appear to need a chapter on network administration. After all, system administrators are hired by most organizations to ensure that a network stays up and running. Most of the time, however, system administrators are presented with a horrendous number of different tools with which to do their job.

To make matters worse, these tools generally have no relationship to one another and have vastly different user interfaces. For the system administrator, this amounts to a significant amount of frustration. For the organization for which they work, this amounts to a significant amount of money spent on training.

What is needed is a simple set of tools that can be used to build a homogeneous environment for the administrator. If the tools have a common interface, then the system administrator needs to learn only the basics of one tool to understand the others. The Java Management API, or JMAPI, provides a robust environment in which you can create administrative tools, provide administrative functionality, and modify your regular Java objects so that they can be administered by the JMAPI.

As the Internet grows, and as programming the Internet becomes more and more accessible, the need for complex network management will be apparent. If you create your Java applications with management in mind, you can prepare for the eventual arrival of Internet system administrators.

Network management at a glance

A long time ago, the notion of a network did not exist. In fact, computers were connectionless entities that resided in a room and did not in any way talk to one another. Soon, the Local Area Network (LAN) emerged and computers in the same physical location could be connected to one another. It enabled information to flow from computer to computer, and even for data to be centrally located on another computer. Then, these little networks began to merge with larger networks and, eventually, the Internet developed and connected them all together (see Figure 9-1).

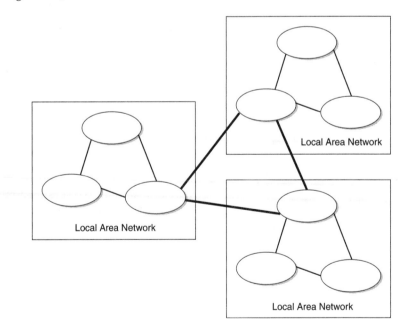

Figure 9–1 The growth of connectivity among small networks eventually gave rise to the Internet.

Some day, our children will hear the tale of the birth of the network as they bounce on our knees, but today we are presented with a very adult problem: how to make sure each one of those computers stays up and running and how to fix them when they do break. This is the high-pressure world of network administration.

To complicate the matter further, network administrators often are asked to handle software concerns as well. To facilitate this, several protocols were developed that hook into applications and determine and/or fix their health. Once again, network administrators are called on to fix ailing applications and bring them back to a usable state.

As Java applications become more and more popular, and JavaStations and the Java operating system gain greater acceptance, a burden will be placed on network administrators to ensure the reliability of applications and the hardware on which those applications run. To assist with this matter, Sun's Solstice network administration group put forth the Java Management API. The JMAPI will be discussed in detail in the next section, but for now we concentrate on traditional network administration problems and how they relate to Java.

Simple network management protocol

One of the protocols created by the Internet Engineering Task Force to assist with local and wide area network administration is the Simple Network Management Protocol. SNMP has several advantages over its competitors, chief among them is its ease-of-use. By setting up something called an "SNMP trap," the network administrator is able to identify crucial components, protect them, and give himself a means to be notified when the component fails.

SNMP exchanges information between the manager application and the managed component through something called a *Protocol Data Unit* (PDU). A PDU contains information about a component and is sent over a network connection to the manager application. The application can read the PDU and determine the health of the component. PDUs usually contain information about an application's name, type, and current state. The SNMP trap we referred to is actually a form of a PDU.

SNMP is in wide use today. Chances are high that your network connection to the Internet uses SNMP in one form or another to maintain its integrity. SNMP manager applications are monitored by network administrators who can determine if and when a component fails, and from there can arrive at a solution to the failure fairly quickly.

It is important to understand that we refer to SNMP in "application" space. The truth is that SNMP can be incorporated within applications themselves. In so doing, a network administrator can pinpoint the exact causes of failures because he or she has a direct hook into the code that failed. In a moment, we will see how Java programmers can create similar applications by using the Java Management API rather than SNMP.

The unique management problems of Java

One of the biggest problems encountered with incorporating SNMP into Java is that SNMP is not Java. Java is a wonderful language, with great ease-of-use features. We want to be able to deploy large-scale Java applications both over the Internet and within our corporate Intranets. In order to do so, and still have control over network administration, we must have a way to hook into Java code and obtain information about it.

In the next few sections, we will examine the Java Management API closely and learn where it can be used appropriately when deployed Java applications are created. As the language gains more acceptance, as Java hardware becomes more and more prevalent, and as applications are shipped that are written in Java exclusively, some form of Java management mechanism must be developed and used if our networks are to maintain a semblance of integrity.

Network Administration Overview

Network administration is often the underemphasized aspect of the Internet revolution. Without a coherent network administration strategy, all networked applications will fall apart, and the network backbone will break. It is because of the importance of this that we will undertake a discussion of its relevance to Java network programming.

Modifying Clients for JMAPI

The client code that is included as part of the Java Management API consists of a series of RMI clients that interact with managed object servers. These RMI objects enable you to communicate seamlessly with the object your client is designed to manage. Your client should be able to affect the performance and activity of the server, provided the managed object follows the JMAPI architecture and implements its core objects.

The JMAPI client architecture also consists of what can only be called a user interface bonanza. From pie charts to line graphs, lists to graphical lists, icons to animation, the JMAPI's Admin View Model (AVM) is nothing more than a layer on top of the Abstract Window Toolkit. In so doing, the AVM is, like the AWT, completely platform independent and AVM does not rely on any windowing system to function.

AVM base classes

The AVM base classes are, as we discussed, an extension of the AWT. They implement several components, including image buttons, scrolling windows and panels, toolbar, image canvases, dialog boxes, and things you can do while your application is busy. There are also several generic tables, HTML browsers, and chart objects for you to use as you see fit. We will not show you how to use each of these individually because they are used the same way the normal AWT classes are used.

AVM help classes

The AVM help classes provide a general-purpose help utility for application programmers. By using the AVM Help functions, your application's help documentation could be used just as easily by other, non-JMAPI, applications and vice versa. Why duplicate documentation efforts when the JMAPI can assist you in creating a uniform documentation structure? AVM help documentation is nothing more than HTML with a few JMAPI authoring tags sprinkled within it. The JMAPI tags are contained in comments within the HTML documentation, so the HTML documentation can be used elsewhere without giving away the fact that the same text is also used by the JMAPI.

The help classes consist of four modules. The first of these modules is the UI-based Table of Contents and Navigator. The TOC/Navigator allows you to survey your documentation and build a hierarchical list of the topics contained therein. It uses the authoring tags within the documentation set to determine the arrangement of the contents list.

A documentation generator also is included to assist you in creating indices, glossaries, and even table of contents files. The documentation generator (jmapidoc) acts on the HTML file, parses the authoring tags within it, and spits out a series of HTML files that can be used by the Help Navigator.

The third module is a series of help files built by the JMAPI documentation generator and refer to the JMAPI itself. This way you can pass on information about how JMAPI operates as part of the documentation for the ManagedObjects you create. A set of help templates that you can fill in yourself is included along with the standard JMAPI help files. They will help you get started with building documentation for your objects.

Last, a search engine is included with the AVM help utilities so that end users can find the information you have created for them quickly.

Managed object interfaces

Let's say we have a series of objects that model each individual employee in our large, monolithic corporation. Traditionally, the solution to poor employee morale is more management. Therefore, to improve our employee's morale, we will add a manager to oversee him.

Our EmployeeManager is based on RMI, so we must include the RMI classes in our file. Furthermore, we must create a StatusObservable object to oversee the object. The StatusObservable object will link our ManagedObject to an event notification mechanism. If we so desire, we can set up a notification link within our client. If any other client fiddles with our employee, we would know about it instantly.

```java
public class EmployeeManager
{
    public static void main(
        String args[]
    )
    {
        // our employee
        EmployeeInterface employee;

        // our observable class
        StatusObservable statusObserver =
            new StatusObservable();
    }
}
```

Once we have set up our `EmployeeManager`, we must go to the `ManagedObjectFactory` to get an `EmployeeInterface` object. The first argument to the `newObj` call is the name of the object, including any Java package containers that are associated with it. The second argument is the name of the object in the name space (in our case "EMPLOYEE").

```java
public class EmployeeManager
{
    public static void main(
        String args[]
    )
    {
        // our employee
        EmployeeInterface employee;

        // our observable class
        StatusObservable statusObserver =
            new StatusObservable();

        // create the employee object
        try
```

```
    {
        employee = (EmployeeInterface)MOFactoryObj.newObj(
            "sunw.jmapi.EmployeeInterface",
            "EMPLOYEE");
    }
    catch(Exception exc)
    {
        System.out.println("Error in create: " +
            exc.toString());
    }
    }
}
```

Now we must set our employee's attributes. We will create a `setTask` method and a `setName` method here and implement them in a few moments. We will then go about adding the object to the management system (in other words, we'll place the employee in our org chart).

```
public class EmployeeManager
{
    public static void main(
        String args[]
    )
    {
        // our employee
        EmployeeInterface employee;

        // our observable class
        StatusObservable statusObserver = new
            StatusObservable();

        // create the employee object
        try
        {
            employee = (EmployeeInterface)MOFactoryObj.newObj(
                "sunw.jmapi.EmployeeInterface",
                "EMPLOYEE");
        }
        catch(Exception exc)
        {
            System.out.println("Error in create: " +
                exc.toString());
        }
```

```
            // assign a task
            try
            {
                employee.setName("Heath");
                employee.setTask("Throw a touchdown");
            }
            catch(RemoteException exc)
            {
                System.out.println("Error in setup: " +
                    exc.toString());
            }

            // add this client to the list of objects listening
            // in on this employee
            try
            {
                employee.addObject(statusObserver);
            }
            catch(Exception exc)
            {
                System.out.println("Error in addObject: " +
                    exc.toString());
            }
        }
    }
```

There are two operations analogous to the addObject method we just employed. We just as easily could have modified the object, then notified any other observers of this change by invoking modifyObject on the employee. If we wanted to remove the object from the management system, we could invoke deleteObject on the employee. Remember, the clients can set and modify attributes, the servers can use those settings to do its business, and the clients can notify other clients that a change has been made.

Setting up notifications

In order to create the notification mechanism in our client, we must implement the MOObserver and create an ObserverProxy within the employee object. We must also implement the update function as required by the MOObserver. The update function will be the callback function. As we have discussed in Chapter 3 on IDL and Chapter 4 on RMI, simply setting up a callback is not enough. We also must create a place for the server to invoke that callback.

```
public class EmployeeManager implements MOObserver
{
    public static void main(
        String args[]
    )
    {
        // our employee
        EmployeeInterface employee;

        // our observable class
        StatusObservable statusObserver =
            new StatusObservable();

        // create the observer proxy
        ObserverProxyImpl observerProxy =
            new ObserverProxyImpl(this);

        // create the employee object
        try
        {
            employee = (EmployeeInterface)MOFactoryObj.newObj(
                "sunw.jmapi.EmployeeInterface",
                "EMPLOYEE");
        }
        catch(Exception exc)
        {
            System.out.println("Error in create: " +
                exc.toString());
        }
        // add the observer proxy to the managed object and
        // tell it to notify on modifications only
        employee.addObserver(observerProxy,
            ManagedObject.OBSERVE_MODIFY);

        // assign a task
        try
        {
            employee.setName("Heath");
            employee.setTask("Throw a touchdown");
        }
```

```
        catch(RemoteException exc)
        {
            System.out.println("Error in setup: " +
                exc.toString());
        }
        // add this client to the list of objects listening
        // in on this employee
        try
        {
            employee.addObject(statusObserver);
        }
        catch(Exception exc)
        {
            System.out.println("Error in addObject: " +
                exc.toString());
        }
    }
    public void update(
        ManagedObject mo,
        Observation observation
    )
    {
        if(observation instanceof ModifyObservation)
        {
            … do our modification stuff here …
        }
    }
}
```

When any other manager client invokes modifyObject on the ManagedObject, we get a notification in the update method. This enables us always to stay in synch with the managed object, even if there are many other clients modifying it at the same time. Now we must set up our servers so that they can be managed by the clients we just created.

Modifying servers for JMAPI

The Java Management API includes a set of objects to be used on the server side of a Java networked system. These objects are known collectively as the Administration Runtime Module (ARM). The ARM is the focal point of all management associated with Java applications. Once Java applications include the ARM, they are essentially instantiated objects that can be readily administered.

The various components of the ARM are discussed in the next sections. Each component contributes a specialized function to the overall goal of administering your clients fully. Your Java applications can be plugged into existing system management protocols and software including SNMP, Solstice, and others using the ARM. Once your Java applications can be administered, you can rest easy in the knowledge that your object system can handle network situations beyond your control.

The admin runtime module

The diagram in Figure 9-2 outlines the various components of the ARM that we will soon discuss. Each of the components are interchangeable. For example, your application may need to use the ManagedObject routines, but you can omit the Notification module easily should you so desire. Furthermore, your managed applications remain fully scaleable and the performance of your system should not be degraded. Figure 9-2 illustrates the modular design of JMAPI applications.

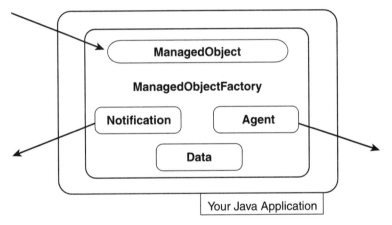

Figure 9-2 Modular design of JMAPI applications.

When a JMAPI client is used to communicate with your server, it can inquire as to its status and overall health. This information may take the form of a notification, essentially a call back set up by the client using the JMAPI server, or the client may inquire of its own volition. This kind of communication and data exchange is the heart of networked computing and is required in order to administer the network with which you communicate.

ManagedObject classes

The ManagedObject class implements a distributed management architecture. It enables multiple clients to obtain links to the same managed server and affect changes on them simultaneously. Its underlying communication mechanism is

Java RMI (see Figure 9-3). Using remote method invocations, the `ManagedOb-jects` residing on the client side can talk to the RMI `ManagedObject` server running within the managed server.

Figure 9–3 RMI is the underlying communication mechanism of JMAPI.

In order for a `ManagedObject` to begin communication with the object it wishes to manage, the management server must be configured. This is done using the RMI paradigm of creating a public interface for the `ManagedObject` clients to talk to first. Here we are going to create an employee object and attempt to manage it:

```
public interface EmployeeInterface extends ManagedObject
{
    // set and get a task
    public void setTask(
        String newTask);
    public String getTask();

    // set and get the employee's name
    public void setName(
        String newName);
    public String getName();
}
```

As you can see, this public interface inherits from `ManagedObject` and, therefore, gets all of the RMI functionality it needs. In so doing, we need not make mention of RMI throughout the server explicitly. Indeed, the RMI network code is part of `ManagedObject`.

Implementing the `ManagedObject`

Once we have created the interface, we must create the implementation of the `ManagedObject` class. This adds the functionality to the interface, so that we have much more than a skeleton. We will add a constructor and implement the functions prescribed in the `EmployeeInterface` object.

```
public class EmployeeImpl extends ManagedObjectImpl
                    implements EmployeeInterface
```

```
{
    public EmployeeImpl() throws RemoteException
    {
        super();
    }

    public void setTask(
        String newTask
    )
    {
    }

    public String getTask()
    {
    }

    public void setName(
        String newName
    )
    {
    }

    public String getName()
    {
    }
}
```

In addition, we must implement the performAction methods that map the creation of ManagedObjects using the ManagedObjectFactory of our implementation. Whenever this ManagedObject is created, deleted, or modified using the factory, one of the performAction methods will be called.

```
public class EmployeeImpl extends ManagedObjectImpl
                        implements EmployeeInterface
{
    public EmployeeImpl() throws RemoteException
    {
        super();
    }

    public void setTask(
        String newTask
```

```java
    )
    {
    }

    public String getTask()
    {
    }

    public void setName(
        String newName
    )
    {
    }

    public String getName()
    {
    }

    public void performAddActions(
        StatusObservable observable,
        CommitAndRollback commitObj
    )
    {
    }

    public void performModifyActions(
        StatusObservable observable,
        CommitAndRollback commitObj
    )
    {
    }

    public void performDeleteActions(
        StatusObservable observable,
        CommitAndRollback commitObj
    )
    {
    }
}
```

The perform methods accept an observable as a parameter. This facilitates notifications, which we will discuss shortly. Perform methods also take a `CommitAndRollback` object in order to keep track of all the operations on the `ManagedObject`. If we encounter any kind of error during the perform method, the `CommitAndRollback` object will allow the `ManagedObject` to backtrack and resume its previous unaltered state. This ensures that the perform methods are always atomic in nature, meaning that either the whole thing is complete or none of it is. In keeping with their implementation, the perform methods are intended for atomic operations (database access, file manipulation, or the like). We have not implemented anything in them here, but they are still required as part of the `ManagedObject` implementation.

Managed attributes

The name and task attributes of our employee need not be created in the `EmployeeImpl` object itself. Instead, we can take advantage of the `ManagedObject`'s attribute mechanism. We can enable the `ManagedObject` to handle persistence and network-related tasks associated with the attribute for us by storing our attributes within the `ManagedObject`'s infrastructure.

```
public class EmployeeImpl extends ManagedObjectImpl
                          implements EmployeeInterface
{
    public EmployeeImpl() throws RemoteException
    {
        super();
    }

    public void setTask(
        String newTask
    )
    {
        setKnownAttributes("employee-task", newTask);
    }

    public String getTask()
    {
        return (String) getAttribute("employee-task");
    }

    public void setName(
        String newName
```

```
)
{
    setKnownAttributes("employee-name", newName);
}

public String getName()
{
    return (String) getAttribute("employee-name");
}

public void performAddActions(
    StatusObservable observable,
    CommitAndRollback commitObj
)
{
}

public void performModifyActions(
    StatusObservable observable,
    CommitAndRollback commitObj
)
{
}

public void performDeleteActions(
    StatusObservable observable,
    CommitAndRollback commitObj
)
{
}
}
```

ManagedObjectFactory classes

In the previous section, we saw how a ManagedObjectFactory enables a client to obtain a handle to the server with which it wishes to speak. The ManagedObjectFactory is no different from the BMW auto factory in Spartanburg, South Carolina. In Spartanburg, BMWs flow off the assembly line one by one. Here, our ManagedObjectFactory enables us to serve up ManagedObjects on demand, creating them on-the-fly, initializing them, and readying them for use. As long as our objects implement the ManagedObject interfaces, they can be created and obtained through a factory.

Notifications

We discussed how notifications are based on the Java `Observer` and `Observable` classes in the client section. Unlike in Chapter 4, "Java RMI: Remote Method Invocation", supporting notification callbacks in JMAPI involves virtually no effort on our server's behalf. The `ManagedObject` implementation takes care of tracking the individual subscribing clients and publishing information when necessary. By using attributes as we did earlier, the `ManagedObject` is able to intercept changes made to the server without the programmer having to supply it with any additional information.

Managed data

JMAPI also enables you to set up your data structures and member variables so that they can be managed from clients as well. You can allow clients to check on the integrity of the data contained within your remote Java servers by registering your data with the `ManagedObject` class. The client then could execute a series of steps if it finds something to act on.

Server agents

Leigh Steinberg is the sports world's greatest agent. He is able to obtain lucrative contracts and signing bonuses for his numerous clients. Similarly, software agents act on behalf of parent applications and obtain information or make invocations when triggered by certain events. The agents are remote objects, so they run in their own process, perhaps on their own machine, perhaps even on a remote network. In so doing, they do not affect the performance of the calling object.

Setting up an agent is similar to setting up an RMI object, but again much of the RMI overhead is handled for you.

Summary

Managing your networked applications is a complex and difficult task. The more objects you introduce into your system, the greater your chances are of things going wrong. JMAPI enables you to plug your applications into a predefined management scheme easily. In so doing, you can start your object system and watch from afar how it behaves. By setting up alerts and "traps," you can make sure that your object system alerts a global manager when a problem arises. Together with JMAPI, your applications can be reliable systems of objects.

Now that we've spent a few chapters discussing how to develop systems of objects using software, let's take a moment to examine how Java-based hardware can change your professional and personal worlds. Someday soon, every computer-based appliance will be Java-powered, fulfilling Java's original intention as a language for embedded systems.

CHAPTER
10

JavaOS

JavaStation

Java Chips

Java Hardware

As Java grows in popularity, it will eventually eliminate the distinction between operating systems and window managers. Even though Windows 95 is pretty and user friendly, it is unstable and frustrating more often than not. Java removes the need for Windows 95 and its successors once an application base is present for it. As Java applications become more and more prevalent, the operating system on which they run will become more and more irrelevant.

Sun Microsystems has put forth several specifications and a few products tailored to this brave new world of architecture and operating system independence. The Java Operating System is a set of core APIs and pseudo-operating system built using them, that can run on any platform with a Java Virtual Machine. The JavaStation and the Java Chips that power it gives Sun a hardware solution designed to run Java and Java-based networked applications with greater speed and security while at the same time potentially negating Microsoft's stranglehold on the client industry.

JavaOS

Every day that you spend reinstalling Windows, fiddling with drivers, and configuring software is a waste. So says Sun Microsystems. The folks at Sun believe strongly in the notion of a networked computer. A networked computer enables you to place the burden of configuration and installation of software on a centralized server. A true networked computer has no hard disk, only RAM. It loads an operating system on-the-fly, always ensuring that you have the latest and greatest version. It enables you to download applications and features of those applications as you need them.

Scott McNealy calls Microsoft Office a "personal activity generator." He is a staunch believer that much, if not most, of the functionality contained within the various productivity software suites is unneeded by the average computer user. With that reasoning, McNealy and Sun created the JavaStation. We will discuss the exact hardware specifics of the JavaStation and the processor that runs it in a moment. In this chapter, we will discuss the Java-based operating system that will run on the networked computer.

Why JavaOS?

In order for the vision of networked computers to become reality, the operating system that is dynamically loaded must have four very important features. First, it must be small. The download of the operating system itself should be relatively fast. Loading the operating system should not take the equivalent of 15 floppy disks or an entire CD-ROM.

By keeping the OS small, engineers can prevent bloat of the operating system. Perhaps we want to build a networked computer that does not download the operating system on-the-fly, but rather stores the OS inside ROM. In order to achieve that goal, the operating system must be small enough to fit inside strictly limited ROM space. ROM also assists the operating system to boot faster.

Furthermore, if the operating system is able to fit within a small space, the performance will be significantly greater than if the operating system were bloated and needlessly large. In fact, the current JavaOS system has had precious little performance enhancements, but is still faster than many existing operating systems. With improved JIT compilation, the performance can only get better.

The operating system must also be somewhat platform independent. Because many vendors, including Sun Microsystems, Oracle, and Intel, will be providing their own brand of the networked computer, a design goal of the operating system would be to ensure that it can run on any of these other machines.

Third, JavaOS had to be able to support the entire AWT and, of much importance to this book, support the full IO and network capabilities inherent in Java. If the networked computer were unable to execute networked code, then JavaOS would be mostly useless. Remember, Java is the Internet language, and should always fully support Sun's notion that "the Network is the Computer."

Finally, the operating system must support the full Java API. Without such support, the JavaOS would be largely useless and negate many of the best qualities of Java, specifically "write once, run everywhere."

High-level JavaOS system architecture

Before we discuss JavaOS itself, let's take a moment to see why Windows has taken off despite being a clearly inferior operating system. As we discussed when we spoke of ActiveX, the name of the operating system game is applications. It doesn't matter if your operating system is the greatest thing since the chocolate covered banana. If your operating system has no applications, it is worthless.

As we are all aware, one of the greatest things about Java is that it is platform independent. It negates the importance of the operating system. So long as the operating system implements the Java Virtual Machine, every Java application can run directly on top of the operating system itself. As Microsoft, Apple, and others embrace Java and incorporate the VM directly into their operating systems, application vendors will be able to write their applications entirely in Java and publish them to the world, knowing that as long as they have adhered to the Java rules their application will run on every machine.

In order for JavaOS to succeed in the operating system arena, it must do the one thing it was created to do: run Java applications. Forget about the performance enhancements, the coolness of writing an operating system for Java in Java, the one great thing about JavaOS is that it doesn't present anything new or different to the application programmer. Programming on top of the JavaOS is as easy as programming on top of any other operating system. Furthermore, JavaOS is fully Java compliant, meaning a Java program that is written on another platform will still execute on JavaOS. JavaOS takes great pains to implement the Java Virtual Machine properly so that you, the application programmer, will need to make no additional efforts to develop applications for it.

The diagram in Figure 10-1 illustrates the nature of a typical Java Virtual Machine embedded within another operating system. Note how applications care only about the Java Virtual Machine, and don't really care about what goes on underneath it.

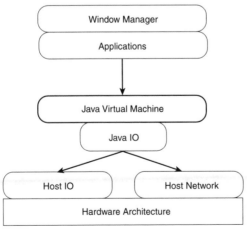

Figure 10–1 The Java Virtual Machine interfaces to the operating system for you and your applications to talk to the Virtual Machine.

Figure 10-2 shows a diagram of the JavaOS architecture. Once again, the same pretty face is presented to developers as in the previous example.

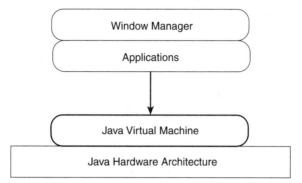

Figure 10–2 The Java Virtual Machine is part of the operating system, but your applications don't know the difference.

The JavaOS architecture implements the core functionality for all of the Java language specification. It leaves the native method calls up to the Java Virtual Machine. As you can see, there is nothing special about this kind of implementation. It follows all of the Java principles we have grown to know and love.

JavaOS Virtual Machine

When implemented within a normal operating system, the Java VM is responsible only for providing Java functionality. The JavaOS requires more from the Java VM, however. The JavaOS specification prefers to divide the Virtual Machine into the traditional Java VM as well as something it calls the Java Kernel. The Java Kernel handles all of the native windowing methods, memory management, and IO routines.

The JavaOS Virtual Machine also handles all of the thread support for Java itself. By splitting this functionality into two parts, the VM and the Kernel, the model of the traditional Java Virtual Machine is retained. Just as in every other operating system, JavaOS makes sure that the low-level functionality is divided from the high-level Java-specific functionality.

Drivers and networking

Because the Java Kernel is capable of executing Java bytecode only, all device drivers must be written in Java. Because writing code in Java only is quite limiting to device driver authors, the Java Kernel provides two helper classes that will enable you to modify memory directly. Obviously, because of the nature of Java, these routines are in no way available to Java objects written on top of the Virtual Machine.

JavaOS also supports a variety of network protocols, as called for by the Java networking specification. The basic transport and routing mechanisms of TCP, UDP, IP, and DHCP are supported by the networking component of JavaOS.

Uniqueness of JavaOS

There are quite a few things that separate JavaOS from conventional operating systems. For one thing, JavaOS does not require a local file system. Instead, the HotJava windowing environment and the HotJava Views desktop environment are essentially Web browsers. These pseudo-browsers go to servers to fetch their information rather than storing the information locally. As a result, no file system is required. Furthermore, JavaOS has no system calls to call its own. It relies on the Java Kernel and the JavaOS Virtual Machine.

JavaStation

The JavaOS is intended to run on the JavaStation. While it can be scaled down somewhat to run embedded within Java-enabled appliances, the JavaStation requires the JavaOS image to implement the virtual machine and AWT-related windowing systems. The JavaStation is a small, portable device that was recently unveiled by Sun Microsystems. Several vendors have promised similar devices in the near future, most notably Oracle. Some vendors plan to use the JavaOS, others are working on one of their own. Microsoft will eventually have an answer to the network computer as well.

In later October of 1996, Sun Microsystems made what could either be a historic announcement, or the most over-hyped pronouncement of the Java Revolution. They introduced their JavaStation. The JavaStation is, in Sun's own words, a "zero client." It takes the hardest part of computer networks today, system administration, and removes it from the hands of ordinary mortals, centrally locating that power and responsibility with network administrators.

As we saw in previous chapters on network administration, system administration is the most important aspect to a deployed set of applications. While this book has concentrated on developing networked applications, we need to take a moment and examine where those applications will be executed and how they will perform on those machines.

Introduction to the JavaStation

Contrary to popular belief, the JavaStation is not intended for home use. The chances of every one of us PC addicts trading in our whiz-bang Intel machine with CD-ROMs, sound cards, and hard disks for a little hunk of iron that only gets its information from a far away place are slim to none. For that, we can all breathe a sigh of relief. After all, if we are composing a letter to our best friends telling them that our boss is a lunkhead, why should we store that information where our boss could read it? We want to keep that kind of sensitive information close to the vest and where we can physically see it.

The JavaStation is intended for what Sun refers to as "task-specific" users. A task-specific user is one who, like a bank teller, uses a computer for one thing and one thing only. The bank teller will retrieve and modify account information, create new accounts, close accounts, and otherwise change your account status from one single application, on one terminal, in one location. If all the bank tellers in the same branch were to use JavaStations running the same bank account Java application, then the JavaStation begins to make sense.

Sun has thought of deploying JavaStations to factory floors, telephone operators, and other groups of people who use a computer for a single purpose. This is the revolution that will change the industry much more than a scaled-down version of Windows from Microsoft.

JavaStation Deployment

Let's say I wanted to deploy a series of JavaStations to the various stations in our peanut butter factory. As far as we can tell, we want to be able to see the progress of our peanut selector, peanut presser, waste disposer, peanut butterer, and butter packager. By creating a Java application geared towards each of the five groups of people, we can create a uniform set of applications for the company. Now, we can locate those applications on a central server equipped with a Web server (see Figure 10-3).

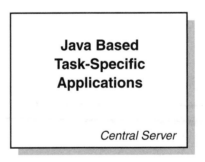

Figure 10–3 Java applications can be located on a central server.

We must then deploy JavaStations to each of these stations and link them to the central server as shown in Figure 10-4. It turns out that the JavaStations all have Java Chips inside of them. We will discuss the Java Chip in greater detail in the next section. They also run the JavaOS that we referred to in the previous section.

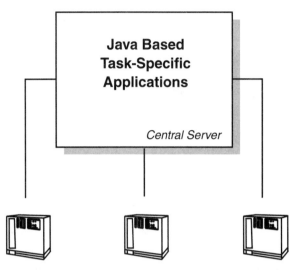

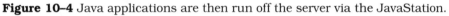

Figure 10–4 Java applications are then run off the server via the JavaStation.

Because of this Java-centricity, our applications will run without a hitch on the JavaStation. The JavaStation runs a desktop system called HotJava Views, which acts as a sort of kind of Windows for the JavaStation. It contains simple applications such as mail, phone books, calendars, and a means to execute stand-alone applications. But, most importantly, HotJava Views includes a Web browser. The Web browser enables us to connect to the central server and execute the factory applications we created for it.

Advantages of the JavaStation

The nice thing about the JavaStation is that you don't have to be a rocket scientist to use it. An administrator comes in, sets up the machine, hooks it to the network, and leaves. The JavaStation itself requires no further administration, and because there are no disks, drives, or controllers to get messed up, administrative costs are projected to be quite low.

The very reason that makes a JavaStation unsuitable for home use is the exact reason that makes it so wonderful for the work environment. With all of the information located on a central server, it is much easier to maintain security over the information flowing through the network. The JavaStation has no local state representation because it has no disk drive and no place to store information for periods longer than the application's execution time. Because of this, all the information is stored and maintained at the server side.

Finally, applications are much easier to administrate and install. Because of the Web browser paradigm, applications need not be installed on every JavaStation.

Simply update the application located on the server, and every browser that downloads the application from that moment on will automatically get the latest and greatest version. Furthermore, modular applications that take advantage of distributed design principles such as those taught in this book will have the ability to be feature rich without drowning the user in features. An application may use a particular feature, such as a spell checker in a word processor, only once in a while. Why load it all at once when it can be done incrementally?

Future JavaStation Advancements

With faster Java Chips and a better JavaOS, the JavaStation will continue to improve. With a native JIT compiler, application execution speed will be considerably faster. Improved network connections will facilitate faster download performance of high-intensity Java applications. This is the future of Java, and perhaps the future of Java Computing itself.

Writing Networked Applications for JavaStation

Because the JavaStation relies on the Web browser paradigm, no real code enhancements are needed to execute programs on the JavaStation. So long as your Java applets conform to the applet restrictions in Java, they should be fine on the JavaStation.

Java applications are an entirely different matter. The Java Virtual Machine present on the operating system (in this case JavaOS, but other operating systems may arrive in the future) will determine the compatibility of Java applications running natively on the JavaStation. As of this writing, JavaOS has minor compatibility problems particularly with the networking components of the Java language. Pre Java Developer's Kit 1.1 implementations of Java RMI were basically unusable on the JavaStation. However, the latest JDK should correct those flaws.

The Java Revolution makes it to your desktop

The JavaStation and the JavaOS are but a few ways that Java hardware can change the way we exist and go about our daily lives. As the Java Chip architecture begins to get a solid foothold in the industry, we will see several devices from Personal Digital Assistants (PDA) to watches, cellular phones, and even home appliances take advantage of both the Java language and its accompanying hardware specification.

Java Chips

Beyond the JavaStation lies a vast expanse of uses for the Java language. Imagine a day when you pick up your cell phone, call your home, and tell your clothes dryer to start. Maybe you are away on a business trip, and you spot a program on television featuring the always enchanting Scott McNealy. You can pick up your phone, call your home, and tell your VCR to begin recording.

Look around your home or office. Look at all the devices that have some kind of computer, no matter how small, within them. Imagine if they were all written in platform-independent Java, if they were all networked somehow, and if creating applications to interface with them were as easy as creating a "Hello, World" application in Java.

This is the world of microelectronics and embedded systems, and Sun Microsystems, not satisfied with creating Java and changing the programming world, wants a part of it too. Their answer is picoJava, the dedicated Java processor. It is designed to run Java code faster than anything on the market today, including Just In Time (JIT) compilers and bytecode interpreters.

These embedded systems will require their own brand of networked communication, but to develop such a mechanism, some understanding is required of the hardware and software issues driving the arena. Embedded systems could mark the most explosive growth area for Java applications in the next five years. While most financial and telecommunication experts are rightfully conservative in their embrace of the Java language, the embedded systems folks see Java as the greatest thing since sliced bread. It is for that reason that the embedded systems arena may be your best bet at making a big splash in Java networking.

The Java Chip family

The picoJava line is designed to be inexpensive, fast, and accessible to all computer manufacturers. There are two kinds of chips, the microJava embedded chip designed to be placed in everything from cellular phones to cable boxes and ultraJava, its bigger desktop cousin. The ultraJava chip is still in its design stages, so we will concentrate on outlining the uses and abilities of the microJava chip.

Sun claims that systems containing the microJava chip can execute Java code around 12 times faster than code executed by Sun's own Java interpreter. While bytecode interpreters are making performance leaps almost monthly, Sun feels that for small footprint hardware architectures, similar to the limited capacity of those processors required for cellular phones and the like, a dedicated software Java Virtual Machine may be too much to ask for. If the hardware itself did the bytecode interpretation for your application, then more of your application can reside in the software end of an embedded system and a software-based VM would not be needed (see Figure 10-5).

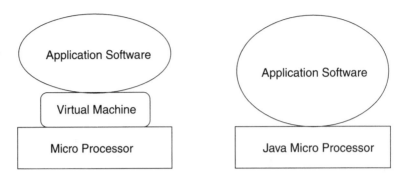

Figure 10–5 The Java microprocessor puts the Virtual Machine on a hardware level.

The problem with these Java chips is not their performance. For their dedicated uses, their performance will likely not be as much of an issue. The chances of a Java chip supplanting your desktop machine, be it a PowerPC or an Intel, are pretty slim. However, for an embedded system, these chips will more likely than not put forth excellent performance numbers and satisfy that need.

No, the problem with these chips is their flexibility. If the Java language were to change or the bytecode structure changes, the hardware, not simply the software, would have to change as well. Yet, for embedded systems this is not usually a worry. System designers of consumer appliance electronics will likely continue to embrace the Java language and the Java Chip as well.

The picoJava architecture

The Java Virtual Machine executes Java bytecodes using a well-defined instruction set, several data types, operands, and memory management routines. Translating that set of routines to a hardware level involved creating a mirror universe of instructions, operands, and memory management schemes on the chip level.

Today, software is compiled into code native to the hardware on which it runs. The Java Virtual Machine itself translates Java platform-independent bytecode into machine language so that it can execute. What if the virtual machine existed on a hardware, rather than software, level? Then, the compact instruction set contained within the Java bytecode specification could be run "directly on the iron" rather than being translated into native code.

Running Java bytecode directly off the chip involves implementing a hardware stack architecture that directly mimics that of the Virtual Machine. Furthermore, method calls and parameter passing were optimized because of Java applications' tendency to make several calls between functions. While the actual specifics of the picoJava architecture are either beyond the scope of this book or a Sun Microsystems trade secret, the end result looks quite promising. Sun claims that a wide range of applications running on picoJava were found to be 15 to 20 times faster than an Intel 486 at similar clock rates, and at least five times faster than a Pentium with a JIT compiler and identical clock rates.

Why Java Chips?

Java Chips are not a new Starbuck's snack food. They are serious attempts by Sun Microsystems to make the Java programming language the ubiquitous language for all computer systems entering the next century. The interesting prospect for Sun is to make an impact on the traditionally subdued embedded systems manufacturers. While conquering the hearts and minds of software engineers was easy because of the extreme volatility of the software industry, forcing major changes on hardware systems has been historically harder.

Java chips enable embedded software systems to be run on any platform, from your dishwasher to your television. Its small footprint and sufficient processing power gives it an advantage. Keep in mind that the Java Chip is much more than the much-hyped and controversial (for the Microsoft camp) Network Computer. The possibilities are endless.

Sun is gambling that the embedded systems market will go beyond expressing their love of Java. It is betting that it can make gobs and gobs of money by licensing the Java architecture to hundreds of embedded systems manufacturers, sparking a hardware revolution in consumer electronics while further fueling the massive hype surrounding Java itself.

Summary

By affecting hardware and the machines that exist in our everyday lives, Sun Microsystems is hoping that the Java processor will spark a true Java revolution. Up until now, the Java software revolution has been contained within the hallowed halls of geekdom, with occasional forays into the mainstream media. By changing the way we do business, go shopping, and run our lives, Sun's Java Chip could mark the beginning of the era of convergence, where all of our appliances and electronics gadgets begin to operate as one. These Java-enabled appliances could be networked computers running the JavaOS, or embedded systems that bring the mundane tasks of our daily routines to the Internet era.

Once we've developed applications and are ready to deploy them to the wonderful world of the Internet, we need to take a second and look at the very real security issues surrounding the new medium. First, do you plan on encrypting data before transmitting it? Do you plan on authenticating clients that talk to your servers? How do you plan on giving access to task-specific users within your intranet? These are but a few of the issues we will discuss in our next chapter.

CHAPTER 11

Java Security

Encryption

Authentication

Governmental restrictions

Java and Security

We have all heard that Java is a "secure" programming language. What exactly does that mean? In this chapter, we discuss the unique features of Java that make it the ideal choice for distributed network programming. Furthermore, we will discuss the nuances of the applet host security model, as well as how security is handled from within your Java applications.

We will also touch very briefly on Internet security and some of the alternatives you may want to explore in your own networked applications, making them safe for cross-network transmission. We begin our examination with encryption, the act of scrambling your data as it is sent across the wire. Another form of security, authentication, makes sure the information received from a network transmission is from an approved location.

Safety in Java

When we refer to Java as a safe language, we are referring to the fact that you cannot "shoot yourself in the foot." There are no memory leaks, no out of control threads, and no chances of ending up in the dark spiral of C++ debugging. Make no mistake—Java is a powerful language, and you will always end up with the possibility of sitting in an infinite loop. You can still freeze your Java code with thread deadlocks, and you can certainly end up accessing parts of an array that aren't really there. In short, Java is safe, but it isn't idiot proof. The fact remains that in order to screw up your Java programs, you still have to make a major effort.

Most Java programmers are pleased that Java has no pointers to memory locations. This makes program debugging much easier and it also makes security verification possible. It cannot be verified at compile time that a pointer will do no harm. It can be loaded at run-time with a naughty address to poke a hole in the password file or branch to some code that sprinkles at-signs all over a disk. Without pointers, Java ensures that all mischief is done within the downloaded applet running inside a Java virtual machine. Moreover, memory is not allocated until runtime, and this prevents hackers from studying source code to take advantage of memory layout because it is not known at compile-time. Attempts to write beyond the end of an array, for example, raise an `ArrayIndexOutOfBoundsException`. This feature alone would have prevented the infamous Morris Internet worm from tricking `sendmail` (running with root privileges) to give root access to the worm.

Garbage collection, exceptions, and thread controls are part of Java no matter how you try to use it. But, security and safety are two entirely different things. Safety refers to protecting ourselves from our own stupidity. Security refers to protecting ourselves from others' stupidity. Because Java objects are loaded dynamically, Java ensures that the objects are "trusted." Java's class security mechanism makes sure that your applications are using the proper objects and not an object someone has surreptitiously slipped into the download stream.

Java Class Security

The designers of Java knew that applets could be downloaded over unsecure networks, so they included a bytecode verifier in the Java virtual machine's interpreter. This checks that memory addresses are not forged to access objects outside of the virtual machine, that applet objects are accessed according to their scope (public, private, and protected), and that strict runtime type enforcement is done both for object types and parameters passed with method invocations. These checks are done by the bytecode verifier after the bytecodes are downloaded but before they are executed. This means the verified code runs faster because it need not perform these security checks during execution.

Each imported class executes within its own name space. There is a single name space for built-in classes loaded from the local filesystem. Built-in classes can be trusted and the class loader searches the local name space first. This prevents a downloaded class from spoofing a built-in class. Also, the name space of the same server is searched before the class loader searches other name spaces. This prevents one server from spoofing a class from a different server. Note that this search order ensures a built-in class will find another built-in class before it searches an imported name space. So, when classes are downloaded, the client's built-in classes are used because they are trusted (see Figure 11-1).

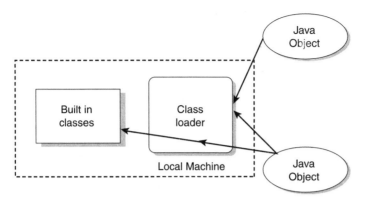

Figure 11–1 Downloaded Java objects use the local built-in classes rather than their own.

Java's networking classes can be configured to allow access in one of four different ways:

1. Access to any host on the network
2. Access outside the firewall only if the class itself was loaded from outside
3. Access only to the host from which the code was downloaded
4. Disallow network access altogether

For example, applets running inside a Netscape browser can access only the host from which it was downloaded, while applets running inside a HotJava browser do not need to have this restriction. Note that the Netscape browser's choice of security level would be impossible if the Java language allowed pointers. How could a bytecode verifier guarantee that a pointer is never used to access a method that deposits a copy of the Redskins playbook into the Cowboy's Web site? Only an exhaustive search of all possible execution paths under all possible inputs could make such a guarantee. This would be possible only for very trivial applets.

Finally, the Java language has been thoroughly field-tested by billions and billions of high school and university students, college dropouts, and professional hackers lurking in the dark alleys of the World Wide Web. Each and every one of their creative minds was confident it could find a flaw in such a seemingly wide-open door to any system in the world! The most publicized security breaches happened early in Java's distribution and all have been corrected in the current 1.0.2 and 1.1 releases. It has been very quiet ever since. The flaws that were uncovered were implementation errors, not design problems. One group was able to insert their own class loader instead of the one loaded from a secure local file system. Clearly all bets are off if an untrusted class loader is used that doesn't enforce the class search order we described earlier. Another implementation bug was exploited by using a bogus Domain Name Server in cahoots with an evil applet. Java 1.0.2 uses IP addresses instead of host names to enforce the network access security levels described earlier.

Details about these early security flaws and their corrections can be found at `http://java.sun.com/sfaq`. You can download a "security validation test suite" of Java programs that test the security of a system from that site. We've included them on the CD-ROM that accompanies this book and there is a link on our Web site to the current suite of test programs on `java.sun.com`.

Here are the contents of the security test suite as of December 1, 1996.

- Files:
  - Can this applet read files on your system?
  - Can this applet obtain information about files on your system?
  - Can this applet write a file on your system?
  - Can this applet use `File.delete()` to delete the file named `/tmp/foo`?
  - Can this applet use the UNIX command `/bin/rm` to delete the file named `/tmp/foo`?

- System Properties:
  - Can this applet read the ten system properties that applets are allowed to read by default?
  - Can this applet read hidden properties like `user.name` or `user.home`?
  - Can this applet replace your browser's property file?

- Sockets:
  - Can this applet connect to port 25 on `www.netscape.com`?
  - Can this applet send data to `www.sun.com`?

- Processes:
  - Can this applet kill your browser?
  - Can this applet run programs on your computer?

- Libraries and name spaces:
  - Can this applet load a library on your computer?
  - Can this applet create its own class loader?
  - Can this applet create a class of its own in the `java.net` name space?

- Windows:
  - What does a window created by an applet look like?

Table 11-1 details the behavior you can expect for certain actions of a Java program given the browser in which it runs and the location from which the program is downloaded.

Table 11-1 Security restrictions of various applet environments.

Action	Download a file using the specified browser from the specified location				
	Netscape Navigator		Appletviewer		Java Standalone Application
	From a Network	From a Local Disk	From a Network	From a Local Disk	
Read a file on a local file system?	No	No	No	Yes	Yes
Write a file on a local file system?	No	No	No	Yes	Yes
Delete a file using File.delete ( )?	No	No	No	No	Yes
Delete a file using a system call?	No	No	No	Yes	Yes
Read the user.name property?	No	Yes	No	Yes	Yes
Connect to a port on the client host?	No	Yes	No	Yes	Yes
Connect to a port on a third host?	No	Yes	No	Yes	Yes
Load a library	No	Yes	No	Yes	Yes
exit (1)?	No	No	No	Yes	Yes
Create a pop-up window?	No	Yes	No	Yes	Yes

Encryption

In this section, we describe some of the techniques commonly used to encrypt data exchanges between two parties. Data traveling through the Internet can be captured (and possibly modified) by a third party. Certainly, you do not want your credit card number to be revealed to a third party and you probably also want the merchandise you purchased to be delivered to your address and not to a different address inserted by a third party. Data encryption ensures that a third party will not be able to decipher any message sent between a client and a server.

A very simple algorithm used to scramble "sensitive" jokes on the Internet is called "rot13" because it rotates each character by 13 positions in the alphabet. That is, "a" is mapped to "n", "b" is mapped to "o", and so on. This algorithm also decrypts a message that was scrambled by it. This is adequate for its purpose: to protect people from reading a joke that they might feel is offensive. This is an example of *symmetric key encryption,* where both sides use the same key (13) to encrypt and decrypt a scrambled message (see Figure 11-2).

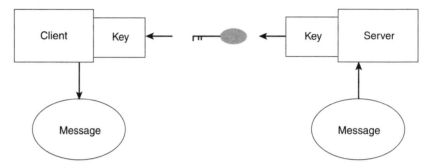

Figure 11–2 Symmetric key encryption decodes messages with a key on both the sending and receiving end.

More powerful mathematical algorithms are used by symmetric key encryption products such as DES (Data Encryption Standard), Triple DES, RC2, RC4, and IDEA. DES uses a 56-bit key to scramble blocks of 64-bits in the message. It was designed for hardware implementation and is relatively fast for encrypting large amounts of data. It is used by Secure Sockets Layer (SSL), but its global use is limited because U.S. law prohibits its export. Recent research has shown that DES can be cracked by a "million dollar machine" (pocket change for Bill Gates). Many companies now use "triple DES," which encrypts each block of data three times with three different keys (No, triple DES cannot be cracked by a three-million dollar machine). RC2 and RC4 use 40-bit keys that make them two and ten times faster than DES, respectively. More important, however, is the fact that RC2 and RC4 can be exported with 40-bit keys. IDEA (International Data Encryption Algorithm) uses a 128-bit key and is very strong encryption!

One problem with symmetric key algorithms such as DES is key distribution. Both ends use the same key and anyone else who knows the key can, of course, decrypt any message encrypted with that key. The key distribution problem is solved by an asymmetric key encryption technique called public/private key encryption. As its name suggests, each user has a public key known by anyone on the Internet and a private key that each user must keep secret. It is based on a strong mathematical foundation with an encryption algorithm that uses two very large prime numbers. The probability of cracking this encryption is so astronomically low that the algorithm can be published without worry because the two prime numbers are computationally impossible to discover.

The beauty is that a single key need not be exchanged. Public keys can be distributed freely; in fact, you want everybody to know your public key. Anyone can encrypt a message with your public key and only you (or someone who knows your private key) can decrypt it! You can encrypt your reply by using the sender's public key. Pretty slick, eh?

A side effect of public/private key encryption is that it can also be used to authenticate the sender. A user encrypts a message with his or her private key and, if you can decrypt it with their public key, then you can be sure it really came from the sender (as long as someone has not published a bogus public key for the person signing the e-mail). In other words, if you can trust the public key you have, then you can be sure the message was sent by the person with the unique matching private key. This use of public/private key encryption is called a digital signature. There are plans to include a digital signature when a Java applet is downloaded so that clients can verify that servers are who they say they are.

A company named VeriSign provides digital authentication products and services. For example, the first time a cellular telephone dealer logs in to enroll with a service provider it is assigned a public/private key pair from a secure server located on VeriSign's premises. Thereafter, a digital signature is sent along with each message between a dealer and the provider, and the recipient verifies the sender's public key with VeriSign at the beginning of each interactive session. Messages can be decrypted only by the owner of the private key. Moreover, clients (dealers) cannot deny having submitted a subscriber registration, and the server (cellular telephone service provider) cannot deny having granted the service subscription.

How are private, signed messages sent? The sender first encrypts the message using his or her private key (signing) and then encrypts the resulting message with the recipient's public key (making it private). The double-encrypted message is sent over the Internet. Nobody except the intended recipient (with the matching private key) can decrypt the message, and then decrypt the resulting message with the sender's public key. Using a secure third-party server such as VeriSign's, all parties can validate the other side's public key, as long as the third-party server is not compromised.

All of this is wonderful, except that public/private key encryption is computationally expensive. A natural way to provide the same security while reducing the encryption overhead significantly is to encrypt the actual message with a single symmetric key, and use public/private key encryption to send the symmetric key to the recipient. The random symmetric key created by the sender is called a message or session key. It is encrypted with the intended recipient's public key. The intended recipient (and only the intended recipient) can decrypt the session key with its private key, and then use it to decrypt the private message.

This is almost perfect! The message is private, but the sender is not authenticated, nor is it certain that the message has not been altered. One way to guarantee the integrity of the message is to compute a checksum at one end and verify it at the other end. A mathematically solid algorithm called MD5 (Message Digest 5) is commonly used to produce a fixed-length checksum (or message digest code) that can be computed at both ends. The message digest code produced by MD5 is sufficiently unique that it is virtually impossible for two messages to have the same MD5 code. Also, it is sufficiently random that it is virtually impossible (computationally unfeasible) to determine the original message from its MD5 code. More important, it is virtually impossible to substitute a modified message that will produce the same MD5 code at the other end.

Now the sender creates a message and computes its MD5 code, which is then encrypted with the sender's private key. The message is encrypted with a symmetric (DES) key chosen at random, and the DES key is encrypted with the recipient's public key. Everything is sent to the recipient. Only the intended recipient can decrypt the DES key with its private key. The DES key is then used to decrypt the message. An MD5 code is computed from the message and it is compared with the one received from the sender (after decrypting it with the sender's public key). If the two MD5 codes match, the message is tamper-free and signed by the sender.

It's as simple as that! Privacy is accomplished efficiently by using a symmetric (DES) key to scramble the (lengthy?) message, authentication is accomplished by using public/private keys to scramble the MD5 code and the session (DES) key, and message integrity is accomplished by computing an MD5 code at both ends and comparing them.

Authentication

In many applications it is important to authenticate the identity of a client making a request for a service. Examples include banking, financial, real estate, medical records, and ISP (Internet Service Provider) applications. An ISP, for example, wants to ensure that Internet access is being provided to a paying customer and not the customer's housekeeper. The on-line stock trading application wants to make sure it is the portfolio owner who is making trades.

The usual way to do this is to require an account number or customer name and a password. This is adequate for work stations and time-sharing systems and client-server sessions such as calling Charles Schwab to manage your stock portfolio account. In a distributed system, however, various services are provided by many different servers. Instead of a single authentication to a single server or application, each service request sent over the network must be authenticated by the server.

One obvious requirement of such an authentication system is that it be transparent to the user. The user does not want to type in a password for each service each time it is requested. Another requirement is that it be available at all times because, if a server cannot authenticate a request, it will not provide the service. When the authentication service is unavailable so are all the services that use it. A less obvious requirement is that authentication must be protected against capture and playback by another user on the network. Capture cannot be prevented on broadcast media such as an Ethernet cable, so the authentication procedure must be able to prevent a playback by an impostor.

One popular authentication system is Kerberos, which is named after a 3-headed guard dog in Greek mythology. It depends on a third party that is trusted by both client and server (see Figure 11-3). Clients request a ticket from the third party. The ticket is encrypted using the server's secret password, so the server trusts the client when it can decrypt the ticket. The server's password is known only to itself and the third party. The third party knows everyone's password! This means that all systems are vulnerable if the trusted third party is compromised.

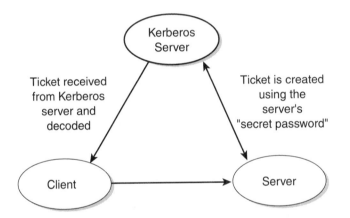

Figure 11-3 Servers can trust clients only if they can decrypt the ticket from the Kerberos server.

A well-known bank has two major data centers, one in San Francisco and the other in Los Angeles. Each center backs up its data at the other site. In this way, the bank can resume operation soon after serious damage to either data center. The Kerberos servers are replicated at both sites and kept behind "the glass wall." In fact, there is a sealed walkway with locked doors at both ends and a badge reader with a video camera in the middle. If your face doesn't resemble the one on the badge, you are not allowed into the room that houses the Kerberos servers. In fact, you are promptly escorted out of the building by two or more very large people.

Playback is thwarted by including a timestamp in the ticket. That is, the Kerberos server encrypts the client's IP address, a session key, and a timestamp *using the server's key.* The client encrypts its service request message with the *session key* and sends it, along with the ticket, to the server. The server uses *its key* to decrypt the ticket. If the IP address in the ticket matches the IP address in the IP packet header **and** the timestamp is within a few milliseconds of the current time, then the server accepts the client's request. It uses the *session key* to unscramble the request and perform the service. It's as simple as that. Playback is impossible because the *encrypted timestamp will have "timed out" before an impostor can capture and try to replay the request*. Also, the IP address of the impostor will not match the IP address encrypted in the ticket.

Governments and Security

The issue of security on our computers is greatly affected by the restrictions on security technology placed on a company by its home government. Because this is not by any stretch of the imagination a comprehensive text on security, we instead outline the two major controversies concerning government intervention in computer security. We attempt not to pass judgment on either the government or the security community; you can make that determination for yourself. Instead, in this section, we simply point out the two sides to the arguments of governmental control of security export and the government's right to possess keys to domestic security apparatuses.

Export control

The United States government is extremely adamant in protecting against U.S. technology falling into non-domestic hands. But, because the Internet is a worldwide medium and social phenomenon, without boundaries and governments to hinder it, the government realizes that some form of security technology must be used to transmit information across national boundaries. Therefore, the U.S. government restricts the level of security found in certain products that are international in nature. For example, the Netscape browser has two versions. One is a U.S. domestic version with full browser security features. The other is an international version that implements the Secure Socket Layer with less security. The international version may be exported outside the United States, while the domestic version may be used only within the United States.

Never mind the inability to actually protect against the dissemination of the more powerful security technology to international audiences, the United States simply makes the distinction. If Netscape were to blindly distribute the domestic version without making a statement such as "Domestic Use Only," they would be breaking the law. Is the law enforceable to end users? Probably not, but the law is there, written as plain as day, and should be followed by "morally upstanding citizens." For you, as application programmers, secure networked applications should follow the same kind of export controls if they are applicable.

The "Clipper" controversy

Historically, the United States government has always known that there are ways for its citizens to keep information hidden from the government. In fact, the

Fourth Amendment to the Constitution of the United States of America specifically outlines this right that all American citizens possess:

> *The right of the people to be secure in their persons, houses, papers, and effects, against unreasonable searches and seizures, shall not be violated, and no Warrants shall issue, but upon probable cause, supported by Oath or affirmation, and particularly describing the place to be searched, and the persons or things to be seized.*

But, over the years a distinction has been made as to what is "unreasonable." The government, in interests of "national security" may, with permission from the Judicial branch, execute a search of one's property and possessions. How does this apply to the digital age?

The entire "Clipper chip" controversy centers around the government's willingness to publish an encryption algorithm for telephones, computer files, and any other form of communication. The transmissions would be encrypted and mathematically impossible to break. However, the government would always be able to have a "back door" to the encryption with its own special key. As outlined in the Fourth Amendment, the government may use the key only with a written warrant, but nevertheless the idea that "Big Brother" may be watching is enough to bring chills down the spines of some people.

Lost in the argument is the fact that there are several other encryption algorithms that could be used instead of Clipper, like PGP for example, that are just as good and do not muck with governmental interference. But, Clipper represents the entire belief that in the end, the United States government, as well as the governments of the entire world, has no idea how to protect itself without sacrificing intellectual freedom in the digital age.

Summary

Secure, networked transmissions are of the utmost importance to many people. If the Internet is truly to become the focus of all our communication into the next century, then we must all have confidence that no one can intercept and decode our innermost thoughts. While we have very briefly outlined the concerns of the United States government, we hesitate to endorse or criticize any one position. In the end, the debate over the involvement of government authorities will be settled in another, more appropriate, forum. For now, as application programmers, you should be keenly aware of the position of your government, whatever it may be, on how you can send secure transmissions.

With this solid base of network programming underneath us, we must now make a decision about which alternative to choose. Each has its advantages and disadvantages, and we will discuss them in detail in the next chapter.

CHAPTER 12

Sockets

Java IDL

Java RMI

JDBC

Other

Making an
Architectural
Decision

Making a decision is difficult, particularly when the fate of your company's entire vision may be at stake. While we make no attempt to salvage the many Titanics of free enterprise, we do offer our thoughts on what the world of Java networking can mean to you. In this chapter, we candidly browse the advantages and disadvantages of each communication alternative. Do you want the heavy-duty power of CORBA or the lightweight simplicity of RMI? Are databases vital to your business process, or do you require customizable protocols?

As we have seen, Java networking is a vast and expansive subject. This book is the tip of the iceberg, and as the industry begins to shake out, more and more information will be brought forward. This chapter will help you separate fact from fiction, reality from hype, and engineering from marketeering.

Java sockets

Many of the alternatives we have discussed in this book involve sockets in some way or another. To recommend that you not use sockets essentially would be to say that you should not use any of the technologies we talk about. Sockets by themselves are useful for quite a few different things. Remember, when you send an RMI or IDL message, you are essentially sending a big chunk of data and the headers to that data. When we discussed our own message format in Chapter 2, "Java Sockets," we were able to put together a small, lightweight messaging system. If speed and efficiency are of the utmost importance to you, then certainly you would be interested in using Java sockets alone.

Flexibility

Remember, we created our own message format and we transmitted it with great speed. Our message format was not inadequate as it transmitted all the information we required. Notice too that we did not have to learn anything new. As long as we know what a socket is and how to use it, we can easily transmit a message to our server.

Servers are equally easy to create. With Java IDL and Java RMI, we needed to create an entire infrastructure for our server. With sockets, converting an application to a server application was not only easy, but extremely powerful. Once again, we lost no functionality by using sockets instead of some other communication alternative.

Furthermore, we could simply convert our connection-oriented socket to a broadcast socket. Then we could use the broadcast socket to send information to a port while allowing anyone else to listen in on that port. Because of this ability to easily and quickly switch between paradigms, sockets can be an excellent choice for both the beginner and the advanced networking guru who wants to build his own infrastructure.

Simplicity

As we saw, using sockets is extremely simple. Once you get the concepts down, actually changing your applications to use sockets is quite an easy task. Using the `ServerSocket`, you are able to build a simple server. By integrating threads, you can make sure your server is efficient in its handling of data. In addition, there is no confusing IDL to learn and no RMI API to understand. By using only sockets, you sacrifice the functionality of RMI and IDL for speed and ease of use.

Because the networking world understands and knows sockets so well, having built and deployed applications that use sockets for years, you will also have a ready supply of applications to use from within Java. Because sockets do not actually send data "over the wire" and instead send strings of information, you can seamlessly plug your Java applications into new or existing applications written in other languages. Just as with Java IDL, sockets give you the promise of being able to easily integrate legacy applications.

Again, there are several trade-offs between sockets and the other alternatives we discuss in this book. Java IDL also integrates legacy applications well, but the "plug and play" ability of Java IDL is a distinct advantage over using sockets alone. With sockets, you have to make sure everyone is speaking the same protocol. With Java IDL, there is no message format or protocol to worry about. Simply invoke remote objects as if they were already on your machine.

Java IDL

Every year for the past three years was touted as "the year CORBA will break out." Every January a flood of articles in trade rags and industry newsletters trumpets the arrival of the Common Object Request Broker Architecture. While it is anyone's guess as to what the future will be, it is a relatively safe assumption that CORBA, or a derivative thereof, will power the forces of the Internet for quite some time. The reasons are numerous, but the fact remains that CORBA technology, although not devoid of major shortcomings, is the most robust, mature, and powerful alternative presented in this book. Any investigation into an Internet communication strategy should place CORBA at the top of the list of technologies to investigate.

Advantages of JavaIDL

JavaIDL is a well thought-out, coherent set of base objects that can be used to create a tightly woven distributed-object system. Because of the maturity of CORBA, many of the questions about JavaRMI and sockets have been addressed in the specification and in the products currently available. In a moment, we will discuss the advantages and disadvantages of the various implementations of the specification that are on the market today. Yet, regardless of the great number of ORBs, JavaIDL is a solidly engineered set of core components that facilitate Java to ORB programming.

As we have discussed, the ORB isolates an object from the underlying mechanisms that ensure a client does not need to know the physical location of a server, how to start the server, or even if it should shut the server down. When you walk into a supermarket, the doors are automatic. You don't have to open them automatically, and you don't have to close them behind you. Similarly, an ORB handles a lot of the internal machinations of networked communication for you.

Beyond its maturity and its handling of much of the boredom of working with networked objects, JavaIDL is also Java. It uses the same memory handling, parameter passing, serialization, and so on, that Java does, and therefore helps to alleviate the learning curve of CORBA itself.

Disadvantages of JavaIDL

JavaIDL's biggest disadvantage is also one of its strong advantages: JavaIDL is CORBA. CORBA is a complex series of rules and regulations (in the software sense) governing how distributed objects should behave. JavaIDL is completely CORBA compatible, and is therefore an extension of CORBA itself. It plugs into CORBA very easily and without much hassle, but at a pretty steep price. In order to use JavaIDL effectively, you must understand CORBA and truly understand the principles of distributed objects. While this book attempts to outline what CORBA is and why you would want to use it, it is not the ultimate resource.

Yet, because of Java, much of the memory management morass and the differences between varied ORBs is rendered moot because the nature of Java removes it. Java is platform independent and requires no memory management on the programmer's part. Even though CORBA programming is hard, thank your lucky stars for Java. Just taking a look at a C++ CORBA program compared to a Java CORBA program will make a Java believer out of you.

JavaIDL implementations

There are three major vendors of CORBA-based products today. The first is Sun Microsystems. Sun is a major proponent of the CORBA revolution, and their NEO product is an extension of their commitment to the industry. NEO is a heavyweight, completely scalable solution for CORBA clients and servers. Visigenic's VisiBroker is a smart, easy-to-use CORBA option that offers strong three-tier client/server capabilities. If talking to a database is of the utmost priority for your software architecture, VisiBroker for Java might be your best option.

The current industry leader is Orbix. Unlike NEO, Orbix exists on every platform. While Orbix may have some problems with speed and scalability, it is a reliable, easy-to-use object broker. Many customers find getting started with Orbix to be a relatively easy task, and discover soon thereafter that CORBA isn't as bad as it was cracked up to be.

JavaIDL is robust

Imagine creating a client application that can invoke a server, get information, and report results without even once having to worry about network code, server-side behavior, or slow system resources. CORBA, and the ORB specifically, handle all of those tasks for you. So long as an ORB is on both the client and the server platform, the request can get through to the server, the server can be started up if necessary, and the server can process information for the client.

The notion of an ORB on every platform is not as far-fetched as you might expect. Sun's Solaris operating system is incorporating Sun's own NEO family of CORBA products directly. When you get Solaris, you will also get the plumbing necessary to create CORBA fixtures. Similarly, OLE and COM have always been present on the Microsoft Windows operating environment, and with CORBA offering a strong OLE/COM to CORBA connectivity solution as part of its specification, the client side on Windows platforms will soon be a reality.

Furthermore, a JavaIDL application also includes its own "mini-ORB" that provides limited functionality so that an ORB need not be present within the Web browser itself. Netscape, however, as part of its ONE series of technology announcements, promises full ORB integration in its Web browser in soon-to-come future versions. In this way, the Web browser can act as a communication mediator between clients and CORBA servers.

JavaIDL is difficult

One of the big gripes we have heard and emphasized in this book is that CORBA is difficult. Well, there's no getting around the fact that in the past you had to be a true C++ expert in order to understand CORBA itself. You could allocate a chunk of memory on the client side, pass it to the server, where it got deallocated, and still have a memory leak on your client side. That was just one of the many, many, many problems with C++ and CORBA.

Yet, that is much more of a C++ problem than a CORBA problem. True, you still need to know much more than the basics of object-oriented programming to use CORBA, but with Java things become much easier. Memory management, for one, is no longer even an issue.

The Interface Definition Language is blasted by critics as just one more thing you need to know in order to program in CORBA. True, the IDL is a sometimes unneeded layer on top of your normal application, but it serves a very important purpose. It prevents your applications from being locked into one language. Who knows? Tomorrow, a new programming language may emerge with its own cool name, its own cult following, and its own list of strengths. The entire world may jump on that bandwagon much as it has with Java. But, CORBA applications still will be important and will not be rendered obsolete because they can be phased into the new language in a short time without affecting the rest of the system.

Language independence, while not of real importance to the subject of this book, is the single most interesting thing about CORBA. It enables you to migrate applications to new platforms, new languages, and even new algorithms without having to adjust the entire object system. Remember, with JavaRMI you are locked into Java until you have a reason to change. That kind of thinking is why many people are trying today to figure out how to migrate from COBOL.

Java IDL is powerful

Java IDL is a flexible, distributed-object environment. With it, you can invoke C++ objects half a world away as if they were both local and written in Java. To you, the application programmer, the Java to CORBA to C++ is hidden. You simply instantiate Java objects and talk to C++ servers on the other end without even knowing. Of course, if you prefer to write Java servers, more power to you.

Remember, language independence is a very good thing for large-scale object systems. You can swap components in and out using the language most appropriate for the task. If you happen to have a CORBA to LISP language mapping (don't panic, there isn't one), you could write all of your artificial intelligence components in LISP, while saving UI or computation components for an object-oriented language like Java or C++. Java IDL is the only alternative we present that can possibly integrate such disparate object components.

But, for many people the simplicity and elegance of Java RMI may be all that is needed. Maybe you don't have any legacy systems to be integrated. Maybe language independence is of no use to you. Maybe all you want is a simple remote object invocation system. In that case, Java RMI is definitely your cup of tea.

Java RMI decisions

After surveying the entire spectrum of Java solutions we offer in this book, it is time to make a decision. Perhaps JavaRMI has piqued your interest. The promise of never having to see C++ again seems like a good thing. Using the fun and robust networking ability inherent in Java may be an even better reason to turn to a Java-only alternative. Whatever the reason, this is the place to get an honest account of what RMI can and cannot do for you.

RMI Advantages

One of the absolute best things about JavaRMI is that you never ever have to see C++ again. C++ is arcane, difficult, and frustrating. Meanwhile, Java is fun, easy, and exciting. Because Java offers the strongest alternative yet to a series of frustrations wrought upon the computer science population, JavaRMI has garnered significant attention from the masses. It follows a simple notion of abstracting distributed implementations by publishing interfaces and linking in implementations of those interfaces later on.

Because we invested a significant amount of time, money, and effort in the Java revolution by learning and promoting the language, we may be tempted to jump directly into an all-Java solution to the communication quandary. Because invocations on Java objects are simple to begin with, JavaRMI makes sure that it is equally simple to make the same kinds of invocations across different virtual machines. It is precisely this simplicity that makes JavaRMI appealing.

RMI Disadvantages

JavaRMI has three significant drawbacks however. For those interested in Java-only programming, these may not be an issue. However, for those interested in rewriting an entire business in Java, JavaRMI may not be much of a solution. Java does not make it easy to integrate legacy applications. If most of your business is conducted using C++ or C, introducing Java may be more trouble than its worth. Your C++ and C modules are used to having unlimited access to system resources, while the Java Virtual Machine may prevent some of that freedom to which you are quite accustomed.

Second, Java is not fast. Indeed, it is an interpreted language, and therefore is subjected to a layer of processing that C++ and C are not. However, the introduction of JIT compilers and other performance enhancements may negate the issue. Still, it is important to realize that if performance is at a premium, Java may not be the language for you; JavaRMI, in particular, may not be the communication alternative for you. While other options in this book place the performance burden on servers that could just as easily not be Java servers, JavaRMI offers no easy out on the issue.

Finally, Java RMI applications are not widely accepted, and there is no industry standard as with JDBC and JavaIDL that will ensure that your applications are interoperable. One day, perhaps far in the future, JavaRMI will get smart and speak the same Internet Inter-ORB Protocol as JavaIDL, enabling programmers to take advantage of the functionality of CORBA without even having to know what it is. After all, a remote object is a remote object, whether it is a CORBA object or an RMI object. Until that time, JavaRMI clients can talk only to JavaRMI servers.

Three-tier applications in RMI

As we discussed in previous chapters, the notion of three-tier client-server computing will not go away. It is the foundation for most of today's distributed systems. MIS weenies love it because it enables them to funnel access to data sources through a central repository. Programmers love it because they can revise and update the various components of their applications without massive overhauls. After all, the business logic contained in servers defines how and when databases are accessed. Client side GUIs are concerned only with getting and displaying information. If a programmer makes a change in the business logic, there is no need to push the change to the client as well.

JavaRMI does not readily facilitate the notion of three-tier client server computing any more than JavaIDL does. Both are, in fact, middle-tier technologies. Sure, client side applications written in JavaRMI are required to communicate with an RMI server, but the client is, essentially, only Java. The real functionality, brains, and resource management takes place on the server end. The data source is nothing but a repository of information.

Once again, the performance problem rears its ugly head. Because the middle tier is intended to be home to all of the business logic in an object system, JavaRMI servers may have to process data extremely efficiently, perhaps more efficiently than possible.

JavaRMI is not robust

Perhaps the most important aspect of RMI is its lack of support for true distributed computing. When invoking across machines and networks, the fact is that a client generally has no control over how processes are executed on the remote end. Indeed, the remote end can very well be an entirely different hardware architecture than expected. JavaRMI offers no ability to allow a client to invoke without knowing the destination of the request. The lack of location independence should be quite a significant factor in making an architectural decision towards RMI.

While JavaRMI is easy to understand, get started with, and design frameworks around, it does not address some of the fundamental network concerns of distributed-object programmers. Location independence is one of these concerns, as is automatic startup. When a client invokes a server for the first time, the request goes through only if the server is already running. This requires the server programmer not only to have the server available, but to provide for fault tolerance. What if the server goes down unexpectedly? Part of the software design specification should be an automatic failover to a backup server, or to automatically restart the server itself. Needless to say, these are difficult tasks to program and may be more trouble than they are worth.

JavaRMI is a fantastic approach to remote object invocations. It is easy, fun, and a logical extension of the Java programming language. However, it is hampered by several severe deficiencies that prevent it from becoming a mainstream solution to distributed object computing. Mission-critical application programmers may find the shortcomings of RMI to be reason enough to search for another alternative.

JDBC

Java Database Connectivity is an enabling technology, not necessarily a communication framework in and of itself. By enabling technology, we mean that it enables you to link other communication strategies with repositories of information and data to form a cohesive network of objects that can communicate vast quantities of information. JDBC is not the answer in itself, but in combination with JavaIDL, JavaRMI, or even Java Sockets, it can be a heck of a powerful answer to the Internet question for the next decade.

Why JDBC is not enough

JDBC alone limits you in what you can accomplish with advanced networking. Every client that talks to a database connects directly with the database. There can be no additional intelligence added in the business logic to assist with routing messages. Basically, your applications are connected to the database, and if that causes some kind of sluggishness between the database and the client, then so be it. In the end, the decision to use JDBC alone or with another technology amounts to a decision between the two-tier and three-tier architectural models.

The two-tier architecture links clients directly with the data repository as shown in Figure 12-1. This means that any kind of processing for the access and any further processing for the data retrieved from the repository is left to the client. Splitting the business logic out of the client is the driving force behind the three-tier model. However, in some cases that trait is not a necessary qualification because if your applications are deployed often, or maybe even deployed over the Web, then updating a client is not a major factor because it will be done no matter what architecture you choose. If you are deploying shrink-wrapped applications written in Java--as will be common in just a few years—then updating applications constantly will be a major pain, and you may want to revert to a three-tier model.

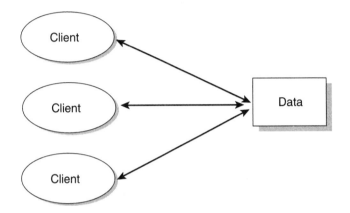

Figure 12–1 Two-tier client to database architecture.

The biggest drawback to the two-tier model is the sheer number of clients that may attach itself to a data repository. Typically, data repositories are not set up to handle the intelligent management of resources that is required to process multiple simultaneous invocations. If your applications ping the database only rarely, then this is not a factor for you. However, if there are to be many instances of your client application, you will want to go to a three-tier model.

A three-tier model is predicated on the belief that business logic should not exist in either a client or a database. It dictates that the client should be a pretty application the sole purpose of which is to funnel information back to the user. The client is typically a rich GUI with simple execution steps that relies completely on the information given to it by the middle tier (see Figure 12-2).

The middle tier is a server that talks to a data repository. The server is written using JavaIDL, Sockets, or JavaRMI, and can talk to the database using JDBC. JDBC acts, as it always does, as the interface from a client (in this case the middle-tier server) to a database. It just so happens that the server is fully capable of handling multiple invocations and requests and houses all of the business logic. The business logic could range from simply adding a number of results from a data-

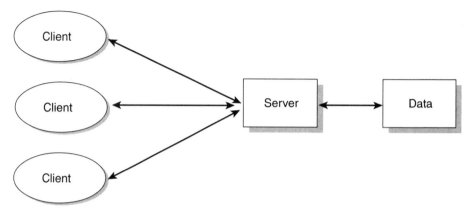

Figure 12-2 Three-tier application architecture with server middleman.

base query and passing it back to the client, to invoking other servers using the same data. Whatever it does with the data it retrieves, the server can manipulate it as it sees fit and pass the information back to the client.

JDBC and JavaIDL or JavaRMI

As we discussed, the middle tier in the three-tier architecture could easily be JavaIDL or JavaRMI. Indeed, IDL and RMI are complimentary technologies to JDBC. JDBC is not their competition because the vast majority of people using JDBC use it within a middle-tier paradigm. This is why JavaIDL and JavaRMI are vital to JDBC's success. Moreover, JDBC lends credibility to JavaIDL and JavaRMI. Without a simple technology to enable database access, JavaIDL and JavaRMI would be largely useless in the business community.

The largest investments made by most companies in their computing infrastructure is contained within their databases. Databases often are used to maintain important records ranging from medical history to employment records and to keep track of business processes from supply purchases to stock maintenance. Most of the time, changing the database to a Java-only application is not only difficult and expensive, but completely unreasonable and unfeasible. For this reason, JDBC can be used to communicate and update the database, while the middle-tier server can be quickly migrated to Java using the techniques in this book.

Client applications can be generated quite easily using the many visual Java builders on the market today. Often, client applications are not only simpler to create, test, and deploy, but are less vital and less error prone than the rest of the architectural model.

JDBC Alone

While using JDBC alone is certainly not out of the question, it is highly discouraged for mission-critical applications. However, for proof of concept applications, applications requiring limited data access, and even for heavy-duty applications with large chunks of data transfer, JDBC may be an excellent option.

What JDBC gives you is a simple, clean interface to a database that requires no additional knowledge of network programming, distributed design, or remote procedure calls. For database programmers, JDBC is a welcome arrival for Java because it means that they need not build special server programs whose sole purpose is to funnel information back to the client. In other words, for those programmers who desire not to use three-tier computing, JDBC is the perfect answer.

Because of its simplicity, you will find that for major application development efforts, JDBC is all you need to affect some kind of persistence for your client applications. Clients can do their heavy computation, cool graphics, or whatever and store their state in a database using JDBC. The next time the client is executed, it can retrieve its previous state from the database and start again where it left off.

JDBC overview

JDBC is a fantastic set of APIs to connect Java applications and applets directly to databases. With its simplicity, robustness, and ability to bring together the disparate worlds of databases and the Internet, JDBC will be a successful venture for Java. By modifying your existing database clients for Java, you can capture all of the usefulness of the Java Revolution without sacrificing the power required to manipulate your data stores.

Other Java technologies

In addition to the four major Java communication technologies, we have shown you three other mechanisms you can use to plug your Java applications into the Internet. Beans, Servlets, and JMAPI give you the means necessary to package, publish, and administer the applications you have written in RMI, IDL, JDBC, or Sockets. While the "big four" are fascinating and powerful in their own right, they need the additional functionality provided by the other Java APIs that have been or will be published in the future.

When to use Beans

Let's say you've created a bunch of gee-whiz Java applications to interface with your hand-held Personal Information Manager. These applications have several modules that translate the data on the device to a format that is readable by your on-disk schedule manager. These modules are for your address book, to-do list, and schedule. By dividing your Java applications into separate, self-contained

Beans, you can publish the components. Moreover, if you were to split out the network component that interfaces the device with your computer, then others can write their own customizable applications that use your network module (see Figure 12-3).

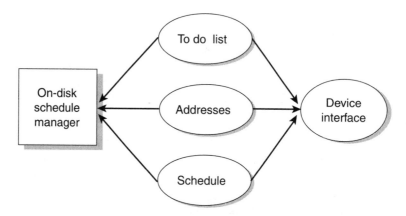

Figure 12–3 Beans enables you to build components such as the Schedule component that can be used by other applications.

This is precisely what we intended to do with our featured application. While we didn't exactly use Beans, we could have done so easily and allowed others to pick out the Beans they wanted and interface with our calendar manager. Currently, the network module talks to a server on a remote machine. The server stores the information on the disk on which it resides.

What if we were to modify our calendar manager to use Beans? It would simply be a matter of encapsulating our various Java objects in Beans containers. Then we could allow anyone who wants to interface to the rest of our calendar manager to do so using the Network module. Remember, Beans supports the notion of introspection which enables people to take our Network module, browse it from within a GUI builder, and then generate their own objects that interface directly to it. Even if they do not like our user interfaces, people still could use the Network module rather than invest their own time and effort into learning the RMI, IDL, or JDBC APIs.

When to use Servlets

Servlets are an information publishing tool. What if we wanted the people in our department to know what our schedule is simply by browsing our personal Web page? We could allow them to do so by sticking the server portion of our calendar manager inside a servlet. The servlet then could be queried via an HTTP request, and the information contained within the server could be displayed on the Web page. Then, when we modify our server, people talking to our servlet would get the latest and greatest list of what we are doing that day (see Figure 12-4).

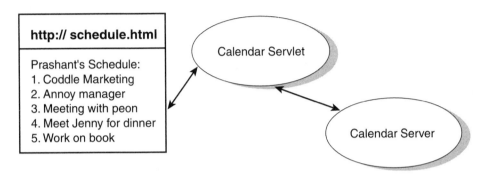

http:// schedule.html

Prashant's Schedule:
1. Coddle Marketing
2. Annoy manager
3. Meeting with peon
4. Meet Jenny for dinner
5. Work on book

Calendar Servlet

Calendar Server

Figure 12–4 Servlets provide dynamic documents via Web servers.

The alternative to servlets is to create a Web page by hand and stick it on a Web server. But, if we were to change the times of our appointment, we would have to generate a new Web page. By incorporating the servlet technology within our server, we do not have to regenerate a Web page every time. Remember, the entire Internet game is about information. How to get, disseminate, and update information constantly. Servlets enable you to publish information contained within servers that get and update that information constantly.

Summary

Whew! There you have it! Several different alternatives, all of which accomplish different things. We hope that this book has been of some help to you as you sort out your information strategy for the next decade. The Internet is a fabulous phenomenon and, as you know, much more than a collection of Web sites, e-mail accounts, and chat rooms. Using the technologies we presented to you in this book, you can begin to harness the power of the Internet to publish and receive information right from within your Java applications.

After all, we firmly believe that Java is the Internet Programming Language, and after reading this book, we hope you will agree.

APPENDIX
A

Glossary

Term	Definition
ActiveWeb	Active Software's publish/subscribe system for Corporate Intranet information publishing.
ActiveX	Proprietary Microsoft component model for the Internet.
AWT	Abstract Window Toolkit. The windowing environment supplied as part of the core Java classes.
BMW	Bavarian Motor Works. Cool car company, and the authors' obsession.
Bytecode	Form Java objects take when they are compiled. Bytecode representations are then washed through the Virtual Machine and turned into native code
C++	Difficult, arcane, and frustrating object-oriented programming language.
Callback	Saving a method with an object in the hopes that the function will be invoked, or "called back," at a later time.
Castanet	Marimba, Inc.'s Internet communication product.
CGI	Common Gateway Interface. The original way of creating executable content on the server side of an HTTP connection. See *servlets*.
Client	Program that invokes another object from a remote location.

COM	Common Object Model. Proprietary Microsoft protocol for platform-independent inter-object communication.
Component	A separate object which can be reused, modified, and redeployed without requiring access to its source code.
Component Model	Next wave in Object-Oriented Programming that promotes the reuse of objects without exposing any source code whatsoever to the end-user or programmer.
Concurrent Access	Occurs when multiple threads get the same piece of data. See *mutual exclusion*.
Constructor	The function of an object that initializes the object and readies it for invocation.
CORBA	The Common Object Request Broker Architecture. Industry standard for distributed-object programming.
Deadlock	Occurs when a thread grabs a mutual exclusion lock and hangs on to it indefinitely, thereby preventing other threads from getting the same lock.
Encapsulation	Object-oriented programming, practice of.
Encryption	The translation of data into unreadable sequences of characters so that untranslation back into its original state is impossible without a "key."
Firewall	Protective barrier between the internal information of a business and the external information it makes available to the world
HTTP	HyperText Transfer Protocol, the de facto standard for Web communication. Specifies the format of transmissions between Web clients and Web servers.
ICE-T	Interprise Communication Environment Toolkit. Java APIs to facilitate communication between Java and C/C++ servers.
IDL	Interface Definition Language. The part of the CORBA language that enables objects and their interfaces to be specified easily.
IIOP	Internet Inter Orb Protocol. New standard for object communication over the Internet. Enables objects to invoke one another over the Internet regardless of the communication mechanism that was used to create them.

Information hiding	Creating objects that provide one set of user interfaces to data while keeping the plumbing of the data hidden.
Inheritance	**The derivation of an object's interfaces or implementations from another object.**
IPC	Inter-Process Communication. Act of programs talking to one another through a link of some kind, usually a socket.
Java	A platform-independent and architecture-neutral programming language from Sun Microsystems, Inc. Also, slang for coffee.
Java Beans	Component model for Java. See *component models*.
Java IDL	The Java binding to CORBA and IDL.
Java RMI	Remote Method Invocation. A means by which to invoke methods on objects that are not necessarily on the same virtual machine.
Java Web Server	The name for the set of components that include servlets and the written-in-Java HTTP server that allows connections to them.
JDBC	Java Database Connectivity. A set of simple APIs used to connect Java objects directly into databases.
Jeeves	Old name for what is now known as the Java Web Server.
JIT	Just In Time. A kind of compiler that, as part of a Virtual Machine's bytecode interpreter, can take bytecodes and optimize them for a machine's native language.
Kerberos	A form of security encryption.
Key	The special incantation that changes encrypted data back to its original form.
Language Mapping	The means necessary to take one language and convert its syntax and semantics to another language.
Layout	Graphical construct in Java's Abstract Window Toolkit that allows components to be placed on the screen.
LiveConnect	Netscape Corporation's series of technologies for advanced Internet/Intranet communication.

Location Independent   CORBA-added functionality that enables a client to invoke a server without having to know where it is or how to start it.

Method   An operation on an object. (See also, Marlon Brando.)

Microsoft   Software company in rainy Redmond, Washington.

Mutual Exclusion   A method used to prevent multiple threads from affecting the same chunk of data.

NEO   Sun Microsystems, Inc.'s implementation of the CORBA standard.

Object Reference   A pointer to an object.

ODBC   Open Database Connectivity. Microsoft-created paradigm and API for communicating with databases. JDBC uses it as a base for interacting with databases from Java applications.

OLE   Object Linking and Embedding. A proprietary Microsoft protocol for inter-object communication.

ORB   Object Request Broker. Component of the CORBA environment that routes requests from the client to the server.

Orbix   Iona Technologies' industry-leading entry in the CORBA market.

Serialization   The act of transforming a Java object into a string representation.

Server   Program that accepts invocations from objects at a remote location.

Servlet   A component of the Java Web Server that allows you to create executable programs on the server side of an HTTP connection.

SET   Secure Electronic Transaction. Major credit card vendors' proposal for secure electronic commerce.

Socket   Fundamental tool for network communication. Defines end points of communication, the origin of the message, and the destination of the message.

SQL   Structured Query Language. The language most commonly used to construct database queries.

SSL   Secure Socket Layer. Web browser functionality that provides encryption of data across a network.

Streams	A flow of data from which you can get information, or to which you can add information.
String Tokenizer	A construct that allows you to search through a string, extracting parts delimited by a token or set of tokens.
Sun	Cool company responsible for the Java programming language. Also, the big yellow ball in the sky.
Synchronized	Java's version of a mutual exclusion lock.
TCP	Transmission Control Protocol. Socket protocol for point-to-point communication.
Thread	A series of executable steps that are executed along with other steps.
Three-tier computing	The philosophy of splitting the client application from the data using a middle man called a server. The server routes requests from one or more clients to the data source and sends information back to it.
UDP	Unreliable Datagram Protocol. Socket for broadcast communication.
Vector	Complex Java data type that allows you to store and retrieve information easily in an array-like construct.
Virtual Machine	Software component of Java that translates Java bytecode into native code that can then be executed on a machine.
VisiBroker	Visigenic's CORBA product. Bundled as part of the Netscape Communicator.

APPENDIX

B

What's on the CD-ROM?

How do I install the CD?

CD-ROM
Installation

Contents

The CD-ROM that accompanies this book contains several of the applications that we have developed in this book. For example, in Chapter 2, "Java Sockets," we created three applications: the pizza tool, the cookie monster, and the featured application. All three applications are included on the disk. The same holds true for all of the chapters. All the source code of the important applications is contained here.

From Chapter 3, we have included the source code from the two Java IDL projects, the Cooler lab and the Calendar Manager implementation. Chapter 4 gives us the StatsServer and a third Calendar Manager implementation. Chapter 5 gives us the source code for the Presidential Election lookup program, the final implementation of the Internet Calendar Manager implementation, and a Microsoft Access database. Chapter 6 contains all of the Servlet code for the Pumpkin recipe application. Finally, Chapter 7 lends us a tribute to our National Pastime and a simple Beans application.

Software Installation

Because our chapters are written without any nod to basic setup and installation of the software we discuss, this chapter will serve as an introduction to setting up Java in your environment and adding the various APIs we discuss. The Java Developer's Kit version 1.1 beta for both Windows and Solaris 2.5 is included on the CD. For Solaris users, simply unzip the file, and read the README. Windows users may run the JDK executable and an installation wizard will guide you through the rest of the process. Any questions or comments about the installation of the JDK should be referred to JavaSoft via their web page: `http://java.sun.com`.

JDK 1.02 to JDK 1.1

Early versions of the Java Developer's Kit did not include RMI, IDL, or JDBC. Because of this, you were required to install those components yourself. Even though this book is based mostly on JDK 1.1, here we will discuss how to install the networking components that we mention throughout this book.

Users of JDK 1.1 need only install Java Management, Java Beans, and the Java Web Server. The other APIs mentioned in this book are included as part of the JDK. The Java APIs, as well as bug fixes, updates, and versions of the Java Developer's Kit are available from the Java Web site at Sun Microsystems:

> `http://java.sun.com`

A note about Java IDL

Java IDL is not included as part of the JDK 1.1 release. Rather, you must purchase an ORB from your friendly neighborhood ORB vendor. We have taken some effort at pointing out the three major ORB vendors (Sun Microsystems, Visigenic, and Iona), but the basic principles and strategies we've outlined will work for any vendor. Because of our own easy access to Sun Microsystems' NEO product, we have implemented our Java IDL code in NEO. We are also leery of recommending one ORB over another because this is a very important decision. After all, choosing the wrong ORB for your needs may turn you off from CORBA altogether. Therefore, we provide the code, but recommend that you discuss with your ORB vendor how to use it properly.

Installation of Examples

The CD-ROM included with this book includes zipped versions of the six chapters from which we supply example code. All of the examples were developed on Solaris 2.5.1, and all the accompanying `Makefiles` and source code structure is there. All the code has been tested on Windows 95, with the notable exception of the Java IDL code. Because the Java IDL code is not especially tailored for any specific ORB, it will require some "tweaking" to work properly on the ORB of your choice.

Index

A

Abstract Window Toolkit
(AWT) 13, 18
Active Information Broker 290
Active software 285
ActiveWeb 290
ActiveX 257, 258, 259, 274, 276, 293,
319
Andreesen, Marc 289
Apple computer 258, 281
asymmetric key encryption 334
Authentication 336

B

Beans 259, 260, 261, 351
Builder support 261
Distributed Beans 261
Event 260
Layout 260
Persistence 260
Bongo and Castanet 285

C

Callbacks 184
Castanet tuner 285
CGI 238, 251
Clipper 338
Common Gateway Interface *(see CGI)*
Common Object Request Broker
Architecture *(see CORBA)*
Common Object Services 102
component model 257
concurrent access 21
Constitution of the United States of
America 339
Constructed data types 109, 116
Constructors 6
Content Type 244
CORBA 95, 137, 251, 252, 281, 290,
293, 341, 343, 344, 345, 347
CORBA Clients 117
CORBA Naming Service 249
CORBA Registration 136
CORBA Servers 128, 249
CORBA servlet 253

Cyberdog 281

D

daemon 236
Daemon threads 28
Database statement object 207
Datagrams 76
DES 334
Download Performance 34
DriverManager object 206

E

Encryption 333
Exceptions 110, 117
Export control 338

F

Files 16

G

Garbage collection 161
GenericServlet base class 242, 243
GUI merging 265

H

HTTP 59
HTTP server 236
HTTP server, 235

I

IBM 279, 292
ICE-T 294
IDEA 334
IDL 345
idltojava 129
IIOP 59, 93, 241, 293
Inheritance 10
Input using the System class 15
Intel 318, 326

Interface Definition Language *(see IDL)*
Interface inheritance 107, 114
Interfaces 106
interfaces 4
Interfaces, modules, and methods 113
Internet Engineering Task Force 301
Internet Inter-ORB Protocol *(see IIOP)*
inter-process communication 47
introspection 265
IOException 243

J

Java Beans 257, 258
Java Chips 317, 324
Java Class Security 330
Java Database Connectivity 205, 348
Java IDL 264, 293, 342, 343, 347
Java Management API *(see JMAPI)*
JavaOS 317
Java RMI 264, 293, 310, 346, 347, 348
Java Sockets 348
JavaStation 317, 321
Java Virtual Machine 317
Java Web Server 235
JDBC 264, 347, 348
JIT compilers 38, 325, 346
JMAPI 299
Just In Time (JIT) compilers *(see JIT compilers)*

K

Kerberos 337

L

Language Mappings 111
LISP 345
LiveConnect 293
Local Area Network 300

M

Macintosh 281

MacOS 281
ManagedObject classes 309
Marimba, Inc. 285
McNealy, Scott 318
MD5 336
Methods 5, 109
Microsoft 258, 259, 276, 278, 279, 292, 293
Microsoft Access 209
Microsoft Excel 276, 278
Microsoft PowerPoint 276
Microsoft Windows 279
Microsoft Word 276, 279
Modules 106
Monster Truck Madness 279

N

Naming Service 102
NEO 121, 344
Netscape 153, 285, 331, 338, 344
Netscape Navigator 292

O

Object Linking and Embedding 277
ODBC driver 212
OLE 277
Open Database Connectivity (ODBC) 208
OpenDoc 257, 258, 259, 274, 281
Open Network Environment (ONE) 292
Oracle 321
Orbix 101, 121, 344

P

Performance 34
picoJava 325, 326
Pizza Hut 61
port 49
PowerPC 326
Protocols 58

public/private key encryption 334

R

RC2 334
RC4 334
Registering callbacks 187
Remote Procedure Call (RPC) 155
RMI 251, 266, 341
RMI Client 163
RMI Factories 178
RMI Registry classes 173
RMI Remote classes 164
RMI Server 170
RMI's naming system 165
Rogue-Wave 102
Runtime Performance 36

S

Safety in Java 329
Santa Cruz Operation (SCO) 61
Secure Socket Layer (SSL) 293, 334, 338
security test suite 332
Serialization 29
server socket 68
Servlet administration 250
Servlet interface 240
Servlet parameters 245
ServletException 243
ServletResponse 243
Servlets 238, 352
Shockwave 238
Simple Network Management Protocol 301
SNMP 301
SNMP trap 301
sockets 341
Solaris Operating System 259, 344
SSL 334
Streams 13
Structured Query Language 205, 209

Sun Microsystems 153, 242, 258, 259, 281, 294, 317, 318, 321, 327, 344
Sun Microsystems' Solaris operating system 299
SunSoft's NEO 96, 101
synchronized methods 27

T

TCP/IP 59
   Protocol 59
   Server 67
   Client 60
The System class 15, 16
The Thread class 22, 237
Thread controls 25
Thread priorities 28
Threads 20
transient 33
Triple DES 334

U

UDP client 75
UDP receiver 83

V

VeriSign 335
VisiBroke 121
VisiBroker for Java 344
Visigenic 344
Visual Basic OCX controls 276

W

Windows 293
Windows 95 317

Y

yield( ), wait( ), and notify( ) 27

Java™ Development Kit
Version 1.1
Binary Code License

This binary code license ("License") contains rights and restrictions associated with use of the accompanying software and documentation ("Software"). Read the License carefully before installing the Software. By installing the Software you agree to the terms and conditions of this License.

1. Limited License Grant. Sun grants to you ("Licensee") a non-exclusive, non-transferable limited license to use the Software without fee for evaluation of the Software and for development of Java™ compatible applets and applications. Licensee may make one archival copy of the Software. Licensee may not re-distribute the Software in whole or in part, either separately or included with a product. Refer to the Java Runtime Environment Version 1.1 binary code license (http://www.javasoft.com/products/JDK/1.1/index.html) for the availability of runtime code which may be distributed with Java compatible applets and applications.

2. Java Platform Interface. Licensee may not modify the Java Platform Interface ("JPI", identified as classes contained within the "java" package or any subpackages of the "java" package), by creating additional classes within the JPI or otherwise causing the addition to or modification of the classes in the JPI. In the event that Licensee creates any Java-related API and distributes such API to others for applet or application development, Licensee must promptly publish an accurate specification for such API for free use by all developers of Java-based software.

3. Restrictions. Software is confidential copyrighted information of Sun and title to all copies is retained by Sun and/or its licensors. Licensee shall not modify, decompile, disassemble, decrypt, extract, or otherwise reverse engineer Software. Software may not be leased, assigned, or sublicensed, in whole or in part. **Software is not designed or intended for use in on-line control of aircraft, air traffic, aircraft navigation or aircraft communications; or in the design, construction, operation or maintenance of any nuclear facility. Licensee warrants that it will not use or redistribute the Software for such purposes.**

4. Trademarks and Logos. This License does not authorize Licensee to use any Sun name, trademark or logo. Licensee acknowledges that Sun owns the Java trademark and all Java-related trademarks, logos and icons including the Coffee Cup and Duke ("Java Marks") and agrees to: (i) to comply with the Java Trademark Guidelines at http://java.com/trademarks.html; (ii) not do anything harmful to or inconsistent with Sun's rights in the Java Marks; and (iii) assist Sun in protecting those rights, including assigning to Sun any rights acquired by Licensee in any Java Mark.

5. Disclaimer of Warranty. Software is provided "AS IS," without a warranty of any kind. ALL EXPRESS OR IMPLIED REPRESENTATIONS AND WARRANTIES,

INCLUDING ANY IMPLIED WARRANTY OF MERCHANTABILITY, FITNESS FOR A PARTICULAR PURPOSE OR NON-INFRINGEMENT, ARE HEREBY EXCLUDED.

6. Limitation of Liability. SUN AND ITS LICENSORS SHALL NOT BE LIABLE FOR ANY DAMAGES SUFFERED BY LICENSEE OR ANY THIRD PARTY AS A RESULT OF USING OR DISTRIBUTING SOFTWARE. IN NO EVENT WILL SUN OR ITS LICENSORS BE LIABLE FOR ANY LOST REVENUE, PROFIT OR DATA, OR FOR DIRECT, INDIRECT, SPECIAL, CONSEQUENTIAL, INCIDENTAL OR PUNITIVE DAMAGES, HOWEVER CAUSED AND REGARDLESS OF THE THEORY OF LIABILITY, ARISING OUT OF THE USE OF OR INABILITY TO USE SOFTWARE, EVEN IF SUN HAS BEEN ADVISED OF THE POSSIBILITY OF SUCH DAMAGES.

7. Termination. Licensee may terminate this License at any time by destroying all copies of Software. This License will terminate immediately without notice from Sun if Licensee fails to comply with any provision of this License. Upon such termination, Licensee must destroy all copies of Software.

8. Export Regulations. Software, including technical data, is subject to U.S. export control laws, including the U.S. Export Administration Act and its associated regulations, and may be subject to export or import regulations in other countries. Licensee agrees to comply strictly with all such regulations and acknowledges that it has the responsibility to obtain licenses to export, re-export, or import Software. Software may not be downloaded, or otherwise exported or re-exported (i) into, or to a national or resident of, Cuba, Iraq, Iran, North Korea, Libya, Sudan, Syria or any country to which the U.S. has embargoed goods; or (ii) to anyone on the U.S. Treasury Department's list of Specially Designated Nations or the U.S. Commerce Department's Table of Denial Orders.

9. Restricted Rights. Use, duplication or disclosure by the United States government is subject to the restrictions as set forth in the Rights in Technical Data and Computer Software Clauses in DFARS 252.227-7013(c) (1) (ii) and FAR 52.227-19(c) (2) as applicable.

10. Governing Law. Any action related to this License will be governed by California law and controlling U.S. federal law. No choice of law rules of any jurisdiction will apply.

11. Severability. If any of the above provisions are held to be in violation of applicable law, void, or unenforceable in any jurisdiction, then such provisions are herewith waived to the extent necessary for the License to be otherwise enforceable in such jurisdiction. However, if in Sun's opinion deletion of any provisions of the License by operation of this paragraph unreasonably compromises the rights or increase the liabilities of Sun or its licensors, Sun reserves the right to terminate the License and refund the fee paid by Licensee, if any, as Licensee's sole and exclusive remedy.

LICENSE AGREEMENT AND LIMITED WARRANTY

READ THE FOLLOWING TERMS AND CONDITIONS CAREFULLY BEFORE OPENING THIS CD PACKAGE, *ADVANCED JAVA NETWORKING*. THIS LEGAL DOCUMENT IS AN AGREEMENT BETWEEN YOU AND PRENTICE-HALL, INC. (THE "COMPANY"). BY OPENING THIS SEALED CD PACKAGE, YOU ARE AGREEING TO BE BOUND BY THESE TERMS AND CONDITIONS. IF YOU DO NOT AGREE WITH THESE TERMS AND CONDITIONS, DO NOT OPEN THE CD PACKAGE. PROMPTLY RETURN THE UNOPENED CD PACKAGE AND ALL ACCOMPANYING ITEMS TO THE PLACE YOU OBTAINED THEM FOR A FULL REFUND OF ANY SUMS YOU HAVE PAID.

1.   **GRANT OF LICENSE:** In consideration of your purchase of this book, and your agreement to abide by the terms and conditions of this Agreement, the Company grants to you a nonexclusive right to use and display the copy of the enclosed software program (hereinafter the "SOFTWARE") on a single computer (i.e., with a single CPU) at a single location so long as you comply with the terms of this Agreement. The Company reserves all rights not expressly granted to you under this Agreement.

2.   **OWNERSHIP OF SOFTWARE:** You own only the magnetic or physical media (the enclosed CD) on which the SOFTWARE is recorded or fixed, but the Company and the software developers retain all the rights, title, and ownership to the SOFTWARE recorded on the original CD copy(ies) and all subsequent copies of the SOFTWARE, regardless of the form or media on which the original or other copies may exist. This license is not a sale of the original SOFTWARE or any copy to you.

3.   **COPY RESTRICTIONS:** This SOFTWARE and the accompanying printed materials and user manual (the "Documentation") are the subject of copyright. The individual programs on the CD are copyrighted by the authors of each program. Some of the programs on the CD include separate licensing agreements. If you intend to use one of these programs, you must read and follow its accompanying license agreement. You may not copy the Documentation or the SOFTWARE, except that you may make a single copy of the SOFTWARE for backup or archival purposes only. You may be held legally responsible for any copying or copyright infringement which is caused or encouraged by your failure to abide by the terms of this restriction.

4.   **USE RESTRICTIONS:** You may not network the SOFTWARE or otherwise use it on more than one computer or computer terminal at the same time. You may physically transfer the SOFT-WARE from one computer to another provided that the SOFTWARE is used on only one computer at a time. You may not distribute copies of the SOFTWARE or Documentation to others. You may not reverse engineer, disassemble, decompile, modify, adapt, translate, or create derivative works based on the SOFTWARE or the Documentation without the prior written consent of the Company.

5.   **TRANSFER RESTRICTIONS:** The enclosed SOFTWARE is licensed only to you and may not be transferred to any one else without the prior written consent of the Company. Any unauthorized transfer of the SOFTWARE shall result in the immediate termination of this Agreement.

6.   **TERMINATION:** This license is effective until terminated. This license will terminate automatically without notice from the Company and become null and void if you fail to comply with any provisions or limitations of this license. Upon termination, you shall destroy the Documentation and all copies of the SOFTWARE. All provisions of this Agreement as to warranties, limitation of liability, remedies or damages, and our ownership rights shall survive termination.

7.   **MISCELLANEOUS:** This Agreement shall be construed in accordance with the laws of the United States of America and the State of New York and shall benefit the Company, its affiliates, and assignees.

8.   **LIMITED WARRANTY AND DISCLAIMER OF WARRANTY:** The Company warrants that the SOFTWARE, when properly used in accordance with the Documentation, will operate in substantial conformity with the description of the SOFTWARE set forth in the Documentation. The

Company does not warrant that the SOFTWARE will meet your requirements or that the operation of the SOFTWARE will be uninterrupted or error-free. The Company warrants that the media on which the SOFTWARE is delivered shall be free from defects in materials and workmanship under normal use for a period of thirty (30) days from the date of your purchase. Your only remedy and the Company's only obligation under these limited warranties is, at the Company's option, return of the warranted item for a refund of any amounts paid by you or replacement of the item. Any replacement of SOFTWARE or media under the warranties shall not extend the original warranty period. The limited warranty set forth above shall not apply to any SOFTWARE which the Company determines in good faith has been subject to misuse, neglect, improper installation, repair, alteration, or damage by you. EXCEPT FOR THE EXPRESSED WARRANTIES SET FORTH ABOVE, THE COMPANY DISCLAIMS ALL WARRANTIES, EXPRESS OR IMPLIED, INCLUDING WITHOUT LIMITATION, THE IMPLIED WARRANTIES OF MERCHANTABILITY AND FITNESS FOR A PARTICULAR PURPOSE. EXCEPT FOR THE EXPRESS WARRANTY SET FORTH ABOVE, THE COMPANY DOES NOT WARRANT, GUARANTEE, OR MAKE ANY REPRESENTATION REGARDING THE USE OR THE RESULTS OF THE USE OF THE SOFTWARE IN TERMS OF ITS CORRECTNESS, ACCURACY, RELIABILITY, CURRENTNESS, OR OTHERWISE.

IN NO EVENT, SHALL THE COMPANY OR ITS EMPLOYEES, AGENTS, SUPPLIERS, OR CONTRACTORS BE LIABLE FOR ANY INCIDENTAL, INDIRECT, SPECIAL, OR CONSEQUENTIAL DAMAGES ARISING OUT OF OR IN CONNECTION WITH THE LICENSE GRANTED UNDER THIS AGREEMENT, OR FOR LOSS OF USE, LOSS OF DATA, LOSS OF INCOME OR PROFIT, OR OTHER LOSSES, SUSTAINED AS A RESULT OF INJURY TO ANY PERSON, OR LOSS OF OR DAMAGE TO PROPERTY, OR CLAIMS OF THIRD PARTIES, EVEN IF THE COMPANY OR AN AUTHORIZED REPRESENTATIVE OF THE COMPANY HAS BEEN ADVISED OF THE POSSIBILITY OF SUCH DAMAGES. IN NO EVENT SHALL LIABILITY OF THE COMPANY FOR DAMAGES WITH RESPECT TO THE SOFTWARE EXCEED THE AMOUNTS ACTUALLY PAID BY YOU, IF ANY, FOR THE SOFTWARE.

SOME JURISDICTIONS DO NOT ALLOW THE LIMITATION OF IMPLIED WARRANTIES OR LIABILITY FOR INCIDENTAL, INDIRECT, SPECIAL, OR CONSEQUENTIAL DAMAGES, SO THE ABOVE LIMITATIONS MAY NOT ALWAYS APPLY. THE WARRANTIES IN THIS AGREEMENT GIVE YOU SPECIFIC LEGAL RIGHTS AND YOU MAY ALSO HAVE OTHER RIGHTS WHICH VARY IN ACCORDANCE WITH LOCAL LAW.

ACKNOWLEDGMENT

YOU ACKNOWLEDGE THAT YOU HAVE READ THIS AGREEMENT, UNDERSTAND IT, AND AGREE TO BE BOUND BY ITS TERMS AND CONDITIONS. YOU ALSO AGREE THAT THIS AGREEMENT IS THE COMPLETE AND EXCLUSIVE STATEMENT OF THE AGREEMENT BETWEEN YOU AND THE COMPANY AND SUPERSEDES ALL PROPOSALS OR PRIOR AGREEMENTS, ORAL, OR WRITTEN, AND ANY OTHER COMMUNICATIONS BETWEEN YOU AND THE COMPANY OR ANY REPRESENTATIVE OF THE COMPANY RELATING TO THE SUBJECT MATTER OF THIS AGREEMENT.

Should you have any questions concerning this Agreement or if you wish to contact the Company for any reason, please contact in writing at the address below.

Robin Short

Prentice Hall PTR

One Lake Street

Upper Saddle River, New Jersey 07458